When Gifted Kids Don't Have All the Answers

How to Meet Their Social and Emotional Needs

Jim Delisle, Ph.D., & Judy Galbraith, M.A.

Edited by Pamela Espeland

free spirit
PUBLiSHiNG®

Works for kids®

Library of Congress Cataloging-in-Publication Data

Delisle, James R., 1953–
    When gifted kids don't have all the answers : how to meet their social and emotional needs / Jim Delisle & Judy Galbraith ; edited by Pamela Espeland.
      p. cm.
    Includes bibliographical references and index.
    ISBN 1-57542-107-0
      1. Gifted children—Education—United States—Psychological aspects. 2. Classroom environment—United States. I. Galbraith, Judy. II. Espeland, Pamela, 1951– III. Title.

LC3993.2 .D36 2002

2002005263

Assistant editor: Jennifer Brannen
Cover and book design by Marieka Heinlen
Index prepared by Randl Ockey

10 9 8 7 6 5 4 3 2 1
Printed in the United States of America

Free Spirit Publishing Inc.
217 Fifth Avenue North, Suite 200
Minneapolis, MN 55401-1299
(612) 338-2068
help4kids@freespirit.com
www.freespirit.com

The following are registered trademarks of Free Spirit Publishing Inc.:

FREE SPIRIT®
FREE SPIRIT PUBLISHING®
SELF-HELP FOR TEENS®
SELF-HELP FOR KIDS®
WORKS FOR KIDS®
THE FREE SPIRITED CLASSROOM®

free spirit
PUBLISHING®
Works
for kids®

Dedication

This book is dedicated, wholly and completely, to my son, Matt. I cherish his love and his laughter, and I admire him for following his heart in everything he has ever done. Matt, I am proud to be your dad.

—*Jim Delisle*

This book is also dedicated to the devoted advocates of gifted youth whose efforts often go unnoticed. There may be days when you're not sure if your work is making any difference, and you may feel discouraged by a society that largely misunderstands the importance of what you do. I hope that, in some small way, this book encourages and helps you. Keep going! Your heart knows the truth: Gifted kids are worth your efforts, and they do appreciate your caring.

—*Judy Galbraith*

Acknowledgments

As we were preparing the final copy for this book, we were both struck by the number of letters, anecdotes, and personal reflections that are included in it. Some were written by colleagues we have known for years, others by students who were in our classes or who crossed our lives for only a brief moment, and still more by individuals close to our hearts due to the personal relationships we have shared with them. In all cases, their words and reflections have added immeasurably to our understanding of giftedness. Even more, though, these excerpts represent both the friendships and professional relationships that have been forged between us and so many generous others. To every individual who has helped to make this book more complete, more "grounded," we thank you with much sincerity.

Contents

List of Reproducible Pages

Introduction

Gifted kids are so much more than high grades and test scores. You probably know that already; that's why you're reading this book. But for teachers just starting out (or burning out, or overwhelmed with the day-to-day concerns of their job), it's sometimes difficult to see past all that achievement and potential to the child, adolescent, or teen who may be filled with anxiety, pressured to be perfect, lonely, alienated, confused, and unsure of what the future might bring.

We can both remember the specific incidents that first called our attention to gifted kids' social and emotional needs.

Jim: Craig entered my life and my classroom at the same time. A fifth grader, he was fascinated by anything intellectual, and his sensitivity often caused him to see life from an altruistic angle seldom observed in boys his age. He drove his teachers nuts, though. He seldom finished anything he started, for once his fascination for a topic was sated, he felt it was time to move on. For two years, Craig was enrolled in my gifted program, and for two years, I had to fight to keep him there. He wasn't your stereotypical high-achieving gifted child, but he was, indeed, a gifted child. I came to realize that the greatest needs he had were not in academics, but in the social and emotional realms of growing up gifted. Craig, and others like him, have guided my life ever since, and they have shown me the importance of looking beyond high achievement and glossy projects to find the gifted child beneath the academic veneer.

Judy: Early in my career as a gifted education specialist I worked with teens. One day, three boys hung around after class, and I overheard them talking. "Now I get to go be my family's identified patient," one said. Another asked, "Have you ever taken a Rorschach test?" The third said, "I'm seeing a psychiatrist." I suddenly realized that all three students had personal experience with mental health issues, and I wondered: What about the others? It was a wake-up call for me. Not long after, another of my students attempted suicide. When I looked at my program with new eyes, I saw that it was based entirely on meeting gifted kids' academic needs. It occurred to me that if a student's mental health is off-center significantly, or even a little, what point is there in trying to push academic challenge when that's usually the easy part of life for gifted kids? I made it my personal mission to educate myself about mental health, and to balance my academic program with life skills—learning about oneself and others.

It's important to know that there isn't a big difference between addressing students' academic and emotional needs. You don't have to be a counselor with a degree. You don't have to have all the answers. We certainly don't! What we do have are years of experience working with gifted kids, studying gifted kids, reading about gifted kids, getting to know them, caring about them, and trying our best to help them.

We wrote this book to share what we've learned, to share what other experts say (including gifted kids themselves), and to give you some strategies, activities, and ideas you can start using right now to support the social and emotional needs of your own gifted students.

About This Book

■ In **Chapter 1: What Is Giftedness?** we describe the general characteristics of gifted children and some problems associated with those characteristics. We present various definitions of giftedness and invite you to come up with your own definition. We spotlight many of the myths and misconceptions about giftedness (including the pervasive, pernicious myth that gifted education is "elitist"), and we consider the "gifted" label. This chapter includes two important information-gathering tools: a "Teacher Inventory" and a "Student Questionnaire." We strongly encourage you to complete the inventory and have your gifted students complete the questionnaire. Both will provide you with valuable insights.

■ In **Chapter 2: Identifying Gifted Kids,** we wonder (as you do) why identification is so complex, suggest ways to improve the identification process, look at some questionable practices in current identification methods, and present common questions about identification—along with answers we hope you'll find helpful.

■ In **Chapter 3: Emotional Dimensions of Giftedness,** we describe some of the challenges gifted kids face from within and without, including super-sensitivity and perfectionism. We talk about different ways of being gifted and focus in on three categories of giftedness which may predict emotional needs: gifted girls, gifted students from ethnic and cultural minorities, and gifted children with physical and learning differences. We point out some trouble signs you can watch for, including symptoms indicating that a student may be deeply depressed or even suicidal.

■ In **Chapter 4: Being a Gifted Teacher,** we empathize with you and the challenges you face in your job. We understand; we've been there! We offer some ideas for explaining gifted education to parents, colleagues, administrators, and others who may not understand what you do or why it's necessary to do it ("Aren't all children gifted?"). We consider what makes a good gifted education teacher and suggest specific actions you might take to build your own strengths. Then we offer strategies you can use to create a supportive environment for your students, both as a group and one-on-one.

■   In **Chapter 5: Understanding Gifted Kids from the Inside Out,** we describe the difference between self-image and self-esteem and identify specific issues gifted children and adolescents face that set them apart. Then we present several activities related to those issues that help gifted kids explore their perceptions, consider their lives, learn more about themselves, be their own advocates, and like themselves more.

■   In **Chapter 6: Underachiever or Selective Consumer?,** we consider a label that's often applied to gifted kids who don't live up to others' expectations: "underachiever." We distinguish between underachievement and nonproduction, which we prefer to call "selective consumerism." We review the literature and research on what has historically been called "underachievement." Then we suggest strategies for reversing patterns of underachieving and selective consumer behaviors through curricular and counseling interventions.

■   In **Chapter 7: Understanding Gifted Kids from the Outside In,** we present a series of group discussions you can use to help students explore and understand the "Eight Great Gripes of Gifted Kids." The "Great Gripes" are problems and feelings that gifted kids have identified as common to their experience: being bored in school, dealing with others' expectations, worrying about world problems and feeling helpless to do anything about them. The "Great Gripes" aren't new; in fact, gifted kids first told us about them almost twenty years ago. It's significant that these issues still loom so large in their lives. Our discussions allow students to explore them in depth and feel more empowered to cope with them.

■   In **Chapter 8: Making It Safe to Be Smart: Creating the Gifted-Friendly Classroom,** we focus on ways to make gifted students feel welcome, wanted, and able to be themselves. We discuss the relationship between self-esteem and school achievement. We introduce the idea of "Invitational Education" and present specific strategies you can use to make your curriculum, grading procedures, student evaluations, classroom environment, and even your disciplinary procedures more supportive. We also talk about ways to feel better about yourself as a teacher.

Our goals throughout this book are to call attention to gifted students' issues, problems, and feelings; to support your efforts on behalf of gifted kids; to answer some of the "tough questions" you may have (or be asked by others); and to provide you with concrete, easy-to-use strategies and activities for meeting students' social and emotional needs. The goals of the strategies and activities are to help gifted kids understand what giftedness means; to invite them to embrace giftedness as an asset in their lives; to inspire them to take more responsibility for their learning and their actions; and to help them build lifeskills for dealing with perfectionism, conflicts with others, self-esteem issues, and other mental-health concerns.

The strategies and activities you'll find here have been used in many classrooms, some for many years. We're confident that you'll have success with them, too. Watch what happens as your gifted students learn to understand and accept themselves, understand and accept others, and realize that being gifted is a blessing, not a burden.

A Few Words of Encouragement

Naturally, we have no idea what kind of gifted program you teach in—or even if you teach in a gifted program. Maybe you're one of the lucky ones, with a full-time program or even a gifted magnet school that's strongly supported, generally understood, and adequately funded (at least for now). Maybe you staff a resource room where gifted students spend part of each day. Perhaps you're a "pull-out" program teacher who travels from school to school, spending an hour or two each week with each group of gifted students (and you have many groups). Maybe you teach an enrichment class, AP (Advanced Placement) classes, or an after-school, weekend, or summer class for gifted students. Maybe you're a mentor to a gifted child.

Or maybe you're a "regular" classroom teacher, where your inclusive, mixed-abilities classroom may include students who range from highly gifted to gifted, "average" students, those who have learning differences, kids at risk, students who are severely disabled, homeless kids, students for whom English is a second language, and recent immigrants who don't yet speak English. If so, you're probably being asked by your administration to differentiate the curriculum, or you will be at some point in the not-too-distant future.

Differentiation means changing the pace, level, or kind of instruction to meet each student's individual learning needs. In a time when gifted programs are being challenged or eliminated, differentiation is a way of ensuring that gifted students are given the learning opportunities they need. Depending on your situation, these opportunities may include curriculum compacting (compressing curriculum material into a shorter time frame, and allowing students to demonstrate mastery of content they already know); ability grouping (putting gifted students together for instruction in a particular subject area); flexible grouping (putting students together on an assignment-by-assignment basis); cluster grouping (putting all identified gifted students of the same grade level in the same classroom, usually one led by a teacher with training in gifted education); or individualized instruction (independent study projects).

Whatever your own situation might be, and however many gifted students you teach, we hope you know how truly essential you are. Over and over again, gifted students have told us about teachers who have made a tremendous difference in their lives. Gifted adults get misty-eyed when remembering grade-school teachers who took the time and made the effort to know them and guide them. Yes, you'll have bad days, maddening days, frustrating days, and days when you wish you'd followed a different career path altogether. Join the club! But please . . . keep teaching.

And please be willing to deal with the emotional lives of your students, not just their intellectual needs. Actually, working with students' affective needs may be (in the words of one teacher) "the best thing we can do for them." In an average busy day, with a tight schedule and loaded curriculum, it seems difficult to depart from the teacher's guide to deal with feelings. But as many people have pointed out, if students don't have good self-concepts and good interpersonal relationships, everything else comes to a screeching halt.

Affective education belongs in the teacher's guide. And that's what this book is.

Stay in Touch

We'd love to hear from you. Please let us know what's been helpful in this book, what works for you (and doesn't). Are there other strategies and activities you've discovered or developed that seem especially effective with gifted kids? We'd appreciate your sharing them with us. Are there stories from your own experience that make a point, illuminate a need, or support the importance of gifted education? Send them our way. We're always learning from "teachers in the trenches"—people like you. You may contact us by regular mail or email:

Free Spirit Publishing Inc.
217 Fifth Avenue North, Suite 200
Minneapolis, MN 55401-1299
help4kids@freespirit.com

We hope to hear from you. And we wish you continued success in your efforts to understand, teach, and encourage social and emotional growth among the gifted students in your care.

Jim Delisle, Ph.D.

Judy Galbraith, M.A.

CHAPTER 1

What Is Giftedness?

To me, being gifted has its ups and downs. I like having a good mind. It helps me to think ahead, and to solve problems. But sometimes I think too much, and in too much depth. This can create problems for me, and it's not easy to talk with people about them. I fear some people just wouldn't understand.

—RUTH, 10 YEARS, 2 MONTHS, AND 29 DAYS OLD

When you hear the word "gifted," what's the first thing that comes to mind? Answer quickly. Don't spend a lot of time pondering or framing the "right" response. This is not a test!

Did you immediately think "genius," "prodigy," "Einstein," "exceptional," "talented," or "precocious"? Did you picture the child in your classroom who always seems to be one step ahead of you (or more)? Who never stops talking? Who's always the first to raise his or her hand? Who has a million questions? Or did you envision the child who spends hours staring out the window in apparent boredom, who seems to have few friends, who won't turn in an assignment until it's absolutely perfect? For you, is the word "gifted" positive—or negative?

Giftedness means many things. It means different things to different people, to society, and to gifted kids themselves. As a helpful starting point for understanding what giftedness is and means, consider the following list from the ERIC Clearinghouse on Disabilities and Gifted Education:[1]

SOME GENERAL CHARACTERISTICS OF GIFTED CHILDREN

These are typical factors stressed by educational authorities as being indicative of giftedness. Obviously, no child is outstanding in all characteristics.

1. Shows superior reasoning powers and marked ability to handle ideas; can generalize readily from specific facts and can see subtle relationships; has outstanding problem-solving ability.

2. Shows persistent intellectual curiosity; asks searching questions; shows exceptional interest in the nature of humankind and the universe.

3. Has a wide range of interests, often of an intellectual kind; develops one or more interests to considerable depth.

4. Is markedly superior in quality and quantity of written and/or spoken vocabulary; is interested in the subtleties of words and their uses.

5. Reads avidly and absorbs books well beyond his or her years.

6. Learns quickly and easily and retains what is learned; recalls important details, concepts and principles; comprehends readily.

7. Shows insight into arithmetical problems that require careful reasoning and grasps mathematical concepts readily.

8. Shows creative ability or imaginative expression in such things as music, art, dance, drama; shows sensitivity and finesse in rhythm, movement, and bodily control.

9. Sustains concentration for lengthy periods and shows outstanding responsibility and independence in classroom work.

10. Sets realistically high standards for self; is self-critical in evaluating and correcting his or her own efforts.

11. Shows initiative and originality in intellectual work; shows flexibility in thinking and considers problems from a number of viewpoints.

12. Observes keenly and is responsive to new ideas.

13. Shows social poise and an ability to communicate with adults in a mature way.

14. Gets excitement and pleasure from intellectual challenge; shows an alert and subtle sense of humor.

Gifted children can also be extraordinarily sensitive. They often feel more than other kids their age. They tend to develop empathy earlier than other children do. They have a social conscience—and an intense awareness of the world's problems. They worry about the world, the environment, wars and conflicts, hunger and homelessness. Their emotions are intense and close to the surface.

Along with these many fine qualities can come various problems related to them.

The child who . . .	may also be the child who . . .
shows superior reasoning powers and marked ability to handle ideas	is impatient; seems stuck-up or arrogant; challenges your authority; has difficulty getting along with less able peers
can solve problems quickly and easily	wants to move on quickly to more challenging problems, despite what the rest of the class is doing; hates to "wait for the group"; gets bored and frustrated
shows persistent intellectual curiosity and asks searching questions	drives you crazy with questions; asks inappropriate or embarrassing questions; is perceived as "nosy"
shows exceptional interest in the nature of humankind and the universe	has difficulty focusing on ideas that are less grand and sweeping; feels that everyday class work is trivial and meaningless; can't "connect" with interests of age peers
has a wide range of interests; develops one or more interests to considerable depth	seems scattered and disorganized; takes on too many projects at once; gets obsessed with a particular interest; resists direction or interruption; rebels against conforming to group tasks; disrupts class routines; is perceived as stubborn or uncooperative
has an advanced vocabulary	talks too much; uses words to intimidate other people; finds it hard to communicate with age peers; seems pompous or conceited—a "show-off"; plays word games that others don't understand or appreciate; dominates discussions; has trouble listening
is an avid reader	buries himself or herself in books and avoids social interaction

continued . . .

The child who . . .	may also be the child who . . .
learns quickly; comprehends readily	gets bored with the regular curriculum; gets impatient with peers for being "slow"; resists assignments that don't present opportunities for new learning; dislikes drill and practice; does inaccurate or sloppy work
grasps mathematical concepts readily	has little or no patience for regular math lessons or homework
is creative and imaginative	goes too far; seems disruptive; lacks interest in mundane assignments or details; wanders off the subject
sustains concentration for lengthy periods of time	has tunnel vision; hates to be interrupted; neglects regular assignments or responsibilities; is stubborn
shows outstanding responsibility and independence	has difficulty working with others; resists following directions; seems bossy and disrespectful; is unable to accept help; is a nonconformist
sets high standards for self; is self-critical	sets unrealistically high goals; is perfectionistic; lacks tolerance for others' mistakes; fears failure; avoids taking risks or trying new things; becomes depressed
shows initiative and originality	resists going along with the crowd (or the class); is a loner
shows flexibility in thinking; considers problems from a number of viewpoints	has difficulty focusing on or finishing assignments; has trouble making decisions

continued . . .

The child who . . .	may also be the child who . . .
observes keenly; is responsive to new ideas	sees too much; becomes impatient
communicates easily with adults	has difficulty communicating with age peers
gets excitement and pleasure from intellectual challenge	expects or demands intellectual challenge; resists sameness and routine tasks
has a keen sense of humor	uses humor inappropriately to gain attention or attack others; becomes the "class clown"; is disruptive
is sensitive, empathetic, and emotional	takes things personally; is easily hurt or upset; feels powerless to solve the world's problems; becomes fearful, anxious, and sad; has trouble handling criticism or rejection; is "too emotional," laughing one moment and crying the next; may seem immature

Just as not all bright kids have all of the characteristics of giftedness, not all bright kids have all (or most, or even some) of the problems associated with those characteristics. In fact, many of the problems they do have aren't much different from those that other children and adolescents experience during the so-called "normal" process of growing up.

But many researchers, teachers, parents, and children themselves are realizing that gifted and talented kids may have special needs that come with being bright. Their view of the world, view of themselves, and other qualities (such as perfectionism and sensitivity) set them apart from peers and family—and at odds with their school—just at a time when desire for conformity is greatest. Only in the last twenty years or so have we begun to address the cognitive needs of our brightest students seriously. To keep them in school and help them mature emotionally as well as intellectually, we must address their affective needs as well.

What Does Giftedness Mean to You?

On pages 37–39, you'll find a "Teacher Inventory" we developed as a think piece—a way for you to focus on your attitudes about giftedness and your concerns about working with gifted students. Try filling it out like a diary or journal you'd want to read in another five years. Write honestly what's on your mind. What do you know or believe to be true from experience? What do you know or believe on a gut level? What makes sense to you personally?

Even if you're feeling fairly comfortable with your perception of giftedness, your role as a teacher, and your relationship with the gifted students in your care, please don't skip this inventory. Your responses will help you prepare for the activities and strategies in the rest of this book.

What Other Gifted Educators Say

We invited some of our colleagues to tell us what they think giftedness means. Here's what they had to say.

> Giftedness is persistence, tenacity, and a willingness to overcome struggle—a drive to succeed when your gift doesn't "fit the box." In my personal and professional experiences, children who "think outside the box" are often unrecognized for their true intellectual abilities. Many of these children are from nondominant cultures and low socioeconomic backgrounds. As educators of the gifted, we have a responsibility to seek out and identify children who don't fit the prevailing definitions of giftedness. We must provide them with the tools to overcome social/environmental and/or academic barriers so they can achieve their fullest potential.

> Some of the brightest children I've worked with possess an internal drive to succeed. These self-efficacious children have developed strong critical and creative problem-solving strategies through real-life experiences and are able to apply them to schoolhouse learning. They are motivated to achieve when their different ways of thinking/doing are appreciated, acknowledged, and accepted by those in authority. We must provide these children with opportunities to explore and utilize their differing gifts to achieve great things.

> —RICHARD M. CASH, ED.D., Director of Gifted and Talented Programs,
> Bloomington Public Schools, Bloomington, Minnesota

So many kinds of giftedness . . .

. . . a cheery, socially "normal" sixth-grade girl who has developed a passion for ants and is auditing a course on insect behavior at the University of Minnesota. Tuesday she wrote her midquarter exam.

. . . an amazing fifth-grade boy who plays jazz piano, without music, continually for eight minutes, then jokes with us that it just "comes to him." (Meanwhile, I struggle with my second year of harp lessons—my first musical instrument ever.)

. . . the quiet boy who sees complex mathematical patterns easily and can explain them to the rest of us.

I've had the honor of working with so many different kinds of gifted kids during my 35-plus years as a regular classroom teacher. Kids who express their excellence well not only have an area of outstanding brain processing, they also have a sense of calmness, comfortableness—call it "okay-ness"—with their specialness. They have the personal skills, the self-management and emotional skills, to pursue their area of excellence and still be kids going through regular developmental stages.

It is a joy to both appreciate students' giftedness and also to facilitate their areas of normal growth.

—LAUNA ELLISON, **Teacher, Minneapolis Public Schools;**
author of *The Personal Intelligences: Promoting Social and*
Emotional Learning **(Thousand Oaks, CA: Corwin Press, 2001)**

Giftedness is natural ability in domains of life such as academics, athletics, the arts, spirituality, and many other areas. But it is far more than innate talent. It is commitment and dedication, diligence, respect for inquiry, and a near fanatical passion for excellence. There are a lot of bright people who clerk at convenience stores. The world-class sculptors, surgeons, and scientists are the bright people who know the secret to great accomplishment: hard work.

—JERRY FLACK, PH.D., **President's Teaching Scholar, University of Colorado**

Sometimes it's easier to say what giftedness is not than what it is. My conceptualization of giftedness is changing all the time. The more I study and think about it, the more questions I ask, and the more I talk with people who know giftedness, the clearer it becomes. I used to think of giftedness as intelligence.

Now I know that giftedness is more than intelligence. It's a way of being in the world. You can be smart and not be gifted. I think it's possible to have an IQ of 130 and not be gifted. I'm less sure about 145.

Giftedness is a way of responding to what goes on around you and within you. There are affective as well as cognitive components. Some people say that giftedness is what you do. I say okay, but isn't who you are a big part of what you're capable of doing? I'm not sure you can separate the two. There seem to be common personality characteristics among people who achieve at very high levels, but you can have those personality characteristics and *not* achieve at very high levels, too. I'm saying that giftedness seems to require both—who you are and what you do. We do a lousy job in general education of paying attention to these psychosocial factors. There's too much emphasis on achievement without providing the psychological supports needed to get there. We tend to demand and abandon.

—MAUREEN NEIHART, PSY.D.

I view giftedness as exceptional ability in one or more culturally valued domains. When most people in our society think of giftedness, they think of precocious intellectual or academic ability—not surprising given American education's emphasis on intelligence and scholastics. However, children can display artistic, musical, athletic, dramatic, interpersonal, aesthetic, leadership, creative, and other gifts. The number of types of gifts is only limited by what a given society recognizes or values.

I might like to add one additional point. I contend that not every individual is gifted, at least not in terms of my working definition of giftedness. If we accept the view that giftedness is exceptional ability or talent—either potential for or already demonstrated exceptional talent—then it logically follows that not everyone can be exceptional. Gifted individuals are unique because of their unusual, culturally valued talents.

—STEVEN I. PFEIFFER, PH.D., Diplomate, American Board of
Professional Psychology (ABPP); Licensed Psychologist;
Executive Director, Duke Talent Identification Program;
Research Professor of Education & Psychology, Duke University

My formal definition of giftedness is very much in line with that of my state. Giftedness means having the potential for performance at a remarkably high level of accomplishment in any area when compared to others of the same age, experience, or environment. I believe we recognize this giftedness in individuals by observing their behaviors. Each gifted person is unique with individual strengths, weaknesses, and emotional needs that require educational services not ordinarily provided by the schools in order to develop their potential. Because gifted behaviors are such a part of who these individuals are all of the time, these social and emotional issues must be at the center of any educational plan for gifted children, taking precedence over all others. While it is important for gifted children to feel successful at school in classrooms that match their abilities, even more essential is being accepted as someone free to express opinions without fear of ridicule or retribution.

Gifted children remind me of diamonds in the rough, tough but fragile in the early stages, with a value/potential not recognized by many. Without caring, understanding adults and supportive peers who recognize this potential, they will be tossed aside. For those who choose to accept the job of "polishing" to help gifted children realize their potential, the reward will be the chance to be a part of the lives of beautiful, rare, unique, and multifaceted treasures that increase in value with every passing day.

—ANN WINK, **Director of Elementary Gifted Education,
Advanced Academic Services, Texas Education Agency**

What Does Giftedness Mean to Society?

It is estimated that about three million children in the United States (or approximately 5.5 percent of the student population) are considered gifted. Sometimes it seems there are almost that many definitions of giftedness and ways of perceiving giftedness.

Dueling Definitions

There is no one right, absolute, or generally accepted definition of giftedness. Instead, there are federal and state government definitions, school and district definitions, researchers' definitions, advocacy organizations' definitions, dictionary definitions, encyclopedia definitions, teachers' definitions, parents' definitions, students' definitions . . . and the list goes on and on. Here's a sampling of definitions currently in use.

From *Encyclopedia Britannica Online:*

> **gifted child:** any of various children who are naturally endowed with a high degree of mental ability. Since little is known about special abilities, the term is usually confined in psychological and educational writings to a child whose

innate general ability rises above a certain specified borderline. The borderline itself is largely a matter of administrative convenience.

From the National Association for Gifted Children:

A gifted person is *someone who shows, or has the potential for showing, an exceptional level of performance in one or more areas of expression.* Some of these abilities are very general and can affect a broad spectrum of the person's life, such as leadership skills or the ability to think creatively. Some are very specific talents and are only evident in particular circumstances, such as a special aptitude in mathematics, science, or music. The term *giftedness* provides a general reference to this spectrum of abilities without being specific or dependent on a single measure or index.

From the *No Child Left Behind Act of 2001:*

The term "gifted and talented," when used with respect to students, children, or youth, means students, children, or youth who give evidence of high achievement capability in areas such as intellectual, creative, artistic, or leadership capacity, or in specific academic fields, and who need services or activities not ordinarily provided by the school in order to fully develop those capabilities.

From the U.S. Department of Education, *Marland Report* (1972):

Gifted and talented children are those identified by professionally qualified persons who by virtue of outstanding abilities are capable of high performance. These are children who require differentiated educational programs and/or services beyond those normally provided by the regular school program in order to realize their contributions to self and society.

Children capable of high performance include those with demonstrated achievement and/or potential ability in any of the following areas:

1. general intellectual ability
2. specific academic aptitude
3. creative or productive thinking
4. leadership ability
5. visual and performing arts
6. psychomotor ability

Note: Although the *Marland Report* definition has been criticized for being limiting and elitist, it has been and continues to be the one most widely adopted (or adapted) by state and local education agencies. If your school has a published definition of giftedness, chances are it's based on the *Marland Report.*

From the State of Pennsylvania:

[Giftedness is] outstanding intellectual and creative ability, the development of which requires specially designed programs or support services, or both, not ordinarily provided in the regular education program. This term includes a person who has an IQ of 130 or higher and when multiple criteria defined by the Department indicate gifted ability.

From three respected experts on giftedness:

Lewis Terman (1925): "The top one percent level in general intelligence ability as measured by the Stanford-Binet Intelligence Scale or a comparable instrument."

Dr. Paul Witty (1940): "There are children whose outstanding potentialities in art, in writing or in social leadership can be recognized largely by their performance. Hence, we have recommended that the definition of giftedness be expanded and that we consider any child gifted whose performance in a potentially valuable line of human activity is consistently remarkable."

Dr. Joseph Renzulli (1978): "Giftedness consists of an interaction among three basic clusters of human traits—these clusters being above average general abilities, high levels of task commitment, and high levels of creativity."

From a group of parents:

Giftedness is that precious endowment of potentially outstanding abilities which allows a person to interact with the environment with remarkably high levels of achievement and creativity.

What can we conclude from the above? Perhaps that existing definitions of giftedness are too general—and too restrictive.

We suggest that the main problem with any definition isn't what it says, but how it's used. When we use definitions of giftedness to develop criteria for identifying students who need more challenging educational opportunities, that's fine. When we use them to include people who really shouldn't be included, or exclude people who really shouldn't be excluded, that's not fine.

Here's another definition of giftedness that seems like a step in the right direction:[2]

Giftedness can be defined as *the ability to solve complex problems in effective, efficient, elegant, and economical ways.* Using this definition, a gifted individual is one who can use existing knowledge when necessary and can apply known methods when appropriate, therefore reaching solutions based on the best available knowledge and methods. However, a gifted individual can also abandon existing knowledge and concepts, redefine problems, devise new methods, and reach entirely different solutions.

Do Definitions Matter?

Why do we need to define giftedness? Because in many schools, a definition serves as a foundation for developing and funding an appropriate educational program for gifted children. No definition, no program.

By listing and describing certain abilities and talents, a definition helps teachers identify children who would benefit from a gifted program. That's why it's important for a definition to be broad yet specific, inclusive yet focused on particular qualities that set some children apart from their age peers and indicate the need for different types of educational opportunities.

Is your school working on a definition of giftedness? Is it reconsidering or revising an existing definition? If you're involved in this process, you might contribute the following suggestions from the ERIC Clearinghouse on Disabilities and Gifted Education:[3]

- The concept of giftedness is not limited to high intellectual ability. It also comprises creativity, ability in specific academic areas, ability in visual or performing arts, social adeptness, and physical dexterity.

- A program for gifted children should be based on the way in which the school system operationally defines giftedness. A definition should be the basis of decision regarding the selection of identification procedures as well as the provision of educational services for gifted children.

- Definitions of giftedness are influenced by social, political, economic, and cultural factors.

- Giftedness is found among all groups, including females, minorities, handicapped persons, persons with limited English-speaking proficiency, and migrants.

Create Your Own Definition

"The bottom line is a deep interest in children and how their minds are different from one another, and in helping them use their minds well."
—Howard Gardner

You've taken our "Teacher Inventory." You've read several definitions of giftedness. Maybe you've worked with (or are working with) your school to create or improve its definition of giftedness. Now we suggest that you create your own personal definition.

Look around your classroom and consider your students. Not just the ones who have been identified as gifted or selected for the gifted program, but *all* of your students. Pay special attention to the following:

Girls. Many girls have learned to cover up or deny their abilities in order to be popular, fit in, or feel "normal." This is especially true in middle school/junior high.

Boys. Boys are more likely than girls to rebel and question authority. Also, boys are on a different developmental schedule than girls. In general, they mature more slowly, particularly in the verbal and reading areas. They may be designated hyperactive, distractible, or disorderly. Add to this the fact that most teachers are women who tend to value conformity and obedience, and you can probably see the need to look again at the "difficult" boys in your class.

Students with disabilities. Physical, emotional, or learning disabilities (we prefer the term "learning differences") may hinder students' capacity to demonstrate their giftedness in accepted, recognizable ways. The traditional methods used to identify gifted kids would have excluded Helen Keller, among others.

Gifted people with disabilities have been called an "unseen minority." Researcher Nicholas Colangelo has observed that when teacher and parent groups are asked to imagine a "gifted child," they rarely picture a gifted child with disabilities.

Troublemakers. Some teachers and administrators associate "good" behavior with being gifted and "bad" behavior with being unwilling or unable to learn. Look beyond these stereotypes to find the students whose acting out may be the direct result of boredom or frustration.

Students from minority or nonmainstream groups. Their gifts may not be measurable by standard IQ and achievement tests, which are often biased to majority (white middle- to upper-class) students. Also, their gifts may lie in areas that are not celebrated or valued by the mainstream society.

Even when minority students are identified for inclusion in gifted programs, they may not succeed. Their behavior may not fit with the teacher's beliefs about what giftedness means or how gifted students should behave.

Native American children are taught to value interdependence, not independence; in their culture, decisions are made collectively. Puerto Rican children learn to seek the advice of their family rather than act independently. Mexican-American children are taught to respect their elders, the law, and authority, not individual competition, initiative, and self-direction. African-American students may have mixed feelings about academic success. High-achieving black students may be accused of "acting white."

These are only a few examples of why minority students are often not identified for gifted programs—and why those who are may end up being mistaught, feeling frustrated, and either dropping out of the program or being asked to leave.

Students who perform poorly on tests. Some gifted kids aren't good test-takers. They may know the material backwards and forwards, but they find the test situation too stressful to perform at their best. Or they may have personal problems that prevent them from concentrating. Since test scores are one of the main methods used to identify gifted students, this clearly puts them at a disadvantage.

Borderline cases. No matter what method(s) we use to identify and select gifted students, and regardless of how hard we try to be fair and inclusive, there are always some kids who fall between the cracks. If a student goes through your core curriculum faster than anyone else in the class; if he or she engages you in a conversation you don't have with most other students that age; if you think you recognize something special about him or her—a spark, a talent, raw potential—pay attention.

If you're not yet familiar with the work of Howard Gardner, a psychologist at the Harvard Graduate School of Education, we recommend that you explore his ideas. Gardner believes that the brain can't possibly have all of its many capabilities measured by a one-time IQ test. He maintains that the brain actually contains *eight* different intelligences. They are:

Linguistic Intelligence: a sensitivity to the meaning and order of words. The student who enjoys writing, reading, listening, speaking, memorizing, building his vocabulary, and telling stories may have this intelligence.

Logical-Mathematical Intelligence: ability in mathematics and other complex logical systems. The student who instinctively puts things in order, comprehends quantities, and loves brain-teasers, logic puzzles, games, and computers may possess this intelligence.

Musical Intelligence: the ability to understand and create music. The student who can detect rhythms, patterns, and tempos, who can "hear" tone and pitch, and who appreciates many kinds of music may be strong in this type of intelligence. Are there any musicians, composers, and/or dancers in your class?

Visual-Spatial Intelligence: the ability to "think in pictures," to perceive the visual world accurately, and to re-create (or alter) it in the mind or on paper. Watch for the student who "sees" symmetry, can draw whatever she sees, is good at taking things apart and putting them back together, and loves games.

Bodily-Kinesthetic Intelligence: the ability to use one's body in a skilled way for self-expression or to achieve a goal. Does your class include any dancers, athletes, actors, or mimes? Is there a student who seems talented at one or more crafts, like carving, sewing, weaving, or making pots?

Interpersonal Intelligence: the ability to perceive and understand other people's moods, desires, and motivations. Who are the "politicians" in your class? The natural leaders? The motivators and mediators? They may have this intelligence.

Intrapersonal Intelligence: the ability to understand oneself and one's own emotions. Who in your class seems especially aware of his own feelings, dreams, ideas, and goals? Who "marches to the beat of a different drummer"? Do you have any students who enjoy journaling? Is anyone writing a novel?

Naturalist Intelligence: the ability to recognize and classify plants, minerals, and animals. Look for students who feel a deep connection to the natural world and its inhabitants, who enjoy experiencing and observing the out-of-doors, and who like to garden and/or cook. Gardner has identified Charles Darwin as a prime example of this intelligence.

Are you ready for more possibilities? Yale psychology professor Robert Sternberg has defined three types of intelligence. They are:

Contextual Intelligence: the one you use when you adapt to your environment, change your environment, or choose a different environment that better suits your needs.

Experiential Intelligence: the one you use whenever you build on your experience to solve problems in new situations.

Internal Intelligence: the one you use to approach a problem, then evaluate the feedback to decide if you should change your approach.

Then there's **emotional intelligence,** which gained national attention when Harvard Ph.D. Daniel Goleman wrote a book about it in 1995. Goleman identified several qualities that add up to "a different way of being smart," including self-awareness, impulse control, persistence, zeal, self-motivation, empathy, and social deftness.

There's also **emotional giftedness.** This term was coined by Michael Piechowski, a professor of education and psychology at Northland College in Ashland, Wisconsin, who studied and translated the work of Polish psychiatrist Kazimierz Dabrowski (1902–1980). When Dabrowski studied a group of gifted children and youth, he discovered that they displayed something he called "overexcitabilities." They perceived things more intensely and thought about them more deeply than their age peers. They lived life to the fullest and experienced emotional highs and lows, joys and sorrows to extreme degrees. They were extraordinarily, exquisitely sensitive to everything around them. Today, overexcitability—OE—is one of the signs of giftedness that teachers who know about it look for.

See Chapter 2: Identifying Gifted Kids for more ideas and suggestions that may help you to create your own definition of giftedness.

Giftedness In Brief

by Susan Winebrenner, M.S., consultant and author

People often ask me for a "short list" of the characteristics gifted children have which make identification easier. I believe that any student who possesses most or all of the following five characteristics is probably gifted.

1. Learns new material faster, and at an earlier age, than age peers.

2. Remembers what has been learned forever, making review unnecessary.

3. Is able to deal with concepts that are too complex and abstract for age peers.

4. Has a passionate interest in one or more topics, and would spend all available time learning more about that topic if he or she could.

5. Does not need to watch the teacher to hear what is being said; can operate on multiple brain channels simultaneously and process more than one task at a time.

To be gifted, one does not have to possess all of these characteristics. However, when you observe students consistently exhibiting many of these behaviors, the possibility that they are gifted is very strong.

From *Teaching Gifted Kids in the Regular Classroom: Strategies and Techniques Every Teacher Can Use to Meet the Academic Needs of the Gifted and Talented*, Revised, Expanded, Updated ed., by Susan Winebrenner (Minneapolis: Free Spirit Publishing Inc., 2001), pp. 9–10. Used with permission.

Mixed Messages

We reward our gifted athletes with pep rallies, scholarships, and multi-million-dollar contracts and endorsements. We reward our gifted musicians with Grammys and our gifted actors with Oscars. What do we do for our intellectually and academically gifted students? We send them mixed messages.

It's good to be smart . . . as long as you're not *too* smart. *Too* smart makes you a nerd, an egghead, and a teacher-pleaser. It can even make you a target for suspicion, resentment, and open hostility. It's good to get high grades . . . as long as you don't talk about them. That's bragging, and besides, you might injure someone else's self-esteem. It's good to score high on tests . . . as long as you keep this fact to yourself, or within your small circle of similarly brainy friends.

We know that children are profoundly influenced by what they see on television and in movies. How are gifted children often portrayed? As solitary loners, loyal side-kicks, social misfits, outcasts, misunderstood rebels, geeks, weaklings, and geniuses in hiding, waiting to be discovered and saved from themselves.

Researchers Tracy L. Cross and Larry J. Coleman have studied the lives of gifted students in school since the middle 1980s. Their many published articles—including "Is Being Gifted a Social Handicap?" and "The Social Cognition of Gifted Adolescents in School: Managing the Stigma of Giftedness"—reveal a troubled and troubling world. One gifted adolescent Cross interviewed:[4]

> . . . *perceived that gifted students are physically weak, socially inadequate, and not interesting people. They are out of touch, unattractive, and have a high propensity for mental problems. While the student knew that many of these descriptors did not fit him, he had come to believe that to be gifted was somewhat limiting.*

In our own interviews with gifted children, many said that neither their parents nor their teachers talk about giftedness. Many kids concluded that it was something secretive and therefore bad, which increased their fears of being different. We suspect that virtually all highly gifted kids know they are different by the time they are five or six years old. This awareness of difference can turn into feelings of being strange or "weird" if the differences are not acknowledged.

Every gifted person we've ever taught, interviewed, talked with, worked with, or lived with admits to enjoying the benefits of being intelligent—knowing how to think deeply, think creatively, feel intensely, understand complex concepts, explore a variety of interests, make connections that others don't see, solve problems, come up with unique ideas, and so on. It's the mixed messages and skewed perceptions of giftedness that make the label more of a burden than a blessing. It's the insensitive, uninformed comments from teachers, peers, and/or parents that make gifted kids want to downplay, deny, or hide their giftedness.

Tracy L. Cross tells of a reporter for the *Chicago Tribune* who interviewed her about Theodore Kaczynski, the "Unabomber":[5]

The reporter had worked for weeks putting together a story about Kaczynski's history that emphasized the fact that he was a gifted student. Several leaders in the field of gifted education were interviewed. The reporter asked me, "Did Ted Kaczynski commit murder because he was allowed to skip two grades in school?" What an amazing assumption! Does accelerating gifted students cause them to become serial killers? My response was, "I hope not, because tens of thousands of students are gradeskipped each year." I was stunned to learn that such learned people could hold such foolish misconceptions. Imagine what messages are sent to gifted students by less well-educated or academically oriented people. Also imagine how gifted students are actually treated if large numbers of adults, including well-educated adults, hold such wild misconceptions about them.

Gifted Kids Speak Out

"Yes, I learn faster than other kids, but I still have normal friends and I'm not a NERD!"

—Angela, 10

"When should I or *shouldn't* I use my vocabulary? I don't use big words on purpose, it's just that I do seem to have a larger vocabulary than my peers. I'm not trying to show off, but I also don't want to degrade myself. People don't seem to understand this, and it's frustrating for me."

—Annie, 13

The Myth of Elitism

"Gifted education is elitist." We've heard this a million times (granted, that's probably a *slight* exaggeration), and chances are you have, too.

Ours is an allegedly egalitarian nation. We're supposed to give all children the same opportunities to learn, grow, and realize their potential. We're not supposed to give some children special, better, extra opportunities. *That's not fair.*

In fact, gifted education is elitist only if that is the attitude of the staff. A good program promotes a positive attitude about self-worth regardless of ability. And, as psychologist and gifted expert Linda Kreger Silverman notes, "Contrary to popular public opinion, when the gifted are placed in classes together, they do not come to the conclusion that they are 'better than everyone else.' Rather, they are humbled by finding peers who know more than they do."[6]

Gifted children should not be asked to sacrifice an appropriate education to the needs of other children. If we make adjustments and provide for students who are having trouble performing to grade-level standards—which we do—then it stands to reason we should also accommodate those students whose abilities and knowledge exceed what's being taught in the regular classroom, and whose performance regularly surpasses those standards. *That's fair.*

Yet the battle over elitism rages. One director of elementary education in a town in Massachusetts said, "I wouldn't want a gifted and talented program [here]. That's elitist. I think the very term 'gifted and talented' is elitist. I think that all children have different gifts and we should be trying to provide for them."[7] In contrast, Sheila Ehrich, legislative liaison for the Minnesota Council for the Gifted and Talented, gave the following argument against elitism to her state's K–12 Education Finance Committee in early 2001:[8]

> *Is a major portion of a section of every daily newspaper devoted to academic achievements? Are a boy and girl scholar lauded regularly on TV stations across the state? . . . Why have we chosen to exalt and nurture one form of giftedness—athletics—and at the same time to routinely neglect others? Why do we devote millions of dollars on sports knowing only one high school athlete in 12,000 . . . will earn a penny playing sports, but not one categorical dime for our best and brightest academicians, when we know all of our students need their minds to succeed? . . . It is time to end the hypocrisy. Everyone wants the best doctor, teacher, lawyer, engineer, and architect when their services are required. The businesses in our state are searching desperately for employees qualified to lead their companies, create new products for their companies, and provide the economic growth and successful worldwide competition Minnesota is seeking. Yet we allow these future professionals to sit in classes bored, frustrated and underchallenged during their critically formative K–12 years. Does this make any sense?*

Even schools that do have gifted programs sometimes seem reluctant to acknowledge or promote them. They worry about the kids who aren't labeled "gifted," and they try to minimize the potential for bad feelings by calling their programs Quest or Explorer Clubs, SEARCH, SAGE, STAR, PEAK, REACH, or GATE, to give a few examples. Instead of "gifted students," these schools have "high flyers" or "high potentials." Other schools open up their gifted classes to all students capable of maintaining a B average; these students are given less threatening labels like "bright" or "high achievers."

As teachers, we've all met some overeager parents who lobby to get their children into the school's gifted program. In contrast, there are parents who feel unsettled by their kid's gifted status and would rather keep it quiet. Some children have refused to join a gifted program because they don't want the stigma or the threat of heavy new expectations. Some parents occasionally say, "I just wish my child was normal!" (Is bright abnormal?)

What these wide discrepancies in attitude and behavior point to are the conflicts which come with thinking about a perhaps innately threatening concept: superior ability. Perhaps these conflicts arise because society is too quick to jump to the conclusion that superior intelligence, talent, or ability means superior *people*, which implies that the rest of humanity is inferior.

As a democratic society, we are still coming to terms with unequal distribution of "gifts" and "unfair" loadings of potential. "If 'superior' people get 'special' attention," the critics ask, "isn't that giving them unfair advantage?" Doesn't the existence of gifted education acknowledge that individual students do not have equal chances to get a piece of the American pie?

As an educational community, we are still very much in the process of defining giftedness, of measuring it, and of accepting the gifted student as a legitimate target for instruction. Part of the challenge of gifted education stems from working in an immature discipline still busy discovering its necessary "truths" and appropriate methods of practice. As Neil Daniel, editor of the *Gifted Students Institute Quarterly*, puts it, "The simple truth is . . . we don't know what intelligence is. We are unable to define giftedness. And we can't say, really, how anybody thinks."[9] This makes gifted education even more controversial and accusations of "elitism" even more likely.

Meanwhile, gifted students keep turning up in our classrooms, their eyes sparkling with eagerness and challenge, their worries pouring out—or locking up within. And highly gifted but underachieving students continue to drop out of school—if not physically, then mentally and emotionally. In some very tragic instances, our brightest young adults commit suicide. These students have a right to education designed for their level of ability. With few exceptions, they cannot and do not find their way on their own.

The Ten Commandments . . .

. . . That Foster Elitism
(How Gifted Children Develop Feelings of Superiority)

I. Thou shalt be told that boredom is part of life and that easy, redundant work must be tolerated.

II. Thou shalt often hear classmates express frustration because the test was hard . . . when thou thought it was easy.

III. Thou shalt procrastinate on long-term assignments until the day before they are due . . . and thou shalt turn them in and get A's.

IV. Thou shalt hear classmates ask questions of thy teacher that thy teacher answered clearly yesterday.

V. Thou shalt receive numerous telephone calls from classmates the night before a test asking how to solve a difficult problem.

VI. Thou shalt consistently get good grades without having to work or study hard.

. . . That Foster Understanding
(How Gifted Children Develop Humility as They Develop Their Talents)

I. Thou shalt regularly experience work that is relevant, stimulating, and challenging.

II. Thou shalt have expectations placed upon thee that are in line with thy aptitude.

III. Thou shalt learn that self-discipline, long-range planning, and hard work are necessary before thou canst produce quality work.

IV. Thou shalt have the opportunity to hear thy classmates ask questions of thy teacher and thyself that are hard questions—questions which require deep thought and careful consideration.

V. Thou shalt find it necessary to occasionally phone thy classmates to ask for their help and perspective.

VI. Thou shalt work hard to earn thy good grades—and come to realize that the excellence of thy work and the quality of thy ideas are more important than grades.

continued . . .

VII. Thou shalt know the answer to every question the teacher asks . . . and can answer the questions no one else can.

VII. Thou shalt experience humility as questions are raised by thy teacher and thy classmates—questions to which thou dost not know the answer (and of which thou never thought).

VIII. Thou shalt have thyself, thy grades, and thy work held up, by thy teacher, as examples to be emulated.

VIII. Thou shalt, through associations and discussions with thy classmates, come to appreciate that talents come in many forms and that no one talent is more valuable than another.

IX. Thou shalt be chosen first by the team captain for spelling, math, and geography bees.

IX. Thou shalt come to realize that thou, too, hast both strengths and weaknesses, as do other students.

X. In short, thou shalt have ample opportunity to believe that aptitude is equated with human value and that if thou art smarter, thou art better.

X. In short, through a diversity of experiences with thy classmates and teachers, thou shalt come to a fuller and richer understanding of every person's worth. Thou shalt come to realize that human value and intellectual aptitude can never be equated.

Adapted from Bruce A. Clair's "The Ten Commandments," *Gifted Child Today* (September/October 1985).

More Myths and Misconceptions

"Gifted education is elitist" is just one of several myths and misconceptions about giftedness. Here are more you'll doubtless encounter—and rebuttals you might find useful.

Myth: Gifted kids have it made and will succeed in life no matter what. They don't need any special services or help in school or anywhere else.

Fact: Everyone needs some help to make the most of their abilities and succeed in life, even kids who seem to "have it all" from the start. As educational researcher Benjamin S. Bloom has said, "No matter what the initial characteristics (or gifts) of the individuals, unless there is a long and intensive process of encouragement, nurturance, education, and training, the individuals will not attain extreme levels of capability."[10] Also, gifted kids may appear to do fine on their own when they're younger. But as the years go by and their schoolwork becomes more challenging, they may have a harder time, especially if they've never faced challenges before.

Myth: Gifted kids should love school, get high grades, and greet each new school day with enthusiasm.
Fact: Most schools are geared for average learners, not gifted learners, which makes it hard for gifted students to get excited about school. Some of the most talented students in the United States actually choose to drop out of school altogether.

Myth: Gifted students come from white middle- and upper-class families.
Fact: They come from all cultural, ethnic, religious, and socioeconomic groups.

Myth: Gifted kids have pushy parents.
Fact: Some do, some don't. Some parents want to make sure that their children get the learning opportunities they need, and they may be very vocal and persistent about it. Other parents worry about calling extra attention to their children and say nothing.

Myth: Gifted kids are good at everything they do.
Fact: Some gifted students are good at many things; others are exceptionally able at only a few things. Some gifted students also have learning differences, which means that they might not be very good at schoolwork.

Myth: Teachers love having gifted students in their classes.
Fact: Some do, some don't. Certain teachers feel uncomfortable with gifted students and get defensive when they suspect that their students know more than they do.

Myth: If gifted students are grouped together, they become snobbish and stuck-up.
Fact: Some do, some don't. What's especially pernicious about this myth is that adults have used it to rationalize decisions about *not* grouping gifted students or providing them with appropriate learning opportunities.

Myth: Gifted kids have trouble adjusting to school and forming friendships.
Fact: Some do, some don't—just like other kids.

Myth: Gifted students don't know they're "different" unless someone tells them.
Fact: Most gifted kids don't need to be identified or labeled before they know that they're not quite like their age peers.

Myth: Gifted students must constantly be challenged and kept busy or they'll get lazy.
Fact: They might get bored, but they won't necessarily get lazy.

Myth: Gifted kids are equally mature in all areas—academic, physical, social, and emotional.
Fact: That would be convenient, but it's simply not true. Asynchronous development is common among gifted children.* On the other hand, it's not reasonable to assume that just because someone is advanced intellectually, he or she will lag behind in other developmental areas.

Myth: Gifted kids need to go through school with kids their own age.
Fact: They may need to play with them and interact socially with them, but they don't necessarily need to *learn* with them. For the child who started reading at age four, a first-grade reading class can be torture.

Myth: Gifted kids tend to be weak and sickly.
Fact: Actually, gifted children tend to be physically stronger than their age peers. They have fewer illnesses and are generally taller and heavier.

Myth: It's easy for teachers to recognize which children in their classes are gifted.
Fact: Teachers without any training in this area have only a 50 percent chance of accurately identifying gifted kids.

Myth: Gifted children are all alike.
Fact: There is no one "portrait" of a gifted student. Talents and strengths among the gifted vary as widely as they do with any sample of students drawn from a so-called "average" population. Some educators distinguish between academically gifted and socially gifted; between highly gifted and normally gifted; and between highly creative and highly talented students. Many other breakdowns and categories exist.

Myth: Gifted children share common psychological traits or personalities.
Fact: Some are outgoing risk-takers, challengers of the status quo. Some are quiet, satisfied with their private world. As learners, some need constant feedback; others

---

* For more on this topic, see pages 146–149.

don't. Some need a tremendous amount of encouragement to perform, or a lot of structure. Others ask for help after class, or look up a special teacher years later to get advice.

Myth: All children are gifted.
Fact: We'll let Nicholas Colangelo handle this one. In his words:[11]

> *If by the phrase "all children are gifted" it is meant that all children are of value, all can do more if encouraged, and all have untapped potential, I am in your camp. But if the phrase means that all kids can do calculus in sixth grade, all students can achieve a composite score of 32 on the ACT, all kids can score 780 on the SAT-M, that all students can be piano virtuosi, or play professional baseball, then I am gone from the group.*

In sum: Most of these myths assume a sameness about gifted children—in how they learn, how they behave, how they think and feel, what they do or don't need. But gifted children are more different from each other than alike. This is one characteristic they share with all other children: their uniqueness and individuality.

What About the Label?

> *"Some degree of 'labeling' is essential if gifted children*
> *are to grow up understanding how and why they experience*
> *the world differently from others."*
> —Draper Kauffman

That "gifted" is a controversial label you know well enough, probably through personal experience. Think back to your first introduction to the term. What did you assume it meant? Think back to your first parent or staff meeting on the topic of gifted education. Can you remember what people's reactions were?

One mother we know had a 5-year-old child who scored above 150 on the Stanford-Binet Intelligence Scale. Both she and the school had suspected that the boy was gifted. When she called her relatives to tell them the surprising news, their response was, "Oh, boy, I bet you're going to have trouble with him now!" Compare this reaction to telling a friend that you had just inherited a million dollars or won the lottery. Imagine your friend saying, "Oh, boy, I bet you'll have to pay a lot of taxes on that load!" How likely is that?

"In general, I don't tell many people," this mother said. "I get the feeling they'd be a whole lot more supportive if I said my son had a learning disability."

The language people use to describe gifted students indicates how comfortable they are with the concept of exceptional intellect or talent. For some reason, it's easier for society to name, praise, and financially reward the outstanding athlete (and the outstanding entertainer) than the brilliant mathematician or poet. The teasing that "brainy kids" endure in junior and senior high school contrasts sharply with the celebration that "jocks" enjoy.

To some people, giftedness suggests elitism in the racial or class sense. They assume that kids selected for gifted programs are well-behaved, upper middle-class, and white. They fear that the inherent cliquishness of ability grouping will invite the "good test-takers" to assume the mantle of moral and intellectual superiority. Both of these concerns are probably true in what we fervently hope are isolated incidences. Whenever gifted programs do drift toward biased selection processes, or infer undue privilege to certain students, they do real damage to the credibility of gifted education. Nonetheless, it's important to realize that resentments come inevitably with the selection process itself. By identifying one group as gifted, does that make all other children "ungifted"? Aren't we all equal, and all special? Well, yes, but . . .

Parents whose children are not selected for the program may question whether gifted students are getting *different kinds* of levels of instruction, or whether they're simply getting *better* instruction. Wouldn't gifted education programs benefit the average child, too? These parents worry that student performance in "regular" classrooms will go down once the top-level students are pulled out. In fact, the opposite is true. Able children may suddenly find themselves blossoming without the presence of clearly advanced students. It's as though the way has been cleared for them to perform.

Disagreement over the term extends to educational professionals as well. Some experts promote more generalized labels and advise against calling any group of students "the gifted." They recommend that schools broaden their assessment processes by testing all students and relaxing cut-off scores. They favor "throwing a wide net in early childhood and later allowing the educational programming to select those students with unusual talent and motivation."[12] Others believe that to water down the definition is to lose whatever momentum the movement has gained; the end result would (again) be inadequate education for the children at the highest levels of ability.

Like it or not, the label "gifted" is here today, and we need to get used to it. In our view, all labels are equally bad, and calling kids "high flyers" as opposed to "gifted" fools no one and imparts a sense of secrecy (shame? false modesty?) as well. Intelligence is a good thing. So is athletic ability. We don't go out of our way to call the football team something other than the football team, or the marching band anything other than the marching band. Why must we call our brightest students something other than bright or talented? Parents who try to protect their child from the label may end up doing more harm than good. Kids will hear the label anyway, yet have no skills for defusing and processing it.

One teacher commented, "I don't think any of us in the field can give up the term [gifted] because we've finally been able to get it accepted and recognized on a national level." This is an important point, because designing curriculum to serve newly identified needs or populations is definitely a political act. As another teacher said, "Politics is right up there next to direct service. You're constantly involved with politics." And a political movement or group cannot survive without a name.

How students feel about their abilities and the label "gifted" (or whatever group name is used) will depend a great deal on how their parents and teachers feel about them, and how they use the term. Therefore, your attitudes about giftedness are critical.

Gifted Teachers (and Kids) Speak Out

When we piloted our "Teacher Inventory" on gifted education teachers, we asked them whether or not they use the label "gifted." Here are some of the responses we received:

- "I use it because it is good to get it into the vocabulary and to become used to it. It shouldn't be a word to avoid."

- "I try not to use it because it is so misunderstood and misused."

- "I haven't felt qualified to use this label."

- "A gift is something you've been given and you shouldn't have to apologize for that."

- "It is appropriate, although it often means different things to each person hearing it."

- "I do not use it all the time because of the problems it creates for kids. I do use it in specific sessions to help them know how to deal with the label."

- "I use it for lack of anything better, but I don't like labeling any student, whether they are slow or advanced. Teachers do need to categorize students, but I don't think students need to hear the labels we place on them."

- "What's wrong with the word gifted? Everyone knows what it means."

continued . . .

When we asked kids how they feel about being called "gifted," here's what they said:

- ■ "It depends on how it is being used. If someone is giving me a compliment, I like it. But if someone is making fun of me, I don't."

- ■ "Sometimes I don't like it because it makes me feel different."

- ■ "I feel proud."

- ■ "I don't like being called gifted that much. I just like being called my regular name."

- ■ "I feel great, but I don't like to show it."

- ■ "I feel happy because my parents are proud of me, but other times I feel embarrassed."

What Does Giftedness Mean to Kids?

When you ask a dozen gifted kids what giftedness means to them, you're likely to get a dozen (or more) different answers. Some won't want to talk about it. Some will toss a succinct phrase or two your way. And some will go into detail because giftedness—being gifted—is at the core of who they are. It affects their school experience, their relationships with friends, families, and teachers, their self-esteem, their future plans, their expectations, their goals, and almost everything else about their lives.

If you want to know what your gifted students think about giftedness—and themselves and their lives—invite them to complete the "Student Questionnaire" on pages 40–45. The purpose of the questionnaire is twofold:

1. It will give you a reading on how your students feel about themselves and others, on what they think being gifted and being in a gifted class means, and how seriously affected they are by problems known to surface among gifted youth.

2. It will stimulate kids to think about these conflicts, their areas of strength and need, and their feelings.

The questionnaire is a good first strategy for discussing these issues because students have the option to remain anonymous. As such, it won't give you answers from specific individuals (although some students may choose to give their names, and you may know the identities of others by their answers). It will give you collective insights into the following:

1. Why do students think they are in your class?

2. What do students think the class is all about?

3. What do students think gifted (or whatever label is used) means?

4. In what ways do students feel different from most other peers?

5. In what ways do students feel the same?

6. What emotional issues and problems do they have in their lives right now?

7. Who are their support systems?

8. What do they do to feel good about themselves?

The questionnaire is designed for all gifted and talented students, but you may wish to modify it in some way for your students. Younger children may need a shortened form and slightly different lists under certain items. Older students may need differently worded instructions.

We've found that the more time we spend introducing the questionnaire and our purposes, the better data we receive. High school students in our pilot group took about 15 minutes to complete the survey, junior high students slightly longer.

We suggest that you *don't* assign the questionnaire as homework (you won't get many back), and that you *don't* give students only five minutes at the end of the day to complete it. Rather, we recommend using this tool as a learning activity and allowing students ample time to fill it out. You might have your students complete the questionnaire at the beginning and the end of the year for comparison, or use a variation as a course or program evaluation form.

Section D of the questionnaire asks students to indicate how often they experience a series of feelings or problems. These feelings or problems are common among gifted kids, as indicated by our own surveys. In fact, they're so common that we call them the "Great Gripes of Gifted Kids." On pages 129–130, you'll find a shorter activity that focuses specifically on the "Eight Great Gripes." Chapter 7: Understanding Gifted Kids from the Outside In presents in-depth discussions of all eight topics that you can use with your students.

Gifted Kids on Giftedness

More than 1,000 gifted children responded to an online survey regarding their gift-edness. Here are some of their responses:

Q. Gifted kids are often described as: easily bored when not intellectually challenged, needing a lot of novelty, craving mental stimulation, and are often overexcitable. In general, how true is this for you?

22% All of the time	41% Most of the time
29% Some of the time	8% Infrequently

Q. Gifted kids are often described as: intuitive, insightful, perceptive, and able to simultaneously see several points of view. In general, how true is this for you?

38% All of the time	49% Most of the time
13% Some of the time	1% Infrequently

Q. Gifted kids are often described as: introverted, preferring privacy, reflective, quiet in large groups, and uncomfortable as the center of attention in a large group. In general, how true is this for you?

24% All of the time	19% Most of the time
21% Some of the time	36% Infrequently

Q. Gifted kids are often described as: possessing a keen sense of justice, non-conforming, and frequently questioning rules and authority. In general, how true is this for you?

49% All of the time	28% Most of the time
18% Some of the time	5% Infrequently

From Steven I. Pfeiffer, "TIPsters Attitudes About Their Giftedness," *Insights* 14:1 (Fall 1999), pp. 1–2. Used with permission.

Notes

1. "Giftedness and the Gifted: What's It All About?" ERIC Digest #E476 (Reston, VA: ERIC Clearinghouse on Disabilities and Gifted Education, 1990).

2. Reported by C. June Maker in "Identification of Gifted Minority Students: A National Problem, Needed Changes and a Promising Solution," *Gifted Child Quarterly* 40:1 (Winter 1996), p. 44. Based on work by H. Gardner, C.J. Maker, A.B. Nielsen, J.A. Rogers, and P. Bauerie.

3. Elizabeth McClellan, "Defining Giftedness," ERIC Digest ED 262519 (Reston, VA: ERIC Clearinghouse on Disabilities and Gifted Education, 1985).

4. Tracy L. Cross, "The Lived Experiences of Gifted Students in School or On Gifted Students and Columbine," *Gifted Child Today* magazine (January 2000).

5. Ibid.

6. Linda Kreger Silverman, Ph.D., "The False Accusation of Elitism" (Denver, CO: Gifted Development Center). *www.gifteddevelopment.com.*

7. Dan Sheridan, "Scant School Accommodation for State's Brightest Children," *Boston* magazine (October 1999), p. 81.

8. Sheila Ehrich, "Rationale for Funding Gifted Education" (Minneapolis: The Minnesota Council for the Gifted and Talented, February 2001).

9. Neil Daniel, "New Questions About Talented People," *Gifted Students Institute Quarterly* 10:15 (1985).

10. Benjamin S. Bloom, *Developing Talent in Young People* (New York: Ballantine Books, 1985).

11. Nicholas Colangelo, "Message from the Director," *Vision* 7:1 (1998), p. 2.

12. Reported in June Cox, Neil Daniel, and Bruce O. Boston, "Executive Summary," *Educating Able Learners: Programs and Promising Practices* (Austin, TX: University of Texas Press, 1985).

Teacher Inventory

1. Personally, I think giftedness means _____

_____

_____

_____

_____

2. I do/do not use the "gifted" label because _____

_____

_____

_____

3. I'm like my gifted students in these ways: _____

_____

_____

_____

4. I'm different from my gifted students in these ways: _____

_____

_____

_____

5. When I tell other people that I work with gifted students, I feel . . .
(Check all that apply, and/or add your own descriptions.)

_____ proud   _____ compelled to explain/justify what I do

_____ embarrassed   _____ eager to talk about it

_____ guilty   _____ nothing in particular

_____ _____   _____ _____

_____ _____   _____ _____

continued . . .

Teacher Inventory continued . . .

6. To minimize the hard feelings between students in my gifted class/group and their friends (or between my class and other classes), I try to_____

_____

_____

_____

7. When I think about my gifted students,

they seem *similar to* other children their age in these ways:

they seem *different from* other children their age in these ways:

_____   _____

_____   _____

_____   _____

_____   _____

_____   _____

_____   _____

8. This is what I expect of my gifted students as a group and individually:

_____

_____

_____

9. The gifted kids I have the EASIEST time with are those who are:_____

_____

or do:_____

or are good in: _____

continued . . .

Teacher Inventory continued . . .

10. The gifted kids I have the HARDEST time with are those who are:_____

_____

or do:_____

or are good in: _____

11. When I can't answer a student's question, or I feel that I'm "losing control" of the class, these are the things I do:_____

_____

12. The best thing(s) I have to offer my gifted students is (are) my:_____

_____

_____

13. I think I could improve my teaching by _____

_____

_____

_____

14. I think that we, as an education community, need to change or improve gifted education programs in the following ways:_____

_____

_____

_____

15. One thing I'd like to change or do differently in the gifted program at my school is:_____

_____

_____

Student Questionnaire

*This questionnaire is about you. I'd like you to fill it out so I can be a better teacher for you and this class. There are no right or wrong answers. The most important thing is for you to think honestly about the questions. You may remain anonymous, and you may choose to skip some of the questions. But I hope you'll try answering them all—you'll get more out of the questionnaire if you do. All answers will be kept strictly confidential, although we'll talk about some of the questions later on as a group. **P.S.** If you need more writing room, turn the paper over and write on the back.*

A. Basic Information

Your age:_____   Your gender *(circle one)*:   M   F

The number of years you've spent in a gifted class or program *(circle one)*:

0   1   2   3   4   5   6   more

B. Questions You May Already Be Asking Yourself

1. What does "gifted" mean to you?_____

_____

_____

2. How do you feel about the "gifted" label? _____

_____

_____

3. How were you selected for this class or program?_____

_____

_____

continued . . .

4. How do you feel about the selection process? _____

_____

_____

5. What do you think the purpose of this class/program is? *(Check all that apply. Add your own ideas, if you want.)*

_____ I don't know

_____ Harder work than other classes

_____ More work than other classes

_____ More challenging or interesting work

_____ Friendships with people like me

_____ Place to have fun

_____ Place where I'm not considered weird

_____ Learn something new

_____ Be stimulated to try new things

_____ Nothing different from other classes

_____ _____

_____ _____

_____ _____

C. Feelings About Yourself

6. In what ways are you the same as most other kids your age? What things do you have in common? _____

_____

_____

continued . . .

Student Questionnaire continued . . .

7. In what ways are you different from most other kids your age? What makes you unique?_____

_____

_____

8. In terms of your popularity . . . *(check one):*

_____ I have tons of close friends and am liked by almost everybody.

_____ I have a lot of close friends.

_____ I have several (four or five) close friends.

_____ I have one or two close friends.

_____ I have no close friends.

9. In terms of how you feel about yourself . . . *(check one):*

_____ I hate myself.

_____ I don't like myself much.

_____ I like parts of myself but dislike other parts.

_____ I feel okay about myself.

_____ Most of the time, I like myself a lot.

_____ I've always liked myself a lot.

10. If you could change one thing about yourself, it would be:_____

_____

_____

11. The best thing about you, as far as you're concerned, is:_____

_____

_____

continued . . .

D. Conflicts

12. How often do you experience the following feelings or problems? *For each, circle 1 (not at all), 2 (hardly ever), 3 (sometimes), 4 (a lot), or 5 (all the time).*

Feeling or Problem	How Frequently Felt?				
a. I wonder what gifted means.	1	2	3	4	5
b. I wonder why they say I'm gifted, and what is expected of me.	1	2	3	4	5
c. School is too easy, too boring.	1	2	3	4	5
d. Parents, teachers, and friends expect me to be perfect all the time.	1	2	3	4	5
e. Friends who really understand me are hard to find.	1	2	3	4	5
f. Kids often tease me about being smart (or for being interested in certain things, getting high grades, etc.).	1	2	3	4	5
g. I feel overwhelmed by the number of things I can understand or do.	1	2	3	4	5
h. I feel different, alienated, alone.	1	2	3	4	5
i. I worry about world problems, or problems in my family, and feel helpless to do anything about these problems.	1	2	3	4	5

13. What's your biggest problem or difficulty in life right now?_____

_____

_____

_____

_____

continued . . .

Student Questionnaire continued...

14. Generally, how do you feel about your life? (*Make a slash somewhere along this continuum.*)

Feel really great,
confident, happy

Feel extremely bad,
upset, worried;
think about dying

E. Support Systems

15. Who do you share your feelings or problems with when you're wondering what life is about, or who you are? Who do you go to—or like to be around—when things aren't so great? (*Check all that apply.*)

_____ friend

_____ mother

_____ father

_____ sister

_____ brother

_____ other relative

_____ pet (dog, cat)

_____ coach

_____ clergy (minister, rabbi, priest, spiritual leader, etc.)

_____ school counselor

_____ camp counselor

_____ psychologist or doctor

_____ official Big Brother or Sister

_____ other adult (example: neighbor)

_____ teacher

_____ I prefer just being alone

_____ I don't think about that kind of stuff

16. What do you do to feel good about yourself? (*Check all that apply. Add your own ideas, if you want.*)

_____ think or study harder

_____ get some exercise (get on my bike, go for a run, head for the gym, dance, etc.)

_____ call a friend on the phone

continued . . .

Student Questionnaire continued . . .

_____ communicate with a friend on the computer
(chat room, email, instant messaging)

_____ write in a journal

_____ paint or do other artwork or crafts

_____ play a musical instrument

_____ work on a project (club, play, newspaper, etc.)

_____ play harder in sports

_____ earn some extra money

_____ go somewhere (mall, park, a friend's house, etc.)

_____ watch TV

_____ talk to my parent(s)

_____ talk to my teacher

_____ listen to music

_____ eat

_____ use relaxation techniques (yoga, meditation, deep breathing, etc.)

_____ _____

_____ _____

_____ _____

17. If you could get this class or program to do or provide one thing for you, it would be:_____

_____

_____

_____

Your name (optional):_____

CHAPTER 2

Identifying Gifted Kids

"A loving, caring teacher took a liking to me. She noticed the potential and wanted to help shape it."

—TOM BRADLEY

Even if you're not old enough to remember watching *American Bandstand*, the TV show hosted by Dick Clark, it's so vivid an icon of our culture that the mere mention of its name conjures up images of poodle skirts, white sport coats, and pink carnations. A memorable feature of every show was the debut of a song by an up-and-coming rock-and-roller. The assembled masses would dance, applaud at the end . . . and then came the drama: Dick Clark, microphone in hand, would approach several teenagers and ask for a vote.

"Well, it's got a catchy beat, and I like his voice," an articulate 17-year-old would say. "I'd give it an 8." More applause, a brief reprise of the new song, then break to commercial.

That was how *American Bandstand* made stars out of singers: a quick vote by a renowned authority—a radio-addicted teen—who knew a catchy tune when she heard one.

If only identifying gifted kids followed this model: Reveal evidence of the gifts, recognize them as extraordinary, defend the reasons behind the decision, applaud, and move on to the next child. But identifying giftedness is not as easy as deciding that "My Girl" deserves to be a #1 hit. The complications are many, and we as teachers are often caught in a place where we may not want to be.

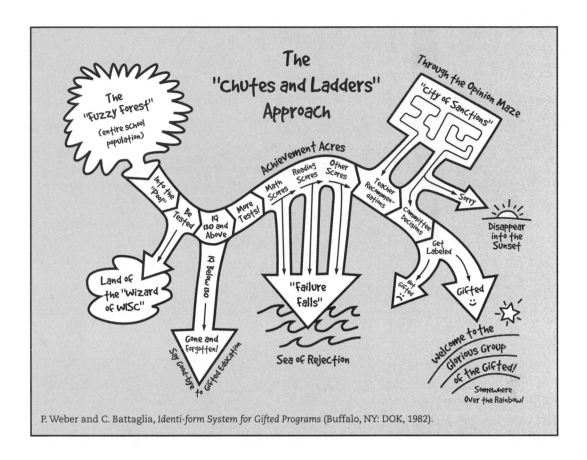

P. Weber and C. Battaglia, *Identi-form System for Gifted Programs* (Buffalo, NY: DOK, 1982).

Why Is Identification So Complex?

Long ago, when a high IQ score was all one needed to be identified as gifted, few people questioned why. If your IQ was 140 or above, you were gifted. If it was 139 or below, you weren't.* It was as simple as that.

This single-score determination of giftedness was as wrong in 1940 as it is today, but almost no one back then voiced strong opposition. So the IQ score reigned supreme, and placement in gifted programs—the few that existed—was based solely on that magic number.

As times changed and the United States became more diverse, educators and others began to challenge the wisdom behind any one number determining a child's

---

* In some versions of the IQ scale, the break between gifted and not gifted is 140. In others, it's 130. Plus, different school districts have different cutoff points for acceptance into gifted programs. For some, it's 145. For others, it's 125. These variations from scale to scale and school to school are reason enough not to use IQ tests alone to determine giftedness (or lack of giftedness).

school placement—and, often, the child's eventual success in life. Teachers (and some parents) started asking:

- What if my student doesn't test well?

- What if some of the questions on the IQ test are biased toward certain ethnic/cultural/socioeconomic groups and against others?

- What if my student speaks a language other than English at home?

- What if my student is shy and doesn't respond well to a stranger asking odd questions?

- What if my student has a reading or writing disability or difference? How does an IQ test compensate for that?

These questions made educators and test-makers squirm. They were good questions, but no one had any answers—at least, not yet. Meanwhile, admitting to the flaws of the esteemed IQ left gaping holes in both the theory and the practice of testing.

It was about then, in the 1960s, that the *American Bandstand* form of identification began to be instituted more widely. Teachers who actually knew children were asked, "Which kids in your classroom do you think are gifted, and why?" This epiphany of common sense—letting experienced observers of children attest to their high intelligence—was disparaged by Ph.D.-types who alleged that teachers:

- were biased

- were ignorant of the traits of a "real" gifted child

- tended to identify kids whose talents most resembled their own

- tended to identify "teacher pleasers" as gifted, instead of those children who were highly intelligent but undermotivated in school

Of course, these Ph.D.-types were also right. Identifying gifted kids based on personal opinion and interpretation is as flawed in its own way as identifying them by test scores alone.

Sounds like a stalemate, doesn't it? The old-guard IQ advocates on one side, and the proponents of teacher-directed identification on the other. In truth, there hasn't been a lot of movement by either faction since the 1960s. IQ tests are rarely used as the sole way to identify gifted children, although virtually every school district we know of uses some type of aptitude assessment as a piece of their gifted identification plan. But teacher nominations are still dismissed by some as being inaccurate, invalid, and inconclusive evidence of high intelligence, especially if not accompanied by high test scores.

More Possible Meanings for the Acronym IQ

I Quit
Some people believe that an average IQ predicts a life of menial jobs and dreary relationships. Wrong! IQ is only one way to measure intelligence, and it's by no means the last word. No one should be sentenced by a test score.

Inane Questions
When you look closely at some IQ tests, you can't help wondering if the people who wrote the questions are really nitwits disguised as experts. Who wants to be judged on the basis of whether they can define "uxoricide"?

Individual Quirks
One IQ test asked students to find the "best, most sensible" word to complete this sentence: "The foundation of all science is _____." The choices are "observation," "invention," "knowledge," "theory," and "art." Which fits best? The test developers had a particular word in mind. A difference of opinion didn't count.

Insufficient Quantity
Some IQ tests last only 20 minutes, which doesn't give students much time to reveal their specific strengths and weaknesses. If kids are going to be selected for (or barred from) gifted programs on the basis of IQ, they deserve more than 20 minutes to show what they know.

Intense Queasiness
Tests have been known to make people anxious. The typical IQ test is administered in a situation that is stressful and constrained by time limits. "Brain drain" isn't uncommon. Students may forget everything they've ever learned—only to recall it all five minutes after the test ends.

Impressive Quality
Although IQ tests are criticized, the fact remains that people with high IQs often do very well in life. The tests appear to do an adequate job of locating overall intelligence; a score of 150 usually isn't an accident or a fluke. But do the tests fail to identify some smart people who just don't perform well on tests? The evidence points to "yes."

Adapted from "Six More Possible Meanings for the Acronym IQ" in *The Gifted Kids' Survival Guide: A Teen Handbook*, Revised, Expanded, and Updated Edition, by Judy Galbraith, M.A., and Jim Delisle, Ph.D. (Minneapolis: Free Spirit Publishing Inc., 1996), p. 51.

How It Should Be

"Teachers can change lives with just the right mix of chalk and challenges."
—JOYCE A. MYERS

It's unlikely that an identification plan (some districts call it an "identification scheme") that satisfies everyone will be developed in our lifetimes. But if teachers and psychologists are ready to admit their own fallibility, identification doesn't have to be an onerous task. Consider the following example.

A growing Midwestern school district is changing from a blue-collar and agricultural enclave to a more diverse suburb filled with homes ranging from $60,000–$400,000. Kids are everywhere—and they come from everywhere—including the nearby urban metropolis, the neighboring towns where apartment dwellers seek their first homes, and neighborhoods where square-foot conscious buyers have $350,000 to spend. Also, a large influx of eastern Europeans has begun to appear, and the school corridors are filled with the colors and languages of our world. Teachers call it "the U.N. in miniature."

Gifted identification in that district, as required by the state, is as test-score based as any: two standard deviations above the norm on an aptitude measure, and the 95th percentile or above on various standardized achievement tests. However, for students whose first language is not English, or for those whose cultural or economic backgrounds may have limited their exposure to the middle-class values and ideas common on IQ tests, the verbal IQ test requirement is lowered to *one* standard deviation above the norm—an IQ of approximately 115–120.

Other corroborating evidence from teachers, a gifted education consultant's observations, or examples of the student's work are accepted as proof of a child's giftedness. When searching for creativity, paper-and-pencil tests (which are never very accurate in measuring creativity) may be replaced by real-world evidence of that creative spark that a teacher, parent, or peer might see.

And what about kids who move into the district from another town where they were in a gifted program? Their entrance is automatic, with a reevaluation (if deemed necessary) occurring within six months to check the placement's "goodness of fit." The program also allows for identification of children with learning disabilities or differences. Their slightly above-average test scores are combined with an interview conducted by the gifted education teacher, who looks for evidence of complex and abstract thinking.

In other words, although criteria are established by the state to locate gifted children in the typical ways (by using test scores), gifts and talents are also sought and identified in children whose life circumstances would otherwise make them ineligible for gifted services.

The result? A gifted program that resembles the ethnic, cultural, and racial makeup of the school district as a whole. It's an even *more* miniature U.N.

Three Tips for Successful Gifted Placement

1. All placements in a gifted program should be considered *tentative,* with the fit between the child's needs and the program's offerings being the bottom-line criterion for continued placement. Bad match? Look for something better.

2. All placements in a gifted program should be considered *voluntary*. No one should have to act gifted if they don't want to.

3. The names of students selected for a gifted program should be *shared with the students' teachers,* who should also be asked if they know of any other children who might be considered for placement. Teachers *cannot* remove a student's name from this list, since this is a sure way to eliminate perceived underachievers and troublemakers.

What You Can Do Right

Classroom teachers are the key players in the eventual success or failure of a child's gifted program placement. It all begins with *proper* identification. Without your keen eyes and ears, it's likely that many gifts will go unnoticed, and many gifted kids will never have the support, encouragement, and opportunities they need to reach their full potential. Here are some proven ways you can help.

Be a Talent Identifier

As a classroom teacher, you interact with your students more than anyone else in the school. When you notice a child with gifted characteristics (see pages 6–7), run, don't walk, to your school's or district's gifted education specialist to document your observations and get the identification ball rolling.

Be a Student Advocate

If you suspect that one of your students is gifted, nominate him or her for the gifted program—and follow up to make sure that your nomination is acted upon. If you're told that "the test scores or grades just aren't there," ask about alternative paths for identification. If such paths don't exist, pave one yourself. Offer evidence of the child's work and thinking that made you suspect giftedness in the first place.

For example, we know one student who spoke six languages and was taking a high school geometry class in eighth grade—but never qualified as gifted because the verbal IQ test he took was administered during his first year of learning English.

You may be your student's strongest advocate. Don't give up without good cause.

Be Supportive and Flexible

If one or more of your students is selected for gifted services, it's likely that this will require some out-of-classroom time with the gifted education specialist. Our experience tells us that if you pile on the make-up work, some gifted students will begin to resent you, your classroom, and the gifted class. After all, if they are gifted, they are probably well-versed in some aspects of the grade-level curriculum.

What can you eliminate so your gifted students don't experience the "double whammy" of needing to do all the gifted program work and assignments on top of your own? The simplest suggestion we can offer—and it works—is to have students complete *one-half* of the week's work or assignments. Their performance will indicate whether they have already mastered a particular skill or need additional practice. You might also consider changing the timing of your assessment, allowing gifted students to take your tests or quizzes at or near the *beginning* of your instructional unit. If they score to your satisfaction (we suggest 85 percent or higher), they are excused from homework and classwork that covers these topics.

Be a Treasure Hunter

Some kids are hard to like. They may announce that "this work is boring" (while you're being observed by the principal, of course). They may refuse to do their homework, declaring that "it's easy and stupid." They may wear old, holey, sweat-stained T-shirts printed with Bart Simpson and his favorite expression: "Underachiever, and proud of it, man!"

Even kids like this might be gifted. You will need—and this is difficult—to look beyond their rebelliousness or nonchalance about schoolwork. Notice, instead, when these students do well. Thoroughly check their school records to see if previous years' teachers noted "a fine mind going to waste" or made other comments ripe with possibilities about the student's giftedness. Get to know them as people, not just students, so you'll be in a position to "discover" talents that perhaps show up in hobby or extracurricular areas. These are important steps toward an academic turnaround in which you can play a part.

Ten Traits and Behaviors That May Prevent Identification

1. Students may get easily bored with routine classwork. Some may say so, often and loudly. Others may tune out and say nothing.

2. Students may work intently on one area or subject, neglecting homework and classwork in other areas of study.

3. Students may use their advanced vocabularies to "retaliate" against those who are not so verbally well-endowed.

4. Students may get so excited about a discussion or topic that interests them that they monopolize the conversation or begin "preaching" about it, even to the teacher.

5. Students may get excited about a particular topic but, once initial interest is satisfied, resist doing additional work that relates to the topic. Their follow-through is weak.

6. Students may dislike or resent having to work with others who are not of equally high abilities, and they may express this dissatisfaction through words or loud sighs.

7. Students may possess a vast knowledge of many topics, and they may correct adults (and peers) they perceive as giving incorrect or incomplete information.

8. Students may use their advanced senses of humor and cunning to intimidate, manipulate, or humiliate others.

9. Students may be self-assured and passionate about particular political, social, or moral issues and state their views openly, distancing themselves from classmates who don't share (or care about) these issues.

10. Students may prefer working independently and resent any adult who wants them to "toe the line" by following a specific procedure with which they disagree.

Some of these negative behaviors may be due to the gifted child having intellectual or emotional needs that are not being met at home or in school. While arrogant behavior should not be tolerated, and academic nonchalance should not be ignored, it's good to know that the source of these issues might be intellectual frustration, not emotional disorder.

What We Sometimes Do Wrong

Nobody's perfect—not even experienced teachers with the best intentions and most comprehensive approach to identifying students as gifted. We all make mistakes and errors in judgment. Let's not forget that our decisions influence our students' futures. With that in mind, here are three mistakes we should all work hard to avoid.

We Assume That "Once Identified, Always Identified"

Giftedness is a lifetime quality. If *properly* identified in childhood, the phenomenon of giftedness will continue to be as immutable a part of one's life as eye color. *Proper* identification is essential—and rare.

For example: Using a group IQ test of suspicious reliability and validity, a second grader is noted as having an IQ of 133, identified as gifted, and placed in a gifted class. All seems well. Subsequent years' testing shows a pattern of widely discrepant scores—110, 121, 108, 113. Is this a problem? Yes and no.

Yes if the child struggles through daily work that provides too much challenge, causing you, the teacher, to lower the level of work expected to be completed by this child. *Yes* again if your gifted program has only a limited number of "slots" and this child, whose placement may be inappropriate, is retained while a more highly gifted child waits in the wings.

Of course, it's uncomfortable to call parents and say, "We're sorry, but it appears that your child is no longer gifted." In fact, *you should never say that. Never even allude to that possibility!* Instead, focus on the reality that the child's needs—intellectual and emotional—will be better met in a setting that's challenging, but not to the point of frustration.

When are wild fluctuations in test scores not a problem? When it's obvious through the child's behaviors and interactions that the level of high challenge is on par with his or her high level of intellect. In this case, the proverbial "match made in heaven" is taking place, and test scores should no longer be the prime consideration in the child's gifted program placement.

Reliability and Validity

Reliability is the likelihood that a test, given once, will produce similar results the next time it (or a comparable instrument) is administered. Example: If you have a group IQ test that gives you a 110 result for a child in October and a 145 in April, that test would not be considered very reliable—statistically or practically.

Validity can have various facets, but the overall concept refers to whether you're measuring what you think you're measuring. *Content validity* concerns whether a test adequately covers enough breadth of information about a subject that the score is a good indicator of one's ability within that subject. Example: If you use a math achievement test that only contains fraction problems, it's not a very valid measure of your students' abilities across the spectrum of mathematics.

We Accept That "Once Not Identified, Never Identified"

This is the equivalent of the Gifted Olympics. A child takes part in the tryouts (group IQ testing) for his particular grade level and, for whatever reason, doesn't make the cut. He's out of the game for life—with no second chances, no opportunity to clear the bar on a second push of his intellectual muscles. He had his chance, and he blew it.

Some people in charge of identifying gifted children see themselves as blockers for kids who "don't belong." What can you do to help a child who deserves another chance? Keep anecdotal records of his giftedness, as you have seen it expressed. For example:

- Save copies of papers or projects that clearly show evidence of the child's advanced abilities or complex thought processes.

- Ask the parents to provide examples of precocious performance or question-asking from early in the child's life. We know one parent whose 4-year-old daughter asked, "Do people feel the same way right before they're born as they do right after they die?" And she demanded an answer. We're not sure what answer her parents gave her, but we do know that this is not a typical question from a 4-year-old.

- Refer to your own examples or vivid memories of times when this child far exceeded the bounds of the usual in terms of journal-writing, question-asking, or the ability to juggle complex thoughts. A young man we're acquainted with was 3 years old when he announced to his mother, "I know that numbers and letters are different." "And how do you know?" his mother asked. "Because," he replied, "when you count, you never get to the end." At 36 months, he had grasped the concept of infinity.

Your role in *properly* identifying gifted students is essential, so don't be content with filling out a numerical checklist (a common identification method) about a child you suspect is truly gifted. Add depth and substance. After all, who knows a gifted child better than an informed teacher who has spent 185 days out of a year observing and interacting with that child?

Gifted? You Decide

Noah wrote this journal entry on his first day of first grade:

School is so difficult for a kid like me. I wish I were a grown-up NOW! (Because grown-ups are allowed to drive cars, which I like.) But, I'm lost in thought. How am I going to afford a car and a house? How am I? How am I? How am I? How am I going to get money? How am I going to get a job? It looks hopeless. Help me, help me, HELP ME! How am I going to pay my financial tax? AHA. Why didn't I think of this before? I'll let my mom and dad help me. The End.

Sara wrote this poem in seventh grade:

NOWHERE
(To the people with nothing inside them)

Where will it take you?
Your shallow pleasure
In making others cry . . .
At their imperfections
And disabilities
Suddenly magnified
For the world to see and laugh?
Where do you expect to get to?
Living off the tears they shed . . .
Life isn't always
That grand.

continued . . .

Screwing up
In front of everyone.
Being tripped
In the halls.
You laugh and point now
"What losers."
I don't see you
In the spotlight
Trying your hardest
Failing, just to be
Laughed at again
By the people with nothing inside them
Who think they'll
Survive?
Us, the legs they stand on.
Us, standing tall above them.
Them, the losers in the back row.
They won't last long.
They're on the road
To nowhere.

We Treat Identification as an "April Event" Instead of an Ongoing Process

Although it's common to identify children near the end of one school year so the next can begin with an intact class of gifted students, there's no reason why a child who comes to your attention at another time should not enter a gifted program during other months. This situation can occur if a child moves into your classroom midyear from another town or school, or when you have a gifted child whose abilities are not initially observable—perhaps the child is shy, quiet, or not screaming out "This is boring!" at the start of each lesson.

Be sure to know the process for nominating a child for your school's gifted program. And if you are told, "We don't identify children until April," state politely (but firmly), "I don't think that when I call Sara's parents about my nomination, they're going to want to wait that long. Sara has intellectual needs *now,* and she deserves to have them met as soon as possible." That should help speed up the process.

Questions and Answers About Identification

"Can giftedness coexist with learning disabilities?"

Yes, which means that the child might benefit from both the gifted and the LD programs, with appropriate modifications made in each setting.

"If a child moves from a gifted program in one town, should he or she be automatically included in the gifted program in another town?"

Yes! If you are gifted in St. Paul, you should also be gifted in Minneapolis (after all, they are Twin Cities!). If, after an appropriate trial period—perhaps one school quarter—it becomes obvious that the placement is not working well for the child, adjustments can be made. But let's assume on the basis of optimism, not pessimism, and give the St. Paul gifted child the benefit of the doubt.

"Should classroom teachers be a part of a gifted selection committee?"

Of course! The perspectives you can offer on typical behaviors and academic expectations of kids in a certain grade level will add valuable insights to placement decisions.

What if your district doesn't have a selection committee, and all decisions are made by one or two people crunching test scores on kids they don't know? For the sake of your program and the kids eligible for it, it's time to insist (or firmly suggest) that a committee be formed.

"How can I make sure that 'atypical' gifted kids are found?"

Gifted programs are often accused of being academic holding pens for middle-class white kids. In many cases, this accusation is accurate.

Don't confuse "gifted children" with "teacher pleasers"—those kids who get straight A's, have good behavior and manners, finish their work on time and ask for more, and always wear the latest styles. Some gifted kids do have these attributes (and clothes), but many don't. Instead, look for kids who:

- are easily bored by routine tasks
- can play and work independently
- prefer complex tasks and open-ended activities
- rebel against conformity
- creatively make toys or tools out of anything
- ask probing questions

■ make connections between ideas that classmates "don't get" (but you do)

■ have an "adult" sense of humor; understand irony and puns

There are many more characteristics, behaviors, and traits that can be used to informally identify gifted children. You read about many of them in Chapter 1: What Is Giftedness? Whichever ones you look for, *make sure to compare them against the characteristics, behaviors, and traits of other kids the same age.* If you keep this caveat in mind, finding gifted children may be as easy as selecting your garden's prettiest rose or choosing your favorite flavor of ice cream.

A Wise Voice from the Past

Long before identification became a hot topic, a pioneering psychologist named Leta Stetter Hollingworth was wondering how to help gifted children. She started researching them in the early 1920s, a time when most other educators believed (as some still do) that bright kids could take care of themselves. Here are a few of her observations:

"When we hear repeatedly, from various people, that a given child is 'old for his age,' 'so reliable,' 'very old-fashioned,' 'quick to see a joke,' 'youngest in his class,' or that he has 'an old head on young shoulders' or 'such a long memory,' we usually find him to be highly intelligent, by test."

"Teachers may judge as 'most intelligent' very dull, over-age children doing good work in lower grades. Thus, for instance, they may not realize that being 'youngest in the class' is an important symptom of superior ability."

"Teachers rate bright children higher in all respects so far reported than their parents do. This is because teachers know a great variety of children, including the incompetent; whereas parents know well only their own children and those of their friends, constituting usually a very restricted range of competency."

"Schools cannot equalize children; schools can only equalize opportunity. It may well be thought to be highly undemocratic to provide full opportunity for the

continued . . .

exercise of their capacities to some, while to others the same offering means only partial exercise of their powers. It is hard for a psychologist to define democracy, but perhaps one acceptable definition might be that it is a condition of affairs, in which every human being has opportunity to live and work in accordance with inborn capacity for achievement."

From *The Child, His Nature and His Needs* by Leta Stetter Hollingworth (New York: Arno Press, 1922), pp. 281, 282, 284, and 298.

A Few Final Thoughts

"The dream begins with a teacher who believes in you,
who tugs and pushes and leads you to the next plateau."
—Dan Rather

Identifying one child as gifted and not another, seeing past negative attitudes and behaviors, advocating for the child who doesn't test well—these aren't easy choices to make. Ultimately, identification is a judgment call based on your own biases and preferences. What can you do? Your best, while acknowledging that no choice will be perfect or completely agreed upon by others.

Of all the issues in gifted education, identification is the most vexing, complex, and frustrating. Once we find the kids, we know how to channel their talents with curriculum and creative experiences. It's the process of selecting the "right kids" that causes gifted education specialists to toss and turn in bed.

It doesn't have to be that difficult. If we see identification as a way to get highly able kids the kinds of education they deserve; if we allow enough flexibility in our identification systems to select children based on test scores *and* the professional judgments of well-informed educators; and if we realize that identification is as much an art as it is a science, then we will do right by those gifted young people who are just waiting to show us the glow of their fine minds.

Is It a Cheetah?

by Stephanie S. Tolan

The child who does well in school, gets good grades, wins awards, and "performs" beyond the norms for his or her age, is considered talented. The child who does not, no matter what his innate intellectual capacities or developmental level, is less and less likely to be identified, less and less likely to be served.

A cheetah metaphor can help us see the problem with achievement-oriented thinking. The cheetah is the fastest animal on earth. When we think of cheetahs we are likely to think first of their speed. It's flashy. It is impressive. It's unique. And it makes identification incredibly easy. Since cheetahs are the only animals that can run 70 mph, if you clock an animal running 70 mph, IT'S A CHEETAH! . . .

Certain conditions are necessary if it is to attain its famous 70 mph top speed. . . . It must be healthy, fit, and rested. It must have plenty of room to run. Besides that, it is best motivated to run all out when it is hungry and there are antelope to chase.

If a cheetah is confined to a 10 x 12 foot cage, though it may pace or fling itself against the bars in restless frustration, it won't run 70 mph. IS IT STILL A CHEETAH?

If a cheetah has only 20 mph rabbits to chase for food, it won't run 70 mph while hunting. If it did, it would flash past its prey and go hungry! Though it might well run on its own for exercise, recreation, fulfillment of its internal drive, when given only rabbits to eat, the hunting cheetah will run only fast enough to catch a rabbit. IS IT STILL A CHEETAH?

If a cheetah is fed Zoo Chow it may not run at all. IS IT STILL A CHEETAH?

If a cheetah is sick or if its legs have been broken, it won't even walk. IS IT STILL A CHEETAH?

And finally, if the cheetah is only six weeks old, it can't yet run 70 mph. IS IT, THEN, ONLY A "POTENTIAL" CHEETAH?

A school system that defines giftedness (or talent) as behavior, achievement, and performance is as compromised in its ability to recognize its highly gifted students and to give them what they need as a zoo would be to recognize and provide for its cheetahs if it looked only for speed.

CHAPTER 3

Emotional Dimensions of Giftedness

"The less a person understands his own feelings, the more he will fall prey to them. The less a person understands the feelings, the responses, and behavior of others, the more likely he will interact inappropriately with them and therefore fail to secure his proper place within the larger community."

—HOWARD GARDNER

How gifted kids feel on an emotional level doesn't always match logically with their intellectual capabilities. Brighter doesn't necessarily mean happier, healthier, more successful, socially adept, or more secure. Neither does brighter necessarily mean hyper, difficult, overly sensitive, or neurotic. In terms of emotional and social characteristics, brighter may not mean anything "different" at all. But while gifted kids don't have common personality traits, they *do* have common problems.

Like members of any minority, gifted students may feel insecure just because they're different from the norm. Teenagers and preteens in particular desperately want to be like everyone else, and any difference, whether positive or negative, is cause for anxiety. But sometimes gifted kids are very different; they may feel isolated, alienated, or "weird" as a result. "They have so many problems connecting with other people," teachers have said, "there's a sense of isolation that gets bigger and bigger as years go by, unless some interventions are made."

The educational community has been quick to dismiss the emotional problems of high-achieving students for many of the same reasons we have dismissed their intellectual needs. Perhaps we have too many other kids with worse problems. Perhaps we think that smart kids don't need our help. Many of us may not realize that some of our brighter students are, in fact, in quite a bit of trouble. They don't necessarily look needy; they seem to have it all together.

Accustomed to conquering intellectual problems logically, students themselves may deny their emotional problems by saying, "I'm supposed to be smart. I should be able to think my way out of this." Or, because they are smart, they can successfully delude themselves or rationalize their behavior.

Finally, many of us may realize that gifted students suffer emotionally, but we aren't sure how to handle it.

Challenges from Within and Without

Evidence is accumulating that certain challenges to emotional balance may come automatically with exceptional intellectual ability or talent. Challenges may come both from within the person and from without. Challenges from *within* include being, by nature, highly perceptive, highly involved, super-sensitive, and perfectionistic. Challenges from *without* come from conflict with the environment. They surface in the "Eight Great Gripes" kids have about school or parents or friends.

Of course, not all students suffer all of the problems described here. Some have few adjustment problems generally and feel fine about life. Others experience difficulty in four or five areas. A student's needs will depend on his or her maturity level, type of intelligence, environment, and a whole host of other personality characteristics.

Extra Perception

Consider, for instance, the effect that being highly perceptive to stimuli (sounds, sights, smells, touches, tastes, movements, words, patterns, numbers, physical phenomena, people) would make in one's daily life. While other people might agree, "These two colors match," the artist says, "No, they don't." The musician hears the difference between a note played perfectly and one played slightly off-key. Howard Gardner speaks of the poet as someone who is "superlatively sensitive to the shades of meanings . . . to the sound of words . . . to the order among words."[1] Whether their medium is one of language, art, social action, or physics, gifted persons are profoundly sensitive to small differences—and those differences make all the difference.

High Involvement

Sensitivity may breed a certain irritation with the "insensitive" and unusual preoccupation with interests, tasks, materials, and questions. While other children seem comfortable letting thoughts come and go and relatively unconcerned with unsolved problems and inexact answers, gifted students dream repetitively of treasured problems, pictures, patterns, or concerns. They are obsessed with the intricacy or beauty of phenomena at hand. The creative composer constantly hears tones in his head. The mathematician dreams of proofs; the writer carries precious fragments of verse in her memory. Gifted individuals perceive greater levels of complexity in the world around them, and they find this complexity interesting and meaningful.

Super-Sensitivity

In addition to being exquisitely perceptive of and receptive to stimuli, sensitivity in the gifted can also mean moral or emotional sensitivity. Many gifted students are super-sensitive to ethical issues and concerns that are considered unimportant by their peers. They may be highly moralistic. They may be quick to judge others. However, this doesn't mean that intellectually precocious children are always emotionally mature for their age. In many cases, kids are both emotionally immature and intellectually advanced at the same time.

The Creative Mind

by Pearl S. Buck

The truly creative mind in any field is no more than this: A human creature born abnormally, inhumanly sensitive. To him, a touch is a blow, a sound is a noise, a misfortune is a tragedy, a joy is an ecstasy, a friend is a lover, a lover is a god, and failure is death.

Add to this cruelly delicate organism the overpowering necessity to create, create, create—so that without the creating of music or poetry or books or buildings or something of meaning, his very breath is cut off from him. He must create, must pour out creation. By some strange, unknown, inward urgency, he is not really alive unless he is creating.

Perfectionism

Perfectionism is not a good thing. It is often misperceived as a good thing, and it has been described as a good thing, but it is not. What is good is the *pursuit of excellence,* which is something quite different.

Perfectionism means that you can *never* fail, you *always* need approval, and if you come in second, you're a loser. The pursuit of excellence means taking risks, trying new things, growing, changing—and sometimes failing. Perfectionism is *not* about doing your best or striving for high goals. Instead, it can block your ability to do well. And it can take a heavy toll on your self-esteem, relationships, creativity, health, and capacity to enjoy life. Because perfection isn't possible, deciding that's what you want—and that you won't be satisfied with anything less—is a recipe for disappointment.

Gifted people of all ages are especially prone to perfectionism. This may be rooted in the awareness of quality. They know the difference between the mediocre and the superior. Once they see how something "ought to be done" (ought to sound, ought to look), they may naturally want to do it that way. And they may drive themselves (and others!) crazy in the process. This is why gifted students need support to persist despite their constant awareness of "failure."

Many of the problems students have with high expectations are reinforced by the environment, particularly if they have had a string of early successes (and a history of lavish praise and encouragement to keep up the stellar work). As Ruth Duskin Feldman, a former Quiz Kid, explains: "Whatever I accomplished, it never seemed enough. I had the nagging feeling I should be up there at the top, as I had been in my youth." She also speaks of intelligence as a trap. When exceptionally bright and capable children (like the Quiz Kids) are:[2]

> . . . accustomed to easy success and . . . are praised for work requiring modest effort [they] may not develop discrimination or learn to meet a challenge. When these children grow up, they seek applause constantly without knowing how to get it. Children held to impossibly high standards and deprived of praise may get caught in a cycle of hopeless, misdirected perfectionism, trying to please parents, teachers, or bosses who never can be satisfied.

Perfectionism At-a-Glance

How a Perfectionist Acts

- Overcommits himself
- Rarely delegates work to others
- Has a hard time making choices
- Always has to be in control
- Competes fiercely
- Arrives late because one more thing had to be done
- Always does last-minute cramming
- Gets carried away with the details
- Never seems satisfied with his work
- Constantly busies himself with something or other
- Frequently criticizes others
- Refuses to hear criticism of himself
- Pays more attention to negative than positive comments
- Checks up on other people's work
- Calls himself "stupid" when he does something imperfectly
- Procrastinates

continued . . .

What a Perfectionist Thinks

- "If I can't do it perfectly, what's the point?"
- "I should excel at everything I do."
- "I always have to stay ahead of others."
- "I should finish a job before doing anything else."
- "Every detail of a job should be perfect."
- "Things should be done right the first time."
- "There is only one right way to do things."
- "I'm a wonderful person if I do well; I'm a lousy person if I do poorly."

- "I'm never good enough."
- "I'm stupid."
- "I can't do anything right."
- "I'm unlikable."
- "I'd better not make a mistake here, or people will think I'm not very [smart, good, capable]."
- "If I goof up, something's wrong with me."
- "People shouldn't criticize me."
- "Everything should be clearly black or white. Grays are a sign of confused thinking."

How a Perfectionist Feels

- Deeply embarrassed about mistakes she makes
- Disgusted or angry with herself when she is criticized
- Anxious when stating her opinion to others
- Extremely worried about details
- Angry if her routine is interrupted
- Nervous when things around her are messy

- Fearful or anxious a lot of the time
- Exhausted and unable to relax
- Plagued by self-hatred
- Afraid of appearing stupid
- Afraid of appearing incompetent
- Afraid of being rejected
- Ashamed of having fears
- Discouraged
- Guilty about letting others down

Adapted from "Perfectionism at a Glance" in *Freeing Our Families from Perfectionism* by Thomas S. Greenspon, Ph.D. (Minneapolis: Free Spirit Publishing Inc., 2002), pp. 9–10. Used with permission.

Uneven Integration

Challenges to emotional peace can also come from within when a student's intellectual abilities are out of sync. For example, a student who has strong conceptual and verbal skills but a reading disability may feel quite frustrated. Someone with strong spatial ability but weak drawing skills is likely to be similarly stymied. A person may be talented athletically, but too shy to compete in team sports. Within each of us, certain abilities may or may not combine gracefully or productively.

Although in the past we've tended to stereotype gifted students as exceptional "across the board," few are actually good in everything they do. This type of integrated ability is both rare and exciting. More typical is the student with demonstrated ability in one academic area, or who can transfer one process skill into a number of different content areas. This same student may be a lousy speller or lazy in math, have terrible handwriting or poor study skills.

Yes, even gifted kids can have poor study skills. As a teacher, you'll need to watch for this and offer help as needed. Regardless of how smart they are, some gifted kids may be clueless about how to organize their time, organize their learning environment, keep track of daily and long-range assignments, take good notes, and more. There are many resources available on how to develop strong study skills, including many written for students. You might want to build a classroom library and hand out books as appropriate. At times, you may need to offer one-on-one instruction.

The Eight Great Gripes

Some of the challenges to emotional well-being come from without—from the individual's conflict with the family, school environment, peers, or society in general. These are the gifted students' common problems—the "Eight Great Gripes" identified through interviews with gifted and talented kids and included in both the "Student Questionnaire" on pages 40–45 and the activity on pages 129–130.

1. No one explains what being gifted is all about—it's kept a big secret.

2. School is too easy and too boring.

3. Parents, teachers, and friends expect us to be perfect all the time.

4. Friends who really understand us are few and far between.

5. Kids often tease us about being smart.

6. We feel overwhelmed by the number of things we can do in life.

7. We feel different and alienated.

8. We worry about world problems and feel helpless to do anything about them.

Activities and discussions for each "great gripe" are found in Chapter 7: Understanding Gifted Kids from the Outside In.

Different Ways of Being Gifted, Different Emotional Needs

With gifted kids so unique, is it possible to generalize about their emotional needs? The answer is yes—with caution, but yes. We can make some generalizations about who is gifted and what their affective needs may be. Moreover, as practitioners, you'll *have* to make some generalizations, even though research has yet to substantiate the bigger picture.

This is where knowing your school's selection process will help. What kinds of gifted students are you working with? Kids with high verbal or math skills? Those who score in the exceptionally gifted range (150–180) on the Stanford-Binet Intelligence Scale? Students whose abilities tend to require enrichment opportunities as opposed to accelerated opportunities (or vice versa)? The types of cognitive strengths your students demonstrate may determine, to some extent, the kind of emotional needs they'll have. Keep in mind, however, that our foremost concern should be for what young people *say* they need help with. Don't deny a child a reaction, an emotion, or assistance because he or she doesn't fit the right category.

There are several frameworks for categorizing students which seem useful to us for predicting their emotional needs. The first has simply to do with the degree of intelligence and the type of intelligence involved.

Quantity and Quality of Intelligence

The degree of difference between the gifted and average student (whether in IQ score, music, language, or chess playing) influences, by itself, the gifted student's self-concept. The young adolescent with a very high IQ (above 150) is likely to feel more different and isolated than kids with IQ scores of 130, simply because he or she is that much more different from the norm. Both are gifted, but because the number of kids in the top 1 to 2 percent of the population is so small, these students are dramatically limited in terms of peer group.

In addition to quantity or degree of ability, giftedness has obvious qualitative differences. Creativity in the visual arts is different than logical-mathematical ability. The interpersonal skills of leadership are different than the linguistic skills of a poet. These areas are equally important; the term "qualitative" suggests intrinsic properties that are unique and special.

Howard Gardner's theory of multiple intelligences is one attempt to consider the qualitative differences in intelligence. Basing his work on a variety of fields—cognitive psychology, child development, neurobiology, and cultural anthropology, to name a few—Gardner has concluded that the classical view of intelligence is too limited. He suggests that there are several ways to be smart, including linguistically, kinesthetically, and interpersonally, and that a single IQ test is not adequate to measure these other areas of human endeavor. (Gardner's eight intelligences are described on pages 19–20.) Gardner contends that the various intelligences operate in relative isolation to each other, and he points to child prodigies as one example of this "specialization" of intelligence. He also believes that the educational strategies which nurture one intelligence may not nurture another.

Gardner's theory of multiple intelligences has been widely accepted as an improvement on the more typical view of intelligence. However, there are some educators who perceive his theory as a relatively simplistic delineation of the various talents that many people possess. These educators are especially concerned about how Gardner's theory is being applied. Some schools and districts are interpreting Gardner's work as a rationale to do away with gifted programs altogether, assuming that if a school "does" multiple intelligences, it is meeting the needs of gifted children. This is not the case. All children can benefit from curriculum that addresses different types of intelligence, but gifted children are not all children, and all children are not gifted.

It may be that Gardner's theory operates better in theory than in actual practice, especially when it comes to determining how the interpersonal and intrapersonal intelligences (two of the eight intelligences Gardner has identified) interact with other areas of talent. We all know students whose vocabulary is so specialized in advanced mathematics or science that they find conversations with their age peers difficult, and we can all point to a student who may not be number one in achievement but is number one in understanding the depth of emotions felt by a classmate in pain. Rather than perceiving these elements of a person's life as separate and distinct intelligences, we might instead consider how they *complement* a more traditional form of intelligence, making it richer and more alive. This avenue of Gardner's theory has yet to be fully explored.

Accelerated and Enriched Learners

Nicholas Colangelo and Ronald T. Zaffrann believe that the terms "accelerated" and "enrichment" actually "describe qualitatively different needs and learning styles of gifted youngsters and not simply methods of how to provide for those needs."[3]

Accelerated gifted students are interested in mastering and integrating increasingly complex material. They have the ability to quickly learn and recall large amounts of information. They are highly efficient information-processors. They crave new information and harder problems. Their sense of fulfillment comes from mastering higher and higher levels of material and applying it to solve problems of increasing difficulty.

Images of the math student solving a difficult problem come to mind. The historian who remembers and interprets long, complex sequences of events; the poet or writer who quotes passages verbatim with ease; the doctor who generates four hypotheses and cites ten particular cases bearing on her diagnosis—these are adult examples of individuals who process, retain, and apply large quantities of knowledge well.

Often, adolescents and preadolescents with this type of ability simply "do well" in school. They are high achievers in a well-defined discipline such as science or literature, and they succeed in curricular systems which stress knowledge acquisition, linear skill-building, and logical analysis. They may also be wholly indifferent to academic subject areas, but suddenly know "everything there is to know" about the Civil War, Michael Jordan, or Tolkien's *Lord of the Rings* trilogy.

Enriched gifted students, in contrast, have the ability to become wholly involved or immersed in a problem, to "form a relationship" with a topic. These students focus on the problem—their relation to it and the learning process—as an end in itself, rather than as a means to accumulate more knowledge.

Enriched students may also be highly emotional, imaginative, internally motivated, curious, and driven to explore and experiment. They tend to be reflective and emotionally mature. Frequently, they have a keen sense of humor. The enriched student becomes passionate about a subject, a project, or a cause, often pursuing it with fierce energy.

Artists, musicians, dancers, writers, and actors tend to fall into this category, although research scientists, political activists, religious leaders, lawyers, and educators are other adult examples. The child who writes, directs, and stars in a play is demonstrating "enrichment" characteristics, as is the student who designs and constructs a futuristic model city, and students who "live and breath" dinosaurs, computers, or entrepreneurial businesses. Enriched students thrive on discovery and experience.

In terms of counseling or emotional need, accelerated learners are most frustrated by lockstep learning. They need to move on and master more material, not do endless drill-and-practice exercises. Because these students have high achievement expectations (for example, they score 100 percent on every test), they may need help setting realistic (or at least humane) goals for themselves. Teachers and parents can "overdrive" achievers in this category, which then reinforces the students' fear of failing. Accelerated learners may also be socially immature compared to their mental peers, and they may need help learning social skills.

Enriched learners, in contrast, aren't especially concerned with achievement (and may never be the top academic performers in a content area), but they invest a significant amount of emotional energy in what they do. In return, they require teachers who are sensitive to their intense feelings of frustration, passion, enthusiasm, idealism, anger, and despair. Enriched students may also need adult support to persist with a single task, or to harness their energies more efficiently.

Other Categories of Giftedness

Other categories of giftedness which may predict emotional needs include gifted girls, gifted children from ethnic and cultural minorities, and gifted children with physical and learning differences. Generally, the needs of these children are related to being simultaneously bright and members of one or more underachieving minorities. They reflect the isolation and conflict of their respective situations.

All of these students need encouragement to be everything they're capable of being, despite the risks of leaving a previously defined role or community. They would especially benefit from more role models, which can be presented in the form of teachers or presenters, graphic displays, verbal examples, biographies, special reports, or projects. When teachers are systematic about being inclusive, attitudes and expectations can change.

Gifted Girls

"Gifted girls assume all sorts of extra burdens that educators need to understand. Few gifted girls know they are talented. They know only that they are different and that this difference is somehow wrong or weird."
—JOAN FRANKLIN SMUTNY

Gifted girls continue to face special conflicts in resolving society's expectations of them as women and as gifted people, despite the impact the women's movement made on role definitions during the 1970s. More than ever before, women are deciding to delay or forego childrearing as a full (or part-time) occupation in order to pursue careers. As of this writing, a majority of women in the United States hold full-time jobs outside the home.

Still, in junior and senior high school, girls are exposed to many deep-seated cultural taboos which make it difficult for them to comfortably display their intelligence and pursue excellence as aggressively as boys. The result of this inhibition can be long-term depression and low self-esteem.

For gifted girls who do express their abilities, further conflicts can result. Bright students are told to develop their talents and be selfish in the pursuit of their goals, but women are expected to be selfless, nurturing, and supportive of others. Gifted students are often active, exploring, and assertive by nature, yet women are supposed to be "sweet, dependent June Allyson types pretending to be overawed by the opposite sex."[4] A gifted female today has more assertive role models than ever before, but women's careers continue to place second to men's in dual-career marriages. Women generally earn less income and (when children are involved) are expected to perform most parenting duties. No one asks high school- or college-age males what they're going to do about day care for their children when they talk about career plans.

For adolescent girls, busy with the work of establishing a sexual identity, sexual confusion may result. The question is how to be feminine and talented at the same time. In the words of one bright woman, "When I was 10 years old and entered seventh grade . . . one of the popular girls took me aside and said, 'Don't raise your hand so much, the boys don't like it.'"[5] As adults, gifted and motivated women literally have to consider rejecting part of their sexuality (for instance, conception and childbirth) if they want to achieve in particularly demanding fields such as law or medicine. Meanwhile, gifted girls have to deal with the biases of some school counselors who are slow to identify them as bright, or who counsel them into sex-stereotyped fields.

Ways to Support Gifted Girls

- Identify them early. The best age for evaluating and identifying gifted girls is between 3½ and 7. For some gifted girls, early school entrance is beneficial.

- Provide special programs that stimulate and challenge them.

- Encourage them to take higher-level math and science courses.

- Use multiple measures of ability and achievement. Females still score lower on the Scholastic Aptitude Test, the College Board Achievement Tests, the Graduate Record Examination, and other examinations critical for college and graduate school admission. Most of these tests underpredict female performance and over-predict male performance.

- Encourage them to take credit for their successes and recognize their own talents.

- Provide material to compensate for the lack of inclusion of women's accomplishments in literature or textbooks.

- Foster friendships with gifted peers who share similar interests.

- Provide role models of women in traditional and nontraditional careers who have successfully integrated multiple aspects of their lives.

- Avoid sex-role stereotyping. Encourage awareness of biased depictions of girls and women in the media. (As recently as January 2000, the Barbie® personal computer for girls came loaded with a little more than half of the educational software on the companion computer for boys.)

- Encourage independence and risk-taking.

- Avoid having different expectations for girls than for boys.

Adapted from "Many Gifted Girls, Few Eminent Women: Why?" by Anita Gurian, Ph.D. (New York University Child Study Center, 2000). *www.AboutOurKids.org*. Used with permission.

Ethnic and Cultural Minorities

A similar dilemma develops for gifted minority students who have to resolve being black (or Hispanic or Native American) and succeeding in a white classroom at the same time. In trying to develop their talents or interests, these students can get caught between two worlds. To illustrate: In one workshop with gifted Native American teenagers, a 15-year-old-boy remarked, "Some of the people in the Indian community think I've sold out because I go to a challenging private school."

Sometimes the conflict stems from peer pressure to resist white authority figures or the white "system" in general. Other times, just being different from one's parents, family, and ethnic or cultural community causes guilt or anxiety. Like children of immigrants to this country, gifted minority students may feel conflicted about being more successful in the white majority culture than their parents. The adjustments and other conflicts may be less painful for Asian students, however, for a disproportionately high number of them are gifted, and many learn quite successfully in American school systems.

Gifted minority students may not be recognized as talented or able because their gifts lie in areas that are celebrated by their ethnic group but not usually by Western society. For instance, minority gifted are often talented in "imagery, creativity, dance, and humor"[6]— areas which American educators have been slow to recognize as legitimate forms of intelligence and which are difficult to measure. Further, when cognitive skills are assessed via achievement tests and English is not their native language, gifted minority students may test below their ability level and be inappropriately labeled and counseled. Intelligence is, as Howard Gardner notes, a culturally defined and conditioned capability.[7] A society that values navigational skills, for instance, shapes its children from an early age to direct a canoe at night by the stars, and considers its best navigators the wise men of the tribe. The spatial ability required by this feat is less prized in American culture.

Because the abilities we value in human beings are very much tied to the products our society needs or cherishes, we can't help but define intelligence in terms of cultural priorities and character. The academic traditions in this country mirror Western concepts of intelligence generally: rational thought and the cognitive domain (normally measured by IQ and achievement tests) are the rule and not the exception. Both in conception and in fact, these notions and these instruments impart a cultural bias.

Minority students may, of course, be talented in similar areas and in similar ways as majority students. But it comes as no surprise that, in many cases, cultural heritage continues to influence how minority gifted students develop and express their talents.

Ways to Support Gifted Minority Students

■ Communicate high expectations.

■ Be sensitive to the experiences and beliefs of people from different cultural groups. Get to know all students and their cultures. Consider the challenges that students may face in school.

■ Continuously and firmly encourage students to go to college. Discuss the necessary coursework, tests, and other preparations with students and parents.

■ Create a multicultural learning environment and make sure the curriculum reflects a variety of cultures.

■ Help students connect with role models and mentors. Organize peer support groups for students with similar interests and abilities.

■ Reach out to parents and family members. Enlist their support in providing encouragement and high expectations.

■ Provide students with a variety of learning options. Create or select activities that are engaging, active, and grounded in reality.

■ Listen to students' concerns, fears, and beliefs about their experiences and their education.

Excerpted from *The Inclusive Classroom: Meeting the Needs of Gifted Students: Differentiating Mathematics and Science Instruction* by Jennifer Stepanek (Portland, OR: Northwest Regional Educational Laboratory, 2000), p. 20. Used with permission. Also available on the Web at *www.nwrel.org*.

Children with Physical and Learning Differences

Research finds high-ability individuals in all segments of society, but traditional identification procedures remain largely inadequate for those with physical and/or learning differences. As a result, this may indicate a small but highly underserved population.

In thinking of Helen Keller, we're reminded of how difficult it was for her to find people and programs to educate and treat her. We remember her intense struggle to communicate with the world, and her emotional isolation before Anne Sullivan became her teacher. We also reflect on how extraordinarily gifted she must have been to learn concepts—the whole meaning and flow of language—through the medium of hand signals alone. For those of us with sight and hearing, it's difficult to separate our knowledge from our visual and auditory perception of the world. Keller's learning, in contrast, was independent of such experiences and relied heavily on sensory, linguistic (in the abstract, not vocal, sense), and spatial intelligence.

Nicholas Colangelo and Ronald T. Zaffrann maintain that students with physical and learning differences may be "high in perception and abstraction but can't translate this to performance because of their handicap." Their inability to "perform a task is associated with the inability to think and understand." In addition, teachers and adults may automatically lower their expectations for these students, who develop even lower self-concepts "because of their situation and the low expectations of others."[8]

Today, gifted children with learning differences are often labeled "twice exceptional" (or sometimes "students with dual exceptionalities"). Like all labels, this one has its shortcomings, but at least it calls attention to students whose giftedness might otherwise be overlooked. For example, a student who is easily distracted and has difficulty completing assignments or concentrating on tests may be passed over when teachers are identifying students for gifted programs. Since school success is often based on graded assignments and test scores, students who don't perform well on these tasks may not be seen as "smart," even though they are, in fact, intellectually, creatively, or otherwise gifted.

Twice-exceptional students may have uneven academic skills and may appear unmotivated. They may have "processing problems" with the way they see and hear, causing them to seem "slow." They may have motor skills problems that affect their handwriting. Because they are often frustrated with school, they may act out and have low self-esteem.

On the other hand, many gifted students with learning differences score in the gifted range on ability, achievement, and creativity tests. They may have a wide range of knowledge about a variety of topics and a fertile imagination. They may have a superior vocabulary and sophisticated ideas.

How common is twice exceptionality? In 1998, according to the U.S. Department of Education's Office for Civil Rights, school districts reported 45,142 students who are considered gifted and who also have a disability. How accurate is this number? Many experts consider it too low. It counts only those students who have been identified, not those whose gifts have gone unnoticed. Some researchers estimate that about 2 to 5 percent of all students are twice exceptional.[9]

Like all students, those who are twice exceptional benefit most when we focus on their strengths, not their perceived weaknesses or deficiencies. These children also need more opportunities to learn and to show what they know in ways that are more natural, comfortable, and effective for them.

Ways to Support Gifted Children with Learning Differences

Identification

- Include students with disabilities in the initial screening phase.

- Be willing to accept nonconventional indicators of intellectual talent.

- Look beyond test scores.

- When applying cutoffs, bear in mind the depression of scores that may occur due to the disability.

- DO NOT aggregate subtest scores into a composite score.

- Weight more heavily characteristics that enable the child to effectively compensate for the disability.

- Weight more heavily areas of performance unaffected by the disability.

- Allow the child to participate in gifted programs on a trial basis.

Instruction

- Be aware of the powerful role of language; reduce communication limitations and develop alternative modes for thinking and communicating.

- Emphasize high-level abstract thinking, creativity, and a problem-solving approach.

- Have great expectations: These children often become successful as adults in fields requiring advanced education.

- Provide for individual pacing in areas of giftedness and disability.

- Provide challenging activities at an advanced level.

- Promote active inquiry, experimentation, and discussion.

- Promote self-direction.

- Offer options that enable students to use strengths and preferred ways of learning.

- Use intellectual strengths to develop coping strategies.

- Assist in strengthening the student's self-concept.

continued . . .

Classroom Dynamics

- Discuss disabilities/capabilities and their implications with the class.

- Expect participation in all activities; strive for normal peer interactions.

- Facilitate acceptance; model and demand respect for all.

- Candidly answer peers' questions.

- Treat a child with a disability the same way a child without a disability is treated.

- Model celebration of individual differences.

Colleen Willard-Holt, "Dual Exceptionalities," ERIC EC Digest #E574 (Reston, VA: ERIC Clearinghouse on Disabilities and Gifted Education, 1999).

Recognizing Problems

Now that we've described some of the emotional dimensions of being gifted, the challenges gifted students face from within and without, and the specific issues particular categories of gifted students might encounter, how would you describe your students? What kinds of problems and needs would you say they have?

If you haven't already asked your students to complete the "Student Questionnaire" (see pages 40–45), we encourage you to do so. Put this information together with what you've just read in this chapter. Then look around your classroom.

Signs of Trouble

It's believed that half of gifted children underachieve in school. (For more on this topic, see Chapter 6: Underachiever or Selective Consumer?) Between 10 to 20 percent of high school dropouts test within the very superior ability range. Of those students who graduate from high school in the top 5 percent of their class, some 40 percent don't matriculate from a college or university.[10]

Poor school performance, dropping out, and not completing college are three ways gifted students can go awry. There are more. As one teacher commented to us about her gifted classes (K–12), "I've always got a kid in trouble." Her examples of trouble included everything from the inability to concentrate to the need for attention, physical closeness, and affection; from poor schoolwork and attendance to disruptions in class.

In terms of everyday sorts of dysfunction, unhappy gifted kids display the same patterns and symptoms as other children do. They brag, tease, put others down, avoid responsibility, develop a "negative attitude," confront adults relentlessly, stop working, stop trying, withdraw. A seriously troubled student is one who seems isolated, who stops participating at school and at home, whose lack of interest seems to pervade every conceivable subject or occupation. Students trapped in this sort of inertia cause some teachers and parents to feel hopeless themselves: "I'm just not getting through to him, no matter what I try." When we asked teachers which types of gifted kids they had the hardest time working with, they frequently answered, "The underachievers, the unmotivated, the apathetic, those full of grudges, the snobs, the ones who have 'given up on the system.'"

Frequently, teachers can recognize low self-esteem or depression most clearly in students' body language. The chin-on-chest, a low or inaudibly pitched voice, habitual mumbling, lack of eye contact, and lethargic body posture are all signs of a poor self-concept.

Similarly, the student who is demonstrably angry, who loses control easily, underachieves, and has no close friends but plenty of "associates in class crime," is also a troubled kid. A sense of powerlessness and rage came through in the words of one teenage boy we observed during a group discussion about school: "What's the point of confronting teachers on how boring the damn school is? The teachers aren't going to change!" As the boy continued to blast away at "the system" and everything else in sight, we noticed how difficult it was for him to use the pronoun "I." Other people were at fault, and other people projected his sentiments. Yet he wasn't able to say what he was feeling. Anger? Fear? Frustration? When asked to use the word "I" so the group could recognize who he was talking about and what he was feeling, the student could not (would not) comply. Inability to own feelings and opinions is a sign of emotional conflict and lack of insight.

Symptoms of the seriously depressed or suicidal teenager have been well-documented. Depressed gifted students may, because of their sensitivity, become "hostages of their own special insights," and need immediate support and help in coping with reality. Some danger signs to watch for are:

- sudden changes in personality or behavior
- severe depression that lasts a week or longer
- concealed or direct suicide threats
- talking about suicide, either jokingly or seriously
- giving away prized possessions

- self-imposed isolation from family and peers; avoiding all social occasions and invitations

- self-imposed perfection as the ultimate standard, to the point that the only tasks enjoyed are the ones completed perfectly

- a perception of failure that differs from others' perceptions of failure

- external pressures to always be #1 and a life orientation that identifies one as a "future leader" or a "mover and shaker of the next generation"

- the frustration that comes when one's intellectual talents outpace one's social or physical development

- the ability to understand adult situations and world events while feeling powerless to effect positive change

- narcissism (total preoccupation with self and with fantasy)

- unusual fascination with violence, or preoccupation with death and death-related themes

- indications of alcohol or other drug abuse, or an eating disorder

- any other rigidly compulsive behaviors—even excessive studying and running marathons (ask yourself, "Have I ever seen this kid relax?")

There is no firm evidence that gifted teenagers are more likely to attempt or commit suicide than less able adolescents. It would be inappropriate to approach every gifted student as a potential suicide. But teachers (and other caring adults) should take all talk of death seriously. Never assume that gifted adolescents are "too smart" to even consider ending their own lives. Some do consider it—and some go beyond considering it to attempting it. If you observe any of the above signs of a teen in trouble, get help. Contact your school counselor, school psychologist, or principal for advice about what to do. Don't wait.

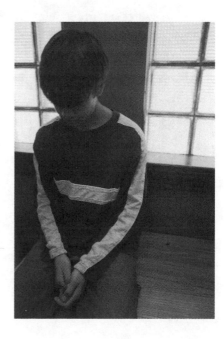

Death with Honors?

According to the Who's Who Among American High School Students *30th Annual Survey of High Achievers, which polled 2,804 high-achieving 16- to 18-year-olds (all of whom have an A or B average, and 97 percent of whom plan to attend high school graduation):*

- 23.1 percent have considered committing suicide

- 4.2 percent have tried committing suicide

- 42 percent know someone their age who has tried to commit suicide

- 17.1 percent know someone their age who has committed suicide

Teens were asked, "If you have considered committing suicide, why did you do so?" These were their top five reasons:

- General depression (76.4 percent)

- School pressures (49.9 percent)

- Fight with parents (35.6 percent)

- Divorce/family problems (28.9 percent)

- Break up of a relationship (14.7 percent)

Teens were asked, "If you have considered committing suicide, what did you do?" These were their top five responses:

- I worked through it myself/started to feel better (81.2 percent)

- I talked to a friend (27.7 percent)

- I talked to a parent (9.8 percent)

- I talked to a hotline/professional counselor (7.7 percent)

- I took antidepressants (5.3 percent)

Who's Who Among American High School Students 30th Annual Survey of High Achievers (Lake Forest, IL: Educational Communications, 2000). *www.eci-whoswho.com.*

Notes

1. Howard Gardner, *Frames of Mind: The Theory of Multiple Intelligences,* Tenth Anniversary Edition (New York: Basic Books, 1993), pp. 73–77.

2. Ruth Duskin Feldman, "The Promise and Pain of Growing Up Gifted," *Gifted/Creative/Talented* (May/June 1985), p. 1.

3. Nicholas Colangelo and Ronald T. Zaffrann, "Special Issues in Counseling the Gifted," *Counseling and Human Development* 11:5 (1979), p. 2.

4. Ibid.

5. Ruth Duskin Feldman, "The Promise and Pain of Growing Up Gifted," *Gifted/Creative/Talented* (May/June 1985), p. 1.

6. Nicholas Colangelo, "Myths and Stereotypes of Gifted Students: Awareness for the Classroom Teacher," in N. Colangelo, C.H. Foxley, and E.R. Dustin, eds., *Multicultural Nonsexist Education: A Human Relations Approach,* 2nd ed. (Dubuque, IA: Kendall/Hunt Publishing Co., 1985).

7. Howard Gardner, *Frames of Mind: The Theory of Multiple Intelligences,* Tenth Anniversary Edition (New York: Basic Books, 1993), p. 13.

8. Nicholas Colangelo and Ronald T. Zaffrann, "Special Issues in Counseling the Gifted," *Counseling and Human Development* 11:5 (1979), p. 2.

9. Reported by Lisa Fine in "Research: Diamonds in the Rough," *Education Week* (October 24, 2001).

10. Sylvia Rimm, Ph.D., "The Pressures Bright Children Feel and Why They May Underachieve," copyright © 2001 by Sylvia B. Rimm, *www.sylviarimm.com.*

CHAPTER 4

Being a Gifted Teacher

"This is definitely not a 'cushy' job."
—Gifted Education Teacher

Have you noticed that teachers of the gifted suffer many of the same stereotypes that gifted students themselves do? Somehow, parents, colleagues, and administrators seem to think gifted education teachers should know all the answers; that life for them is probably easier than it is for the rest of us; that gifted education teachers probably think they're better teachers. Like gifted students, gifted education teachers may also lack supportive peers, either because they are physically the only person in the building (or district!) working in their field, or because they are subtly ostracized. As one teacher managing 120 gifted kids from 12 grade levels told us, "No one wants to hear about my problems."

Contrary to these misconceptions, teaching gifted students is an extremely demanding job. The kids have tremendous physical and psychic energy, and they are "on to you" in a minute—they know when you're unprepared. Yet gifted education teachers are capable of making mistakes, just like any other human being. Furthermore, it's not possible to know all the answers when working with little "content experts." By training and experience, you may be better prepared to work in certain subject matter areas than with others. But no matter what your training, a tremendous amount of preparation is necessary before each class, and few substantial curricular materials exist. In the words of another experienced teacher, "There's no workbook out there, and whatever you use has got to be good or you're dead!"

As for feeling like gifted education teachers are "better teachers," the comparison is irrelevant. One hopes that we are good teachers, that we have chosen to work with gifted students because we feel most successful with or drawn to this group. One also hopes that teachers working with other populations will be best for their assignments. We all have the potential to fail with particular assignments in which we're simply not interested, or for which we're unprepared.

Gifted Education Under Fire . . .

As a gifted education teacher, it's likely that you have more challenges to deal with than misconceptions about your program and your role. Chances are your job is threatened with each new administration (federal, state, and local) and each new budget cycle. When cuts must be made—and increasingly, that's the case—legislators and administrators tend to look first at gifted programs.

In recent months, we've heard from several colleagues whose jobs are in jeopardy and whose programs have been eliminated (in one case, after twenty years). Others are facing larger classes (of thirty students or more) and are being told to differentiate the curriculum to meet everyone's needs.

The *Jacob K. Javits Gifted and Talented Students Education Act of 1994* is under siege. President George W. Bush's budget request for fiscal year 2002 specified zero dollars for the act; Congress allocated $11.25 million. Responding to a $1.3 billion shortfall in the Pell Grants program, the president suggested that Congress rescind funds for the *Javits Act,* among other education "earmarks" and "low priority" programs. His budget request for fiscal year 2003 once again omitted funding for the Javits program.

The *No Child Left Behind Act of 2001,* which President Bush signed into law on January 8, 2002, focuses—as its name implies—on children who need help learning. One of its main goals is to close the achievement gap between disadvantaged and minority students and their peers. We agree that no child should be left behind. We also believe that no child should be *kept behind* because his or her learning needs aren't being met.

. . . and How One Parents' Group Fought Back

In February 2002, a new bill was presented to the Tennessee legislature. The bill proposed moving the gifted program from under the "special education" umbrella and placing it under the "general education" umbrella.

On the surface, that sounds like the right thing to do. Special education services are designed for students with disabilities, and giftedness is not a disability. But when Tennessee parents looked more closely at the bill, they saw what might really happen if it were passed.

continued . . .

Gifted children would lose significant legal rights and protections. Identification and services would no longer be mandated. The Individual Education Program (IEP) would be abolished. Existing gifted programs would be left with no formal structure or funding and could easily be cut. And all general education teachers would have to receive special training to teach gifted students.

Led by the Tennessee Initiative for Gifted Education Reform (TIGER), a nonprofit advocacy group for gifted programs, parents fought back. Through their Web site, email newsletters, and press releases, they actively lobbied against the bill and kept parents across the state updated. In March 2002, the bill was officially taken "off notice"—removed from the legislative calendar.

Are You Gifted?

Suppose we were to ask you this question: "Are you gifted?" How would you answer it?

You may not know whether you're "officially" gifted. As an education descriptor, this term wasn't coined until the federal guidelines appeared in 1976. But suppose you do know that you're not "officially" gifted. Your IQ score is below 130, you were an average student and developed no outstanding abilities, you failed to get into an Ivy League college, and you didn't complete four years of college ahead of your time. Is that bad? Does that make you an inadequate teacher? Does that mean you have nothing to offer, no special qualities? Does that make you a less valuable person? Of course not!

Many important jobs in the world don't require genius-level intelligence, and they may require attributes that other people have in abundance. According to one theory,[1] the optimum range of intelligence runs from 125–145 on the Stanford-Binet Intelligence Scale. People who score in this range are able to master most tasks, work in any occupation they choose, and may function more easily in the world than people with profoundly high IQ scores. And let us not forget that high intelligence is also only one set of personal characteristics that we value. Loyalty, honesty, humor, joy, and enthusiasm are important, useful qualities.

But suppose you are—or think you may be—in the upper 3 percent of the population in intellectual ability. Would you stand up in a meeting with school colleagues (everyone from the principal and secretaries to regular teachers, coaches, and luncheon staff) to be identified? Would you want your name in the paper? How would you tell your friends or relatives . . . or would you? Would telling them help explain what you're all about, or merely intimidate them? Are you comfortable with your abilities or anxious? If you're ambivalent about it, imagine how confused young students are.

Perhaps, you say, recognition for a job well done is okay. What's not okay is the effect of the "gifted" label—the calling-to-attention of an abstract quality that people can't really define but resent or envy anyway. On the other hand, it may be the "packaging" of your personal abilities you resist. "What am I," you ask, "a commodity for others to trade on?" And then there's your sense of justice (and injustice): Perhaps you know plenty of people who have been labeled "gifted," but for the life of you, you can't see why.

These are some common reactions you (or others) may have when thinking about the "gifted" label. Because many of us haven't lived through this ability grouping, we can only guess what it is like to be told in second, fifth, or tenth grade that one's abilities are extraordinary and require special instruction. We do know that it is a label students will live with for the rest of their lives. If they can't talk about it with their gifted education teacher, who can they talk about it with?

Explaining Gifted Education

As a gifted education teacher, you'll need to become comfortable with the "gifted" label sooner or later. (You may want to read or review "What About the Label?" on pages 30–33.) You'll first have to define it for yourself, because you can count on having to explain it to parents, students, other teachers, possibly a coordinator, and other administrators as well. You'll have to be able to explain to students how they were identified for the program ("How come I'm in this class and Johnny isn't?"), why their needs can't be met through traditional instruction, and how your class is different than other classes. You'll want to make sure for yourself that the school's selection process identifies students for programs that are targeted for these abilities, and that your strengths as a teacher match what you are assigned to teach.

On pages 111–122, we'll outline some tactics for discussing the label with small groups of students. They have a right to know why they are in the program they're in, yet they need help putting the label in perspective and making neither more nor less out of it than is appropriate. Having students complete the "Student Questionnaire" on pages 40–45 will prepare them to approach this issue.

Questions and Answers About Gifted Education

Following are some of the "tough questions" you may be asked by kids, parents, your colleagues, and others who are curious about gifted education, along with some possible answers you can try.

"What does 'gifted' really mean?"

■ "'Gifted and talented' are words used to describe kids who are exceptionally capable in some way. Usually this means they are more advanced than other kids their age in terms of intellect, creativity, artistic ability, leadership, or a specific academic subject, like math or science."

■ "'Gifted' means that a student learns very differently than most other children. A gifted student is capable of learning more and faster at school, and can usually perform at a really outstanding level in some area."

■ "Actually, there are six so-called 'categories' of gifted children. There are those with general intellectual ability—in other words, they're smart at almost everything. There are those with specific academic aptitude, meaning they're exceptional in a particular subject or field. There are gifted kids who shine in creative or productive thinking, and those who excel in leadership. Some gifts come out in the visual or performing arts. And some kids are gifted in terms of psychomotor ability—the way they use their bodies."

For other ideas, you might also review the definitions of giftedness in Chapter 1: What Is Giftedness? If you created your own definition, you might respond with that instead.

"How are children selected for the gifted program?"

■ "At this school, we include children in the gifted program if *(choose the appropriate response):* they score in the top 3 to 5 percent on the Stanford-Binet Intelligence Scale; they score in the 95th percentile or above on achievement tests; they are recommended because of artistic, creative, or leadership skills; or . . . *(a combination of the above, or whatever method your school uses)."*

■ "We select students for this program when they have unusual academic or creative potential, and they need learning opportunities that aren't usually available in the regular classroom. We use a combination of teacher and parent recommendations along with achievement and ability tests."

"How come Joey (Janey's brother) didn't get picked for the program?"

■ "I don't know Joey, so I can't tell you why he isn't in the program. I do know Janey, and she's in the program because . . ."

■ "Joey may do well on classroom tests, and that's really good. This program, however, was developed for kids with high overall learning potential, as measured by intellectual ability tests. The difference between achievement and ability is that achievement tests measure what you have learned—what you have been taught. Ability tests measure what you are capable of learning in certain areas. If Joey is working up to his potential and scoring well on classroom tests, he's probably in the right place."

■ "It's probably because Janey scored higher on some tests of general ability, or on tests of creativity or achievement. Although no test is perfect, and we're still learning a lot about how to identify children with special talents, these tests are the best tools we have to work with today."

"What's the best way to teach students with high ability? Isn't it better for them to stay in the regular classroom?"

■ "Depending on the child, her age, maturity, and type of ability, it may be best to move her ahead in a particular subject, or even a whole grade. Or she may need enrichment classes that go beyond the regular curriculum. What's best for her will depend on the type and degree of ability she has and what we as a school have to offer."

■ "A 'pull-out' or 'cluster' class for only gifted kids may be best if a student is ready to move on and work more deeply, at higher levels, for longer periods of time. Gifted students who stay in regular classes often don't get enough of a workout. They get bored, frustrated, and can suffer emotionally as well as intellectually. Some develop behavior problems. Others actually fail school, or they fail to make connections with meaningful work and friends."

■ "Kids at this level of ability simply learn faster and have different learning needs than other students. They need different materials, different kinds of supervision, and different goals set for them. They are also ready to work more on process skills, such as critical thinking and learning skills. Finally, it's important for them to be with other students like themselves—kids who share their interests, who are closer to their mental age than their actual peers. For these reasons, it's best to provide a separate class for them."

"What will my child be learning or doing differently in this gifted program?"

■ "Depending on the options chosen for your child, he may work in an advanced class or with advanced materials. Or he may work on projects demanding higher-level thinking skills. Or he may work on special creative, musical, or problem-solving skills."

■ "In addition to more challenging courses or a broader curriculum—meaning more courses to choose from—students in this program are expected to take more responsibility for their learning. They are expected to help set goals, monitor their own learning, and manage independent time."

■ "The work in this class is demanding. We cover more complex concepts in greater depth, and we require students to do several kind of assignments. We encourage them to work in a range of media or presentation modes, such as writing, speaking, music, a staged or filmed documentary, audiovisuals, and Web sites."

"Should I tell my child that he or she is gifted?"

■ "Yes. Depending on the student's age, you might explain that she did very well on a particular test, or that she's been recommended for the program because of her work (performance or whatever) in a certain area. Show that you're happy or pleased for her. And even though it's tempting to look ahead to a glorious future, try to limit your expectations to the present. For example, instead of telling your child, 'You should really be able to make something of yourself now,' you might say, 'This program sounds like a good opportunity for you. I hope you like it.'"

■ "Yes. Tell her that the class is designed for kids who learn especially well in math (or English, science, or whatever), and that you're really proud of her for qualifying."

■ "Yes. Tell your child how he was selected for the program, and explain that some kids need extra enrichment classes to think about subjects more deeply or explore projects in a number of different ways. Reassure him that he may also find other students with similar interests in the class."

"How do I cope with the feelings (such as jealousy) of other siblings in our family (or other children in my class) who aren't selected for the gifted program?"

■ "Focus on the individual differences and achievements of both (all) children."

■ "Show each child that he or she is valued. Show by your words and actions that many different qualities are important to have, including humor, honesty, loyalty, and caring."

■ "Reinforce all children equally in public. Save some of your praise for the gifted child to deliver in private."

■ "Make sure that you give each child as much one-on-one time as possible. Don't let the gifted child's talent take up all your time."

"Are YOU gifted?"

- "Yes."

- "No."

- "I don't really know, but I suspect that I may be in some areas."

- "I would probably come out very close to the top in math, but I'm only average in other subjects."

- "I'd like to think I'm a gifted teacher, but they haven't come up with a test to measure that yet!"

- "Children weren't tested in exactly this way when I was growing up. But somehow I've always known (or people have always told me) that I was unusually talented or bright."

- "I've always been a high academic achiever, but my IQ is not in the gifted range, so it's hard to say. I think I'm gifted in some things."

"It must be nice having all the smart kids in your class."

- "I really do like these kids. They are a challenge for me, however."

- *(Depending on how the remark is said):* "To be honest, it kind of upsets me to hear you say that. I wonder if you think I don't work as hard as you, when in fact I work very hard."

- "I do have some unusual kids in my class, but I'm sure I don't have all the smart ones—there are plenty in other classes, too! Besides, all kids have something to offer."

- "It's very different working with gifted students. They can be extremely demanding, and they don't automatically succeed at everything they do."

"Shaundra isn't doing very well in my math class this year. Are you sure she belongs in your gifted program?"

- "Have you talked to Shaundra about her performance in your class?"

- "Gifted students aren't usually exceptional in everything they do, and math has never been Shaundra's strong point."

- "Would you like to sit down with me and Shaundra and discuss this?"

- "Are you sure that Shaundra needs to do the work you're assigning her? Is it something she could test out of, or do an independent study on?"

You may want to think through some of these issues in more depth and detail. Write down the questions you most frequently hear and experiment with different answers. Imagine all the parents who have ever confronted you. What were they asking you? What were they worried about? What did they really want to know or be told? Consider the questions and comments you've heard from teachers and administrators over the years. Do they understand what you do every day? Do they grasp the special challenges you face? (And are you sympathetic to the special challenges *they* face?) Think back to the questions you've heard from students. What do they ask you in the hall? Before school? After school? Between classes? In notes or emails?

Why Even Have Gifted Education?

You may be asked this question by people who are confrontive (as in "Aren't all kids gifted?" and "Isn't gifted education elitist?") or merely curious ("What is gifted education all about, and why do we need it?"). You may be challenged to defend gifted education in a time of budget cutbacks, when anything considered "nonessential" is at risk. Following are some reasons why we think gifted education is necessary—today, tomorrow, and always.

- Gifted kids need a place where they can be themselves. That can mean almost anything: brainy, impatient, show-offy, moody, obsessed with a particular interest, off in a mysterious direction. America has traditionally been a society that values equality. Often, that translates into favoring conformity and people who don't stand out from the crowd.

- Gifted kids need a place where they can feel safe and supported. Many high-achieving students actually hide or cover up their abilities to improve their chances of being accepted as "normal" or to win popularity with their age peers.

- Like all kids, gifted kids have the right to the best education *for them*. They need opportunities to learn at their own speed, opt out of work they already know and understand, study things that interest them, go beyond the basics, work with abstract concepts that require more than simple thinking, work with peers who share their interests and abilities, and participate in options that connect their learning to the "real world."

continued . . .

■ By the time they reach their senior year of high school, gifted kids will have spent more than 12,000 hours in school. Shouldn't at least some of those hours be challenging, rewarding, stimulating, meaningful, and enjoyable?

And here are more detailed reasons from the National Association for Gifted Children:

1. Gifted learners must be given stimulating educational experiences appropriate to their level of ability if they are to realize their potential. Giftedness arises from an interaction between innate capabilities and an environment that challenges and stimulates to bring forth high levels of ability and talent. These challenges must be available throughout the individual's lifetime for high levels of actualization of ability and talent to result. According to research on the nature of intelligence and the brain, we either progress or we regress depending on our participation in stimulation appropriate to our level of development.

2. Each person has the right to learn and to be provided challenges for learning at the most appropriate level where growth proceeds most effectively. Our political and social system is based on democratic principles. The school as an extension of those principles must provide an equal educational opportunity for all children to develop to their fullest potential. This means allowing gifted students the opportunity to learn at their level of development. For truly equal opportunity, a variety of learning experiences must be available at many levels.

3. At present, only slightly over one-half of the possible gifted learners in the United States are reported to be receiving education appropriate to their needs. There is physical and psychological pain in being thwarted, discouraged, and diminished as a person. To have ability, to feel power you are never allowed to use, can become traumatic. Many researchers consider the gifted as the largest group of underachievers in education.

4. Traditional education currently does not sufficiently value bright minds. Gifted children often enter school having already developed many of their basic skills. Almost from the first day they sense isolation, as others consider them different. Schools are not sufficiently individualized or flexible to allow modification in structure and organization. Most schools seek to develop skills that allow participation in society, not the re-creation of that society.

continued . . .

5. When given the opportunity, gifted students can use their vast amount of knowledge to serve as a background for unlimited learning. When the needs of the gifted are considered and the educational program is designed to meet these needs, these students make significant gains in achievement, and their sense of competence and well-being is enhanced.

6. Providing for our finest minds allows both individual and societal needs to be met. Contributions to society in all areas of human endeavor come in overweighted proportions from this population of individuals. Society needs the gifted adult to play a far more demanding and innovative role than that required of the more typical learner. We need integrated, highly functioning persons to carry out those tasks that will lead all of us to a satisfying, fulfilling future.

Reasons 1–6 are from the National Association for Gifted Children, "Parent Information: Why Should Gifted Education Be Supported?" (Washington, DC: National Association for Gifted Children, 2001). *www.nagc.org*. Used with permission.

What Makes a Good Gifted Education Teacher?

"Outstanding teachers of the gifted, as identified by their colleagues, as well as average teachers of the gifted, agree that the most important characteristic of a successful educator is to like gifted children."
—LAURIE CROFT

Contrary to what you might expect, veteran teachers of the gifted tell us that what is needed most of all to survive in gifted education is a sense of humor. Humor—plus a strong self-concept, a high energy level, and a sincere liking for gifted students. Rather than in-depth content knowledge or terrific analytical powers, an underlying commitment to students and a positive attitude about learning seem to be most essential. In the words of one elementary-school gifted education teacher, "I'm not an expert in anything. What I have to offer is an attitude of lifelong learning. I like to learn anything."

For the elementary homeroom or enrichment teacher, the ability to "learn along with the students" is probably more important than standing up in front of the class and "disseminating knowledge." As another teacher observes, "In gifted education, you have second, third, and fourth graders who are content-area specialists. They already know more facts than you." What they don't know, necessarily, is how to put things in perspective, how to organize their learning, and how to chart where they want to go.

Requirements for successful teaching change somewhat when the classes are subject-specific and designed for accelerated students. A high school course in Chinese must be taught by someone competent in that language, and advanced calculus needs a well-versed mathematician. But even here, teachers can expect to be challenged by students. A sense of humor, strong self-concept, and a positive attitude about their own continued learning are the qualities which enable teachers to handle challenges gracefully. Teachers should have a solid mastery over their material, but also know their limitations, and be willing (we would hope eager) to continuously expand their knowledge.

Aside from the personal qualities mentioned above, several didactic talents may be particularly useful to gifted education teachers. Primary among these is versatility with a range of teaching strategies. If you heavily favor one mode of teaching, such as lecture-discussion, you may find yourself in trouble. To work with gifted students, you need to be very flexible, capable of individualizing instruction, and adept at managing small- and large-group activities as well. Gifted students particularly thrive on student-centered instruction, yet they need variety in their daily instructional diet. You can't assign them to independent study all year long. You'll therefore need to be capable of designing small-group discussions, large-group projects, tutorials, and other learning activities to foster either content knowledge or process skills.

When we wrote *The Gifted Kids' Survival Guide: A Teen Handbook,* we surveyed hundreds of gifted students, asking them to identify their questions and concerns about growing up gifted. The one thing students said they wanted *most* from their teachers was flexibility. Good gifted education teachers also need considerable communication skills. By this we mean a whole cluster of "people skills" including:

- observation skills: listening, watching, picking up verbal and non-verbal cues
- intuition: sensing needs or issues
- empathy: communicating concern and interest
- role-modeling: demonstrating positive attitudes, appropriate behaviors
- verbal presentation skills
- writing skills
- group leadership and counseling skills

When two teachers asked students in a special project for gifted and highly-able learners (ages 6–16) to describe their concept of a gifted teacher,[2] over 50 percent of the responses listed someone who:

- understands them
- has a sense of humor
- can make learning fun
- is cheerful

Thirty percent listed someone who:

- supports and respects them
- is intelligent
- is patient
- is firm with them
- is flexible

Only 5 to 10 percent listed someone who:

- knows the subject
- explains things carefully
- is skilled in group processes

It may be that the most relaxed, cheerful, and confident teacher is also most knowledgeable (and can therefore afford to be relaxed and cheerful!), but it's interesting that students pick up on these affective qualities faster than expertise.

The Qualities of Teachers

by Susan Winebrenner, M.S., consultant and author

Do teachers have to be gifted themselves in order to teach gifted students? I worried about that the first time I attended a national training program for teachers of gifted students. I was always a competent student who worked very hard in all subjects, but I was never considered gifted by myself or any of my teachers.

I have since learned the answer to my question: No! However, teachers who are successful with gifted kids tend to possess certain qualities that gifted children respond to positively. Those qualities are:

- Enthusiasm about teaching and the joy of lifelong learning.

- Flexible teaching style. Comfort with situations in which some students are doing different activities than others and in which students are flexibly grouped for learning.

- Strong listening skills. Keeps inquiry open.

- Knowledgeable about the unique characteristics and needs of gifted students and willing to accommodate them.

continued . . .

- Able and willing to set up and nurture a learning environment in which risk-taking and mistake-making are expected and encouraged.

- Respectful of students' strengths and weaknesses. Able to encourage students to accept both without embarrassment.

- Willing and eager to expose students to new ideas and provide opportunities for exploring those ideas.

- Able and willing to connect the curriculum to students' learning styles, interests, and questions. Good at empowering students to follow their passions.

- Well-developed sense of humor about themselves and their students.

- Well-organized though not necessarily "neat." Able to do multiple tasks simultaneously with effective time-management skills.

- Comfortable providing a wide range of learning materials, including those that are appropriate for older students.

- Able and willing to locate and organize resources or to steer gifted kids to other people who know how to do this.

- Aware that gifted students need less time with practice and more time with complex and abstract learning tasks.

- Comfortable communicating with students about their individual progress.

- Able and willing to advocate for what gifted students need.

- Able and willing to encourage parents of gifted students to find and take advantage of experiences available for their children through college and community resources.

From *Teaching Gifted Kids in the Regular Classroom: Strategies and Techniques Every Teacher Can Use to Meet the Academic Needs of the Gifted and Talented*, Revised, Expanded, Updated ed., by Susan Winebrenner (Minneapolis: Free Spirit Publishing, Inc., 2001), p. 193. Used with permission.

Seven Tips for Gifted Education Teachers

The focus of this chapter thus far has been on you, the gifted education teacher. Your attitudes about yourself, about giftedness, and about your gifted students are fundamental to the strategies and activities that follow in this book. If you're uncomfortable with gifted students, or unsure of what the label does and doesn't mean, your students will pick up on that discomfort.

Before we proceed, we'd like to suggest some specific actions you might take to strengthen your own abilities as a gifted education teacher, build support for gifted education, and take care of yourself. We have found them helpful, other teachers we know have found them helpful, and we think that you will, too.

1. If you don't have specific training in gifted education, get it—any way you can. If you're able to take the time and can afford a master's program, do it. If not, try to get whatever in-service training is available. Meanwhile, read as much as you can, observe other classrooms or programs, and research your own students.

2. Advocate that all staff at your school take at least basic in-service training on the gifted. Everyone should understand more about these students, even if they're working with them for only a few hours a week. (Gifted kids are, after all, gifted 24 hours a day.) You set yourself up for a lot of problems if you allow yourself to become the only "expert" in the house. You'll find that other teachers become more cooperative once they learn more about gifted students and what you're doing with them.

3. Get a support group going for yourself. Don't expect "regular" classroom teachers to provide the support you need; your problems and issues are different. You may actually have more in common with teachers in special services. But isolation is not good. Join a network at the district or state level. Form your own informal club, or find a few other gifted education teachers to talk with routinely.

4. Keep parents informed of your program's goals. Particularly if the program is new, parents will need a certain amount of education. Try to build a strong parent group in the first years, but don't "take over." Let them become responsible for the ongoing management of the group. You may find parents can be effective advocates and important sources of support if budget cuts or other political issues threaten your program.

5. If you're new to gifted education, give yourself time to grow into your job. Gifted education teachers have been known to burn out quickly. Many of us suffer from the same need for perfection as our students do, and we set unrealistic goals and unreasonable deadlines for ourselves. Take care of yourself by limiting the number of hours you work overtime. Realize that you won't turn underachieving kids around in a year, that you can't guarantee each kid will reach her or his potential, and that you'll make many of the same "mistakes" other teachers make. (But remember, as one gifted child wrote us, "There's no such thing as a mistake; the only mistake is one not made.") Don't expect miracles from your students, and don't expect them from yourself.

6. Give yourself permission to assert yourself and defend your students' rights. Becoming an advocate is not easy. You may feel at odds with a lot of people. Use your support group and parents to help you keep your balance.

7. Enjoy your students. Enjoy the subject you're teaching. Enjoy your own ability to learn and to grow.

Creating a Supportive Environment

Picture the following scene: a special class of young teenagers in a large urban public school.

First, there's Gregory, who is sitting on the edge of his seat, with his lank hair falling in front of his eyes. His foot taps the floor in a nonstop staccato rhythm. His eyes are shining; he is busy explaining the proof he wrote on the board for an advanced calculus class. Several people are talking at once.

Most audible is Janine, who is loudly groaning for help. "Ms. Petroff, I'm totally lost! If you want to know why we're not asking questions, it's because we don't know enough to ask questions!"

Another student goes to the board, demonstrating her method for solving last night's homework. Does Janine get this? "Heck, no! I'm drowning! Send in a life preserver!"

A young boy with braces and thin arms, well under five feet tall, confers with his neighbor—a muscular giant whose face is in full hormonal flower. The small boy grins wickedly as he whispers, "I actually did number 21! I'm so proud! As a matter of fact, I have this incredible desire to write it on the board."

"Well, go for it!" his friend replies, tossing a crumpled ball of paper in the corner wastepaper basket.

Across the room, various conversations overlap as students review their answers, question the teacher and each other vigorously, and recalculate their figures.

"You call that a life preserver?" Janine says to Gregory, whose proof has still left her in the dark.

"Try saying that in English," another kid suggests. (Gregory is a foreign student but obviously well-spoken.)

"Who sees this now?" the teacher asks, as she demonstrates a critical step in notation on the board. Silence lasts but a second.

"Hey! That's slick! That's so slick I'm going to write it down!"

"I'm gonna write home about it!"

"I'd say there's a *real lack of life preservers* here! They all have holes in them!"

The three-ring circus begins again, with kids teaching other kids, kids working at the board, the teacher questioning students, checking for comprehension. Students appear to be capable of attending each of the "three rings" simultaneously, integrating the information without much trouble and moving on. Their questions are answered once, they understand, and they want more.

All eyes return to the teacher as she writes a new problem on the board. She says very little about it, mentioning only which theorems might come into play. Once the problem is posed, students pounce on it like lions on raw meat. Immediately, arguments and questions break out. Just when they seemed to reach an impasse, Janine asks—and then answers—her own question (the teacher silences Gregory in time with a "Shhh, Gregory, let's see if she can figure it out"). Janine does get the right answer, and the class applauds her with "high-fives" hand slaps.

When the class is over, we ask the teacher to talk about two of her students: Gregory, who (as the youngest of the class) seems so obviously precocious, and Janine, who struggles dramatically to keep up with the group. The teacher responds that Gregory certainly is bright; he already knows all the material she hopes to cover in the coming year and is enrolled in her university math class. But Janine . . . Janine is probably the next brightest student in the room.

This example comes from but one class in the country for gifted and talented students. It was an exceptional class in all respects. The students were intelligent, highly motivated, well-behaved, gregarious, and supportive of one another. The teacher was impressive both in terms of math knowledge and pedagogy; she knew how to teach bright students, knew how to guide and support their learning as well as how to stimulate them. Yet even within this small, homogeneous, well-defined, and apparently well-adjusted group of kids, interesting differences in ability and affect could be seen.

Gregory's obvious facility with terms, computation, and problem-solving enable him to perform years ahead of his chronological peers. Janine's math intelligence, on the other hand, may have been the product of intuition, originality, or intense interest. Some educators distinguish between academically gifted and socially gifted; between highly gifted and normally gifted; and between highly creative and highly talented students. As we noted in Chapter 3: Emotional Dimensions of Giftedness, many breakdowns and categories exist.

Ms. Petroff not only notices and addresses her students' academic and intellectual needs. She also is alert and responsive to their social and emotional needs. For example, she perceives that Gregory sometimes gets impatient with Janine, who can't keep up with his lightning-fast thought processes. And she's aware that Janine, despite her abilities, is something of a perfectionist; it's rare when she risks giving an answer of which she's not 100 percent sure. Ms. Petroff's other students include those who are occasionally rebellious, sometimes obsessed with projects that aren't part of the curriculum, overly sensitive, and not always receptive to criticism. In many ways, they keep her on her toes.

How Supportive Are You?

You may feel like there's not enough time in the day to add an entirely new component (affective education) into your curriculum, but it's already there anyway. You may not be addressing emotional issues directly, but indirectly you're already sending messages that guide or impede students' search for self-knowledge—messages that broaden students' understanding of others or not.

We've provided you with background information on giftedness, and we've asked you to take the "Teacher Inventory" (pages 37–39) and give your students the "Student Questionnaire" (pages 40–45), because knowledge of yourself and your students is vital in determining how you behave in the classroom. A supportive attitude is built into (or not built into) the many small things you do every day—the gestures and remarks you make, the amount and type of physical and eye contact you have with your students, the comments you write on paper, the verbal instructions you give. To communicate expectations clearly, to give honest and supportive feedback, to reward learning processes as well as products, to involve students in decisions, to take time to listen, to see yourself as facilitator and not just "knowledge disseminator"—all of these attitudes and techniques affect your students' emotional well-being as much as (or more than) any single group discussion of feelings. Certainly, they go together.

Creating a supportive environment begins the first moment of the first day when students walk into your classroom, and runs concurrently with every instructional task you undertake. Support stems from truly liking and enjoying your gifted students. But support involves more than smiling, showing enthusiasm, and offering words of encouragement, although these are requisite ingredients. Support is also conveyed by setting clear expectations; giving constructive criticism; being honest; being flexible; and providing your students with structure, tangible rewards, comfortable classrooms, accommodating schedules, and routine times for sharing or relaxing.

Some of the strategies we suggest may seem obvious to you. If that's your initial response, take a moment to consider how often you put them into practice. Do you periodically check out how well you're coming across in these areas? Some of the simplest strategies are also the best.

For more strategies and activities that will help you create a supportive environment for your gifted students, see Chapter 8: Making It Safe to Be Smart: Creating the Gifted-Friendly Classroom.

What to Aim For: Gifted Program Standards for Socio-Emotional Guidance and Counseling from the National Association for Gifted Children

In 1998, the National Association for Gifted Children (NAGC) defined a set of standards for gifted education programming. They include specific standards for socio-emotional guidance and counseling. As you work to create a supportive environment that addresses your students' social and emotional needs, you may wish to consult these standards from time to time.

Description: Gifted education programming must establish a plan to recognize and nurture the unique socio-emotional development of gifted learners.

Guiding Principles	Minimum Standards	Exemplary Standards
1. Gifted learners must be provided with differentiated guidance efforts to meet their unique socio-emotional development.	**1.** Gifted learners, because of their unique socio-emotional development, must be provided with guidance and counseling services by a counselor who is familiar with the characteristics and socio-emotional needs of gifted learners.	**1.** Counseling services should be provided by a counselor familiar with specific training in the characteristics and socio-emotional needs (i.e., underachievement, multi-potentiality, etc.) of diverse gifted learners.
2. Gifted learners must be provided with career guidance services especially designed for their unique needs.	**2.** Gifted learners must be provided with career guidance consistent with their unique strengths.	**2.** Gifted learners should be provided with college and career guidance that is appropriately different and delivered earlier than typical programs.

3. Gifted at-risk students must be provided with guidance and counseling to help them reach their potential.

3. Gifted learners who are placed at-risk must have special attention, counseling, and support to help them realize their full potential.

3. Gifted learners who do not demonstrate satisfactory performance in regular and/or gifted education classes should be provided with specialized intervention services.

4. Gifted learners must be provided with affective curriculum in addition to differentiated guidance and counseling services.

4. Gifted learners must be provided with affective curriculum as part of differentiated curriculum and instructional services.

4. A well-defined and implemented affective curriculum scope and sequence containing personal/social awareness and adjustment, academic planning, and vocational and career awareness should be provided to gifted learners.

5. Underachieving gifted learners must be served rather than omitted from differentiated services.

5. Gifted students who are underachieving must not be exited from gifted programs because of related problems.

5. Underachieving gifted learners should be provided with specific guidance and counseling services that address the issues and problems related to underachievement.

From "National Association for Gifted Children Pre-K–Grade 12 Gifted Program Standards: Socio-Emotional Guidance and Counseling" (Washington, DC: National Association for Gifted Children, 1998). *www.nagc.org.* Used with permission.

Strategy: Clarify Your Role as Teacher and Your Students' Roles as Learners

Read your students this famous saying:

**Give a man a fish, he eats for a day;
teach a man how to fish, he eats for a lifetime.***

Invite them to talk about this in terms of knowledge and learning. Is it more important for teachers to tell students the facts, the answers ("knowledge"), or to teach them how to learn facts and answers for themselves? Generally, we know that knowledge is "exploding" so fast that much of the information we learn today will be out-of-date before long. Many specific jobs and careers will require different sets of knowledge and even different skills by the time students are ready to enter the workforce. We also know that people's memories are limited, and learning itself can be a pleasurable process. These are arguments for "learning how to learn."

Ask your students if they can think of other arguments—both pro and con. Ask them if they have already experienced learning something only to find it out-of-date. Perhaps their parents have changed jobs, gone back to school, or been retrained by their company.

Reinforce that while human beings need fish (or other food) to satisfy their immediate hunger, they also need to learn how to fish to survive beyond the day. Similarly, students need to know certain facts, concepts, and procedures, but they also need to learn how to learn and think on their own.

Ask your students what they think your job as teacher entails, and what their job as learners is. Are you to give them the information they need in order to progress, but also to teach (or encourage) them to learn on their own? Should students learn how to ask questions, analyze problems, research topics, evaluate their own work and the thinking of others? Should they try to just memorize what the teacher says is important? Talk about how teachers can communicate information and function as a resource and coach at the same time.

At some point during this discussion, try to articulate whatever role you define for yourself. You may wish to let them know your limits by saying something like, "I make mistakes, too. I have strengths in these particular areas [give examples], but I don't know everything."

---

* Although the original author refers to "man," we interpret his meaning to include all human beings.

Strategy: Clarify Expectations—Yours and Theirs

What do you expect students do to in your class? You'll want to state this as clearly as possible. At the start of the year (or semester, or week), prepare a handout explaining what you want from your students and what you hope to accomplish. State your expectations in terms of the following:

- **learning objectives** (examples: understand the components of a research paper; master the procedures for dissecting vertebrates and invertebrates; communicate ideas and feelings about one's own ethnic culture in a creative project; compare autocratic and democratic decision-making

- **content** (examples: reading assignments—including titles and page numbers; films or tapes to review; Web sites to surf)

- **products** (what's due when)

- **methods** (examples: how students are supposed to proceed; an overall schedule with a list of activities)

- **evaluations** (examples: the type of evaluation—self-evaluation, teacher comments, tests; purpose of measures; policies such as those regarding retests)

- **intangible outcomes** (examples: to start from wherever you are and make progress; to make work personally meaningful; to feel pride in oneself and one's group; to compete in the state spelling competition)

Go over the handout with your students and allow time for questions. If possible, indicate options they may have under content, products, and evaluations. For instance, they may choose to work with different content or materials, or pick from three suggested final projects: prepare a photo essay or stage a debate, write a paper, or some other project. Indicate how you want students to negotiate with you for different options, and at what time.

When addressing intangible outcomes, try to express what signs of learning are really most meaningful to you—what you would be most pleased to see in your students and what you can realistically expect. This is where understanding your own expectations of gifted students comes into play. Be as fair and honest in your expectations as you can.

Also check out expectations students may have of you or the class. See if there are other topics they'd like to cover, other methods or materials they'd prefer to use.

Explicitly stating objectives and expectations has a known impact on students' learning. Given an overview of where they're going and what they're responsible for, they can focus their learning energy better and evaluate their own progress.

Even when assignments are "open" and evaluation consists of measures other than grades or tests, teachers (and other adults) still have expectations—we just take them for granted or assume kids understand them. Making your expectations known causes a stir at first, but public goals cause less anxiety in the long run than hidden or ambiguous goals.

Alleviating the concerns students have about assignments, grades, grading criteria, team assignments, books, and other materials helps build a supportive atmosphere. Checking for these concerns should be done periodically, if not almost every session.

Strategy: Set Ground Rules

> *"A successful teacher doesn't get down to the students' levels, but raises them up to his."*
> —FRANK DAVIES

All students need help learning and understanding how to behave in a group. They need help improving their social skills and developing trust for each other and their learning environment.

Every classroom has rules, whether stated or implied. Often, these rules suggest (or dictate) how students should behave, what supplies students should bring to class, or what the consequences are of misbehavior or late work. But rules don't have to be punitive. Instead, they can be inviting and affirming. Some can even get "disguised" as indirect ways of perceiving the class as a functioning assembly of good people.

Discuss the "Class Rules (Grades K–5)" or the "Class Rules (Grades 6 & up)" on the facing page, depending on the age of the class you're teaching.[3] You may want to list the appropriate rules on a chart and post them ahead of time, or elicit your own set of class rules (with student input) in a group discussion.

Class Rules (Grades K–5)

There are no dumb questions or dumb answers.

It's OK to say "I don't know."

Sometimes it's OK to listen and not talk.

Keep asking until you understand.

No one is perfect.

You can TRY NEW THINGS here.

If you don't agree, say so, and explain your thoughts.

Teasing, bullying, and put-downs are NOT allowed.

It's good to have a MIND OF YOUR OWN.

From *Class Rules Poster: Grades K–5* (Minneapolis: Free Spirit Publishing Inc., 1999). Used with permission.

Class Rules (Grades 6 & up)

There are no dumb questions or dumb answers.

This is the place to TAKE RISKS and learn from mistakes.

Teasing, bullying, put-downs, and sarcasm are NOT allowed.

If you don't agree, say so, and explain your thoughts.

It's OK to say "I don't know."

No one is perfect.

Keep asking until you really understand.

Don't criticize people—agree or disagree with their ideas.

During discussions, sometimes it's OK to listen and not talk.

It's good to have a MIND OF YOUR OWN.

From *Class Rules Poster: Grades 6 & up* (Minneapolis: Free Spirit Publishing Inc., 1998). Used with permission.

Whatever rules you decide to use, talk with your students about what they mean. Talk about how they will be reinforced in your classroom. Look for opportunities to role-model ways to respond to criticism, offer criticism, and respect someone's privacy.

Here are more examples of rules you might want to share with your students, drawn from several classrooms:

Fourth Grade Rules

1. Walking in halls prevents accidents.

2. Be mature and serious during fire drills.

3. Enjoy chewing your gum at home.

4. In groups, talk in six-inch voices.

5. Ask before you use.

6. People can be hurt by both words and actions. Use both carefully.

Remember: Kindness is contagious. You can get it from your classmates.

Notice the positive spin on each rule, the lack of negative phrasing, and the alternative behaviors that are mentioned.

Fifth Grade Rules

Find the answers.
Invite yourself to take a challenge.
Forget what you don't know; focus on what you do know.
Take time to laugh.
Hear what others say.

Gain independence.
Reach new levels.
Answer confidently.
Decide to take a challenge.
Express your thoughts respectfully.

Notice that fifth grade is about more than adding fractions and memorizing state capitals. It's also about becoming a better person and a more avid learner.

Sixth Grade Reminders

Let's all work at . . .

Trying our best.
Organizing our thoughts.
Getting work done on time.
Expressing our ideas respectfully.
Thinking in new ways.
Helping each other learn.
Enriching our minds and hearts.
Regarding one another as learning partners.

TOGETHER much can be accomplished. The wise teacher knows this and communicates it to students.

Eighth Grade Supply List

Things to Bring to Class

1. A positive attitude.
2. A pleasant voice.
3. Restrained feet.
4. Productive hands.
5. An inquiring mind.
6. Equipment to complete your lessons.
7. Assignments due (or overdue!).

This list begins with the most essential ingredient—a positive attitude—and simply builds from there.

Tenth Grade Rules

Rules of the World

1. The world is not fair.
2. Everybody has a boss.
3. Living involves hassle.
4. Nobody is entitled to anything.
5. True pride is self-respect and must be earned, not given.
6. Being loved is only free for babies. After that, reciprocity is required.
7. Everybody goofs a lot.

8. Everybody is laughable.

9. Staying happy involves work.

10. Success is dependent on personal initiative.

You already know something about this teacher's wit as soon as you arrive in class. You can't help but smile at these ten truths—especially number six.

A Request

In an open letter to teachers, a Holocaust survivor offered these moving and powerful words:

I am the survivor of a concentration camp. My eyes saw what no man should witness: Gas chambers built by learned engineers, children poisoned by educated physicians, infants killed by trained nurses, women and babies shot and burned by high school and college students. So I am suspicious of education.

My request is:

Help your students become human. Your efforts must never produce learned monsters, skilled psychopaths, educated Eichmanns. Reading, writing, arithmetic are important only if they serve to make our children more humane.

Quoted in Haim G. Ginott, *Teacher and Child* (New York: Collier, 1995), p. 317.

Strategy: Decide What to Reward and How

What kinds of student behavior (other than compliance, good test scores, and complete homework) do you want to reinforce? How will you reinforce them?

Observe your students for several days. Note the behaviors you'd like to reward and those you'd like to discourage. Write them down so you don't forget them. Include any other behaviors you can think of which may not have surfaced during your observations.

Think about this collection of behaviors. If you wish, share it with a colleague and get his or her feedback.

Here are examples of positive behaviors to look for (or include in your written list):

- following through on tasks
- sharing something personally meaningful
- supporting a friend
- time spent on-task
- asking good questions

- taking initiative
- demonstrating patience or self-control
- exploring something new
- appropriate use of humor

Your list could go on and on.

Now come up with specific ways to reward students who demonstrate positive behaviors. Here are some suggestions for you to consider:

- praise
- public recognition
- formal awards
- permission to do other things
- class celebrations
- opportunity to present work at a parent night or in a variety show
- free time
- individual attention

- special class events (speakers, films, field trips)
- red-letter day
- opportunity to "collaborate" with you or another mentor
- roster of "stars"
- progress charts
- thank-you notes (public or private)

Never underestimate the power of positive verbal messages. Here are several you may want to try:

- "This looks like you've learned a lot. How do you feel about these marks?"
- "I'm glad you're helping your friend."
- "You tried something new today. That took courage."
- "Congratulations on finishing this."
- "I think this group is ready for the state spelling championships."

- "You did a good job of standing up for yourself in that discussion."
- "I'm glad you asked that question, because I'll bet there are ten other people who want to know the same thing."
- "I believe you can do it."
- "I think it's great how you took the initiative to . . ."
- "You showed a lot of patience (or compassion, or self-control) today."

Gifted students need straightforward feedback on their accomplishments, but they also need lots of reinforcement for simply being—for relating well to one another, for relaxing, showing compassion, following through, or taking criticism well. They need encouragement when they demonstrate positive social behaviors and emotional maturity (or progress).

One additional point you may want to check on immediately: Some gifted classes don't "count" in terms of credit. Depending on the type of class you have, the number of hours and types of work accomplished, this may be very inappropriate and discriminatory. Gifted students should not have to complete all required coursework and activities on top of their gifted classes for no additional credit. Participation in advanced or enriched classes should be rewarded. Otherwise, some kids regard gifted education opportunities as a punishment for being bright.

Gifted Kids Speak Out

When we asked gifted students, "How can teachers help gifted kids?" here's what they said:

"Gifted kids like being creative and thinking outside the box. Offer us creative activities instead of always giving things like reports. There are a lot of projects that are more fun than reports."
—Stephanie, 12

"You should let gifted students test out in certain areas by giving them pretests. If they get A's on the pretests, they can work on other work while the people who don't test out can work on what they got wrong."
—Anonymous, 11

"Let us work ahead and independently. What a teacher teaches out of a math book in 45 minutes, I could learn in 10. With the extra time, we could do the next lesson."
—Shanay, 12

"Accept that some students may know more than you do and do not feel intimidated by this. If they know something, let them teach it to you. You can't challenge us if you are afraid of us."
—Ted, 13

continued . . .

"Remember that gifted kids are not sleepless, working machines."
—**Danny, 12**

"Gifted students may be fast learners, but their ways of learning might be totally 100 percent different than yours. I learned to read by doing math! I made a letter equal a sound and made a math problem with sound. I am not a skilled reader, so I learned to do it through math."
—**Jon, 12**

"Do not treat us like aliens that are super-smart, because we are just like any other kid. After we finish our work, we are not anxious to do more. We just want to sit and do what we want. Some other kids think that all we do is study and do homework after school. Ehhh . . . wrong! I am involved with a good deal of activities."
—**Christina, 12**

"You should forget about those silly State tests and just teach us what you think will help us grow. We'll do fine."
—**Amber, 11**

Supporting Gifted Kids One-on-One

The four preceding strategies, and those found in Chapter 8, will help you to establish a supportive classroom environment for your gifted students. But what if you need or choose to work with students individually on social or emotional issues? You may have a mixed-abilities classroom with only a few gifted students. Or you may have students with unique or challenging needs, or students who don't respond well in large groups.

The following strategies are ideal for working with students one-on-one or in smaller groups. Of course, you can also adapt them for use with larger groups.

Strategy: Use Questionnaires and Surveys

When you ask students to complete the "Student Questionnaire" on pages 40–45, the answers you get may not seem all that significant, especially the first time around. What *is* significant is that you asked the questions in the first place. You've opened the door for kids to tell you something about themselves, and you've let them know it's okay to communicate with you on a personal level.

On most days, in most schools, students aren't encouraged to express or clarify their feelings. They're probably not used to identifying conflicts, sources of stress, and sources of support in their lives. Some kids who feel uncomfortable with this process at first may ridicule the questionnaire as "silly" or "a waste of time." Yet for students to mature emotionally, they need to examine their perceptions, even when it's awkward or painful. Posing the questions via the questionnaire is a good first step. It stimulates thinking in a relatively safe way and requires no public response.

Surveying students is, in general, a good strategy for getting individuals to address sensitive questions. Unlike open-class voting (which is a useful group strategy), surveys demand anonymous yet personal answers, and they can be much more explicit. You may wish to instigate very brief weekly surveys on questions concerning academic pressures, careers, or social pressures, and post the results. For example: "In answer to last week's survey on choosing a career, 78 percent of the girls anticipate having a full-time job outside the home as adults, compared to 99 percent of the boys." Again, surveys can engage students individually to reflect on personal traits, values, and attitudes.

A variation on the idea of surveys is found in *100 Ways to Enhance Self-Concept in the Classroom* by Jack Canfield and Harold Clive Wells.[4] Their strategy, "Weekly Reaction Sheets," consists of quick, ten-item inventories that help students examine how they are using their time. Some sample questions: "What was the high point of the week?" "What did you procrastinate about?" "What unfinished personal business do you have left?" After six weeks of recording their weekly reactions, students are ready for a discussion on what they've learned. By changing the focus of the content, you can use weekly reaction sheets to address a broad range of growth issues.

Strategy: Use Journaling

> *"I write entirely to find out what I'm thinking, what I'm looking at, what I see and what it means. What I want and what I fear."*
> —JOAN DIDION

The possibilities for personal growth are almost unlimited when journal writing is approached as creative self-examination. Frequent, private writing has both therapeutic and technical value (in terms of language skills development—although journals shouldn't be assigned for this reason). Journals have become commonplace in classrooms, but their real benefits aren't always tapped.

Often, students are given inadequate direction ("Write something down every day"; "Write about anything, just make it at least three lines long"). Lacking the drama of Anne Frank's story, students quickly become bored with the tedium of their lives and of their writing. Fortunately, there are several concrete journaling techniques which give enough form and direction to the process to make the writing revelatory—even without the drama. (More about this in a minute.)

Unlike surveys, journals require individual readings from teachers and some sort of personal response, preferably in writing. Teachers reading student diaries should respond to each entry with a simple statement which acknowledges the student's feeling without judging it. In spoken counseling, the equivalent is, "Yes, I hear you. It sounds like . . ." Or you may wish to provide comments, suggestions, words of encouragement, or drawings.

Because responding individually to student journals takes time, you may need to limit how often you assign journals, or assign them only to students who seem to enjoy them the most. Journals may work best for students who already like to write or seem inclined to introspection. A shy student who tends to observe rather than participate may flower with this type of individual assignment.

We don't believe that journals should be graded. Neither should they be required if, after a mandatory trial period, they seem unnecessary, duplicative, or nonproductive for the writer.

Excellent sources for writing techniques are *Write Where You Are: How to Use Writing to Make Sense of Your Life, A Guide for Teens,* by Caryn Mirriam-Goldberg and Tristine Rainer's *The New Diary: How to Use a Journal for Self-Guidance and Expanded Creativity.* Rainer describes four basic diary devices—"natural modes of expression" which serve different purposes. They are:[5]

1. Catharsis. This consists of emotional outpouring—a let-loose, tell-it-like-it-is burst of intense feelings. The focus is not on objective reporting or analysis of joy, anger, jealousy, or melancholy (that comes later), but simply on expressing the feeling.

2. Description. In contrast to catharsis, this device calls for a reality-based rendition of events and scenes as perceived by the writer. Here, events, places, and people that are important to the writer can be selected and highlighted with personal comments.

3. Free-intuitive. This third device springs from deeper consciousness. Language from this mode is comprised of abstract, unedited "free associations of the mind." This form of writing expresses the immediate present—what's currently on the writer's mind—and can be helpful for overcoming writer's block. People who are interested in language, psychology, and the unconscious often find stream-of-consciousness writing most intriguing.

4. Reflection. With this final device, the writer engages in retrospection. After taking a semi-detached perspective, the author recalls the past in order to analyze and synthesize events.

These four modes of expression can be translated into guided assignments for the diarist (if guidance is needed) or simply presented so students can expand upon already established styles. For hesitant students, Rainer also describes seven specific techniques for triggering writing, from "list-making" to "portraiture," from "altered points of view" to "secret buddies" and "unsent letters."

Although many of these devices would be useful to any student, some may be particularly provocative for gifted students trying to come to terms with their differences. For example, you might ask a gifted student to:

- Write an entry from the point of view of someone not in the gifted program.

- List your favorites—books, songs, food, clothes, whatever.

- Describe the traits of an imaginary friend.

- Compose a portrait of yourself as you are now and as you expect to be in ten years.

- Describe a tranquil, beautiful, or particularly stimulating place to be; invent an episode which could take place there.

- Reconstruct an angry dialogue you had with a friend or relative.

- Write an imaginary conversation with a favorite (talking) pet.

Journal assignments can be supplemented by readings from other famous diarists such as Franz Kafka, Anaïs Nin, Anne Frank, and Zlata Filipovic. Some autobiographies and memoirs provide excellent models of journal-style approaches. Students benefit from learning about the authors' lives, and they also gain permission to examine their own lives more deeply and thoughtfully. Certain authors can also function as positive role models for students.

Ask your local librarians or media-center specialists to help you identify diaries and autobiographies you might recommend to your students.

Strategy: Use Bibliotherapy

> *"Why are we reading, if not in hope of beauty laid bare,*
> *life heightened and its deepest mystery probed?"*
> —ANNIE DILLARD

Bibliotherapy, simply defined, is the use of books to help people solve problems. Through guided reading, students learn to understand themselves and their environment, build self-esteem, meet the developmental challenges of adolescence, and form coping skills. Bibliotherapy is not about sending kids off on their own to read books and think about them (or not). It's a structured interaction between a facilitator (you) and a participant (your student). In other words, if you're going to suggest books to your students, and you want to have meaningful discussions about them afterward, you need to read the books yourself. Judith Wynn Halsted, author of *Guiding Gifted Readers from Preschool through High School*, explains:[6]

> *Rather than merely recommending a book to a child, [bibliotherapy] includes three components: a reader, a book, and a leader who will read the same book and prepare for productive discussion of the issues the book raises. To be effective, the leader must be aware of the process of bibliotherapy: IDENTIFICATION, in which the reader identifies with a character in the book; CATHARSIS, the reader's experiencing of the emotions attributed to the character; and INSIGHT, the application of the character's experience to the reader's own life. The leader then frames questions that will confirm and expand on these elements.*

For gifted students, bibliotherapy is an effective way to introduce them to fictional peers and mentors—people like them (or like them in certain ways) whose lives, struggles, and decisions are revealing and affirming. It certainly does this more positively than the usual depictions of gifted kids in the media (TV and movies) do. For some gifted kids, reading about "someone like me" is their first exposure to the fact that they're not alone and they're not "weird." Stephen Schroeder-Davis, Ed.D., Professor of Education at St. Mary's University, Minneapolis campus, notes that:[7]

> *For many students in junior and senior high school, being gifted and talented is a double-edged sword. While their inner lives and academic worlds can be exceedingly rich, the social stigma and peer resentment that often accompany outstanding ability and achievement can be extremely painful. . . . Books can fill a need for these highly able children and their advocates.*

Schroeder-Davis has prepared an annotated bibliography of books for gifted readers—a "best of the best" list based on extensive research.* When identifying books that are "authentic" in their portrayal of various aspects of giftedness, he found the following dominant themes:[8]

1. multipotentiality

2. a mentor relationship

3. a desire for autonomy

4. physical isolation

---

* To request a copy of Stephen Schroeder-Davis's annotated bibliography, contact him by email or telephone: ssdavis@smumn.edu or (763) 241-3449.

5. psychological alienation

6. intensity and exclusivity of focus

7. coercive egalitarianism

8. heightened sensitivity and awareness

9. perfectionism

10. familial and/or peer rivalry

What kinds of questions can you formulate and ask your students about a particular book you've assigned? That depends on the book, your student, and what you hope to achieve through bibliotherapy. For example, if your student needs help with relationships, you might choose a book with that theme. As you read it, jot down questions you think of along the way. Try to come up with questions that lead to thoughtful discussion as opposed to simple "yes" or "no" answers. Helpful question-starters are: "What did you think when . . . ?" "How did you feel about . . . ?" "If you were [a character in the book], what would you have done differently?" You might also ask your student to comment on, evaluate, or journal about a character, event, or turning-point in the book.

Strategy: Schedule Weekly Conferences

Weekly conferences may provide just the right amount of attention, in just the right format, for certain students in need of temporary or periodic counseling. Naturally, if the student has serious emotional or psychological problems, he needs to see a professional counselor in addition to talking with you. But as a classroom or special services teacher, you should be rightfully concerned if a student is having trouble in your class. And before you refer a student to someone else, the weekly conference is a good first recourse. Regular office hours can be set up after school for any student to visit you on an as-needed, first-come, first-served basis. Or you can ask particular students to come in for scheduled appointments.

The purpose of student conferences changes, of course, with the student. For some kids, the issue may be breaking away emotionally from parents who don't understand their need to be independent. (Independence, for them, may be symbolized by being different—or, in some cases, by being totally average. A kid who's been pushed too hard for too long will assert his independence by being "ordinary.") For others, it may be trying to rekindle interest in school, or slowing down and focusing on only a few tasks at once. For still others, it may be the pressure of grades, lack of friends, or lack of role models. Students may be weighted down by heavy-duty expectations, or multiple college or career options. The outcomes of your conferences will vary, from improving their academic performance to tempering their productivity; from chang-ing (or individualizing) assignments to recommending extracurricular activities or psychological testing. Although the specific goal will change from student to student, individual conferences can accomplish several things.

- They give kids a chance to ventilate, beyond group discussions (which they may not be participating in fully anyway), about whatever personal problems are interfering with their work or life.

- They give you a chance to confront the student whose grades or level of partici-pation is slipping; the student who is becoming increasingly negative; the student who seems anxious and depressed. Confrontation, in this sense, means communi-cating this message: "I see that something is going on with you. Will you tell me about it? We're going to have to work something out here. . . ." The act of inter-vention alone tells the depressed student that his feelings have been noticed; the irresponsible student that her "act" isn't fooling anyone; and the passive student that his lack of participation is cause for concern.

- They show that you care about the student as a person. You're listening; you're taking his feelings seriously.

- They enable you and the student together to problem-solve different situations.

- They provide direction and support as students go about implementing solutions.

Condensed guidelines for weekly conferences are difficult to suggest when the issues at stake, and the age and type of learner, are so variable. But perhaps the sim-ple approach described here will lend direction to your already evolving practices. Keep in mind the common problems of gifted students. Keep in mind their particular needs for self-knowledge, acceptance by others, and understanding of others. Your observations, questions, feedback, and especially your affirmation of them as people will help them gain these forms of knowledge. Specifically, you may wish to:

1. Use the first session (or two or three) as a time to "get the full story"—to hear and understand the student's perception of herself, her conflicts, and all that is related.

2. Clarify what you (the teacher) feel may be misperceptions on the student's part. Feelings depend in part on cognitive reasoning. Sometimes they are based on percep-tions and assumptions which may or may not be correct. Ask the student to clarify fuzzy statements by rephrasing them. Ask for examples and verification.

3. Suggest ways in which a student might test his own perceptions. For example, you might ask: "Have you asked your mother directly whether she cares about you attending an Eastern college?" "If you're convinced that the English teacher thinks you can't write, perhaps you ought to ask for a conference and get a fuller evaluation." "You say other kids don't like you. Is there any way you could test that conclusion and find out if it's really true?"

4. Ask the student what she wants to do about the problem—what she would like to see happen.

5. Get a sense of when the student is ready to think about solutions. Even after gathering new information and new insights into a problem, the student may not be ready to let go of it. Chronic problems can give people a sense of identity, and changing them (or changing one's response to them) can cause anxiety. But when students seem ready to admit that there just might be a solution to their problem, brainstorm like crazy. Back up the ideas with measurable goals, concrete plans, and dates for keeping in touch. During the follow-up conferences, find out what happened: Did the solution work? Why or why not? Does the strategy need readjustment? Or does the problem need to be reanalyzed and redefined?

6. Set behavioral guidelines for some students while they work on problems that can't change overnight. Students may not be ready to work on solutions for quite some time, but they still need to conform to certain expectations now. For example, it may take years to turn a really discouraged kid around. Perhaps the underlying problem is perfectionism, transfigured into fear of failure. You might meet with him regularly to reinforce his efforts, and to reinforce your minimum expectations (staying in school, not missing class, maintaining a C average, doing required work, whatever).

7. Ask the student what she is learning about herself by having this conflict, by experiencing the emotions it causes, by examining the perceptions she forms, and by testing the solutions she generates. Conflict in life is not always avoidable. What matters is how she deals with it and uses it to grow internally. Some of our greatest opportunities for growth come from conflict, if we only have the courage to meet it with both eyes open.

If deeply-rooted issues such as chemical dependency, family conflict, child abuse, or suicidal feelings emerge, refer the student to more formal evaluation and make sure it happens. Continue to be a listener and an advocate, but demand honesty. You may not be the person to work with him on a deeper emotional level, but you can at least confront him on behavior in your class, and his delusions. You might say, "I may not know the answer to your problem, Jake, but you and I both know that's not true." You can also reinforce him for the positive steps he takes. Stay committed to your course of action, which is to observe, set limits, provide encouragement, respond to needs when possible, and tell the truth.

Strategy: Use Growth Contracts

Growth contracts are written agreements between individual students and teachers, specifying a plan for personal change or growth within a set period of time. Goals generally focus on affective issues of concern to the student. In this respect, they differ from learning contracts, which are essentially academic. (Changing one's attitude about school, or improving performance in a particular area, would be an appropriate growth contract goal, however.) Both the high achiever, wishing to meet new friends, and the underachiever, wanting to find something that holds his or her interest (a goal which inevitably involves risk-taking), can benefit from the process of setting intentions and strategies down on paper.

Growth contract timelines may be as short as one week or as long as a year. Contracts can be initiated by either the student or the teacher. Whether you'll require them of all students, use them only with kids meeting with you for weekly conferences, or for a single student in a special situation will depend upon your own set of circumstances.

One key to making growth contracts successful is helping the student to articulate something that is really important to him or her. The goal of the contract should reflect a felt need. A second key consists of finding strategies that are reasonably small and concrete, easy to monitor and evaluate. A third key is a time commitment from you; the teacher must stay involved. Even the most motivated student needs the reinforcement of having someone to talk to about his or her progress and problems.

A reproducible "Growth Contract" is found on pages 123–124. You might use this as is or adapt it as you see fit.

Along the way, you'll want to talk with the student about the progress being made on the contract. Here are some suggested questions:

- How easy or how difficult for you is (was) it to work on this contract?

- Is the goal still worthwhile to you? Have other goals replaced it?

- If you had to do this over, would you take different steps? Why or why not?

- Do you need to think of other ways to overcome these obstacles? What can you do? Who can help you?

- What has come as the biggest surprise to you while working on this contract?

- How do you feel about the reactions you've been getting from other people, now that you're making these changes?

- How are you feeling about yourself these days?

- Do you remember how you felt when you first started to work on this contract? Have there been any changes?

In summary, keep in mind that whether students fulfill their contracts down to the letter is less important than the information and skills they gain in the process. Achieving complete success is wonderful, but any measure of progress is worth celebrating. Meanwhile, setting goals, designing strategies to meet those goals, working on those strategies, improvising, and seeing what works are skills students will use throughout their lives in an infinite number of settings.

Strategy: Form Peer Alliances

For the gifted student who is emotionally troubled, socially "ungifted," or withdrawn, large groups may seem safe because they're large. Small groups seem threatening when sharing and participation are required, and one-to-one partnerships the most threatening of all. But small groups and peer teaching (or "alliances") may also give the loner the individual attention he needs. They may offer the best, most private arena for him to try out his newly-acquired social skills and to learn about other people.

Partnerships can be short-term (limited to the length of one learning project or exercise) or long-term (as with a year-long study partner). They can be formed between students at the same academic or age level, or between students of different ages and abilities. Tutoring younger or less-advanced students is a good variation of one-to-one learning.

Using assigned partners or small teams (of three or four members) can build social awareness and skills either directly or indirectly. If addressing communication skills, values, attitudes, or feelings directly, start partners off with low-risk activities and work toward exercises requiring more intimacy and self-disclosure.

In our experience, there are several factors that seem to affect the success of peer alliances. They include:

- **Compatibility of members.** Age, sex, and personalities are all important. Students of various ages can be grouped together, but not indiscriminately.

- **Awareness and acceptance of ground rules for working together.** Students can help develop these rules. They usually appreciate having established guidelines.

- **Length of time allowed for the relationship to develop.** Kids can't become close immediately just because they're gifted.

- **Expected outcomes of the alliance.** Not all partners will necessarily benefit or get along. Determine in your own mind what minimum outcomes you're looking for.

When given the option, kids usually rush to be with their friends when choosing small groups or partners. As you know, this is not always a good thing. Use your discretion when placing students together; ideally, their strengths and limitations will balance each other out. Students should have some rapport (or the potential for it) but not be so close as to preclude any challenge or opportunity for new experiences.

Think ahead of time about guidelines your students will need to work together productively. How long will the students be working together? What is the purpose of the alliance, the task? What terms will they have to work out themselves (such as division of labor, agreement on topics or methods), and what will they need to work out with you? What should they do if and when they get stuck?

Keep in mind that short-term partnerships are very useful for serving immediate purposes, but they won't make long-term changes in a withdrawn or antisocial student. You may not always be able to find the right person to team up with a particularly lonely, socially inept kid, but when you do, give them enough time to get to know each other and become more comfortable working with each other. On the other hand, don't be afraid to terminate a partnership that isn't doing either student any good.

Ask yourself what you expect to happen for the students as a result of the alliance. Better study habits? More confidence? A friendship? Learning to work in a team? Support for each other? What are the signs of success, and the symptoms of dysfunction?

Strategy: Refer Students to Counseling

Although this option is the last one described here, it by no means should be considered the option of last resort. Referring a student for professional counseling or therapy does not mean he's beyond other forms of help, or has even exhausted the alternatives. Therapy is more than a form of treatment for the emotionally conflicted; it is potentially a unique form of education in the interpersonal and intrapersonal realms. Any introspectively inclined person can benefit. Professional individual counseling or psychotherapy is undoubtedly one of the best ways gifted students can learn more about themselves and their conflicts with the world, whether these conflicts are severe or not.

But individual (or group) psychotherapy is expensive and not always covered by medical insurance. School psychologists may or may not be qualified or available. In large urban public schools, they typically have heavy work loads and limited time. For these reasons alone, you probably should explore a number of options for students in addition to psychological counseling.

You probably should also keep in mind that for some students, the referral to therapy itself greatly affects their self-concept. They may see it as a punishment or feel there really is something wrong with them ("I must be really weird"), and therefore be doubly ashamed and angry. Others will approach it fearfully but also with relief.

Your own attitude about therapy is very important here. If you communicate by your words, actions, attitude, or body language that therapy represents failure or disgrace (either yours or the student's), it will be more difficult for the student to accept it. It helps if a teacher can say, "I was once helped greatly by a counselor," or "I'm really happy that you're going to be getting some help with this. Good for you for having the courage to work on it."

If your school does not already provide counseling for the gifted, strongly encourage them to do so. The proper arena for support groups for the gifted is really in the counselor's office. Psychologists or counselors are better equipped to sort out the variety of problems in students' lives, whether they're related to the home, career options, finances, drugs, peer group or identity, gender, or school and intellectual concerns. These problems are inevitably intertwined, particularly when one or more is chronic.

As was mentioned earlier in the section on weekly conferences, your job will be to maintain contact with the counselor while continuing to meet with the student and problem-solve the school problems together. Resist the temptation to feel overly responsible for your students. It's easy to become too wrapped up in their lives and affected by their struggles. And although teaching is a caring profession, you'll need to define the limits of your involvement and not feel guilty for doing so. Don't hesitate to refer a student to a professional counselor when you feel there is something going on that needs to be looked at, and which requires more time and more specialized training than you've got.

Notes

1. Leta S. Hollingworth, *Children Above 180 IQ: Stanford-Binet Origin and Development* (New York: Arno Press, 1975; reprint of the 1942 edition).

2. A. Kathnelson and L. Colley, "Personal and Professional Characteristics Valued in Teachers of the Gifted," unpublished paper presented at California State University, Los Angeles, California, 1982. See Barbara Clark, *Growing Up Gifted*, p. 370.

3. Both "Class Rules (Grades K–5)" and "Class Rules (Grades 6 & up)" are available from Free Spirit Publishing as colorful posters. You can view and order them online at *www.freespirit.com*.

4. Jack Canfield and Harold Clive Wells, *100 Ways to Enhance Self-Concept in the Classroom*, 2nd ed. (Englewood Cliffs, NJ: Prentice-Hall, 1993).

5. Tristine Rainer, *The New Diary: How to Use a Journal for Self-Guidance and Expanded Creativity* (Los Angeles: J.P. Tarcher, Inc., 1978), pp. 51–114.

6. Judith Wynn Halsted, "Guiding the Gifted Reader," ERIC Digest #E481 (Reston, VA: ERIC Clearinghouse on Disabilities and Gifted Education, 1990).

7. Stephen Schroeder-Davis, "Giftedness: A Double-Edged Sword," *Book Links* (March 1994), p. 25.

8. Stephen Schroeder-Davis, *The Gifted Child in Contemporary Fiction: An Annotated Bibliography* (Minneapolis: The Minnesota Council for the Gifted and Talented, 1992).

Growth Contract

1. *Target area for growth:* Something I want to change about myself or my life.

I'd like to be _____

_____

_____

_____

2. Steps I'll take to reach my goal:

a. _____

_____

b. _____

_____

c. _____

_____

3. Resources that will help me along the way (including people I can turn to for support):

a. _____

_____

b. _____

_____

c. _____

_____

4. Possible road blocks I'll need to get around:

a. _____

_____

continued . . .

Growth Contract continued...

b. _____

_____

c. _____

_____

5. *Evaluation:* How will I know when things are better?

I'll know when _____

_____

_____

_____

How close to my goal did I come? Explain: _____

_____

_____

_____

_____

Did I achieve as much as I hoped or expected? Explain: _____

_____

_____

_____

Did I achieve less than I hoped or expected? Explain: _____

_____

_____

_____

CHAPTER 5

Understanding Gifted Kids from the Inside Out

"Each of us is a being in himself and a being in society, each of us needs to understand himself and understand others, take care of others and be taken care of himself."
—HANIEL LONG

When she was 15, Christine was asked to share her views on what it means to be a gifted adolescent. "The thought did cross my mind," she said, "to write profoundly on the topic, but I quickly dismissed it. I'm trying to cut down on the number of deep and meaningful thoughts I have before breakfast." Instead, Christine talked about herself and her giftedness by posing a series of questions, including:

- "Why is giftedness linked to achievement—that is, what I can or cannot do—instead of what and how I feel?"

- "Why do teachers act as counselors if they can't listen or stand not having a quick solution?"

- "Who says that growing up gifted necessarily means wanting to get high grades, going to college, and getting a good job?"

- "Have you noticed that adults expect kids to wear the label 'gifted' when they won't?"

Like many who came before her (and many who will follow), Christine was struggling with issues of self-image and self-esteem. But isn't that true of all adolescents? Don't all teenagers question their place in the ocean of existence?

Of course they do. (So do many younger kids, especially younger gifted kids, who tend to be more sensitive, perceptive, and introspective than their peers.) But when giftedness is added into the "Who am I?" and "Where do I belong?" equation, the need for answers may be more intense, powerful, and acute.

Being smart doesn't inoculate a person from the fear of being bypassed by friends or overshadowed by self-doubts about success. Indeed, the gifted child may be more aware than others of the need for these issues to be resolved if one is to have a happy and fulfilling life.

Self-Image vs. Self-Esteem

If you can't tell the difference between a $50 cabernet and a $5 bottle of rotgut red, your self-image as a wine connoisseur may be low. Likewise, if your trigonometry skills are limited to knowing that a cosine isn't the person who underwrites a loan, your self-image as a mathematician might be lacking. Still, if you're not a wine drinker, you probably don't care that your palate is poor, and if sines and cosines don't play a major role in your professional life, it may not matter to you that you can't determine the area of a right triangle.

Herein lies the difference between self-image and self-esteem:

- **Self-Image** = your perception of your ability to do a certain task, like cook a meal, write a term paper, or make a friend.

- **Self-Esteem** = the importance you place on your ability (or inability) to cook a meal, write a term paper, or make a friend.

Even if your self-image as a mathematician is lower than absolute zero, this might not impact your self-esteem in the least. However, if your self-image for doing math is low and it's important to you to do well in math, your self-esteem could be negatively affected.

It's important to know and understand this distinction, and to explain it to your students. Here's why:

- Counselors or teachers may talk about a student's high or low self-esteem as if it were a singular, all-encompassing trait when, in fact, it's content-specific. To say that "Maria has low self-esteem" is a generalization, and, like all generalizations, isn't accurate.

- Gifted kids often tend toward perfectionism,* so helping them see both the connections and distinctions between self-image and self-esteem may allow them to see the importance of being selective in their quest for excellence.

- Knowing the difference between self-image and self-esteem often helps students understand their motivation (or lack thereof) to improve a certain skill. For example, a student may wonder, "Why should I work hard to improve my social relationships if I don't believe that friendships are worth the hassle?" While this might be a sad admission on the part of a potentially lonely person, at least it helps us to understand the reasoning behind his actions or inactions.

---

* For more on this topic, see pages 64–66 and pages 199–202.

Explaining, through example, this fine-line distinction between self-image and self-esteem to parents of gifted kids is also a good idea. Not only may it help them to understand their smart kids a little better, it may also make for more pleasant and productive dinnertime conversations about achievement, motivation, and setting priorities.

Gifted Kids Speak Out

We asked gifted kids, "What are some things adults do and say that are supposed to help you—but they don't *help?" Here's what two respondents said:*

"Oh, it's okay, Eric." (No, it's not.)

"Good try, Eric!" (Yeah . . . right.)

"You'll do better next time, Eric." (As if.)

"Get the football, Eric!" (I'm trying.)

—Eric, 10

"There's always a next time!" (In truth, I really don't care about next time yet. I wanted to do well now!)

"You're smart. Don't worry." (Okay, I'm smart, but that doesn't automatically guarantee that I know the answer or will get an A. I still need to work and worry.)

—Erin, 19

What are some other things adults say to help—but they don't *help?*

"Don't be so hard on yourself."

"Don't take everything so personally."

"Lighten up once in a while."

"Don't work harder. Work smarter."

"You're too (smart, sensitive, opinionated, etc.) for your own good."

"You'll get over this in time."

Gifted Kids Are Different

"Differences challenge assumptions."
—ANNE WILSON SCHAEF

More than half a century ago, psychologist Abraham Maslow proposed a hierarchy of human needs. He defined our most basic needs as physiological: food, water, sleep, exercise, and other essentials of life. Our highest needs have to do with self-actualization: developing our talents, being true to our goals, and becoming everything we're capable of being.

Maslow understood that self-actualization (and, just below it, self-esteem) are possible only when we've had enough to eat, we feel safe, and we have formed close, accepting relationships with others. Once these needs are covered, the higher needs such as self-esteem and self-actualization take on increasing importance.

For gifted children, the desire to belong and to be accepted is as strong as in other children, but they may experience more anxiety about it. As one student expressed:[1]

> I wondered daily about college. How high does one have to go to get 90s at this particular college? At Harvard? Yale? Oxford? Could I reach these heights? How much effort would it take? Just how good am I? Just how smart is smart? The questions constantly plagued me.

Some of the specific intellectual issues gifted children and adolescents face include:

1. **Understanding and accepting what it means to be gifted.** ("Everybody tells me I'm gifted, but nobody tells me what that means—Help!")

2. **Evaluating one's life relative to different measures of success.** ("If I don't become a doctor or a lawyer, will I be perceived as a failure?")

3. **Recognizing the difference between "better at" and "better than."** ("Does my being able to do things other kids can't do make me a more valuable member of society?")

4. **Coping with the frustration of having too many options.** ("There are so many things I'd like to become, and I'm good in many areas. How will I ever select a career or a college major?")

5. **Overcoming the barriers of others' expectations.** ("No matter how well I do, there is always someone telling me that I could have done better.")

6. **Understanding the concept of asynchronous development.** ("I'm 12 years old with the mind of a 16-year-old, the body of a 10-year-old, and the social skills of a 1,000-year-old Druid. Where do I fit in?")

7. **Becoming an advocate for one's own self-interests.** ("I find school so boring, but nobody seems to care. There's got to be a better way to learn.")

8. **Understanding the role of socialization.** ("All of my good friends are older or younger than I am. Why is this? Is it okay to have friends of varying ages?")

It's probably obvious that these intellectual issues also carry over into the social and emotional realms. That's to be expected. How many of life's uncomfortable or unclear situations inhabit only one domain of our existence? Each of us is both a thinker and a feeler. To disassociate one element from the other is an artificial separation, at best.

What this means for you, the teacher who's trying to understand the gifted students in your classes, is this: Be ready to talk about and explore issues with your students that begin as school issues but end up as life issues. The academic world of gifted students is often the one in which they have experienced the most success; therefore, they feel most comfortable talking about it. But as you reveal other layers of your students' lives—social, emotional, vocational, intellectual (as opposed to academic)—you'll likely notice more vulnerabilities than you ever saw in that comfortable classroom context where A's often come easily and homework is a breeze.

Following are several activities that will start you on the path of getting to know your gifted students from the inside out—and helping them to know and understand themselves.

Understanding and Accepting What It Means to Be Gifted

What does it mean to be gifted? This is the springboard from which all other discussions of giftedness are launched.

Activity: *Great Gripes*

One of the best (and easiest) ways to initiate discussion on the meaning of giftedness and its frequent misinterpretation by others is with a list of "Great Gripes." Gifted kids first spoke about these nearly 20 years ago,[2] and many still speak about them today.

Give each student a copy of the "Eight Great Gripes of Gifted Kids" on page 155. Once they've read the list, have them rank-order the items in relation to how strongly each one affects their lives. They may cross out any they haven't thought about or that have had no impact on them, and they may add more gripes of their own (if they have any) that aren't on the list.

From this point, you can begin a discussion on the gripe that solicited the most attention from your students, then continue with those gripes that were seen as less important. In this way, you'll be addressing some concerns that your students see as real, while opening the door to other topics that are more specific to your school or your students.

Activity: Ups and Downs

One of our favorite ways to get children to consider their personal reactions to being gifted is to ask them to complete a bubble chart.

Give each student a copy of "Everything Has Its Ups and Downs!" on page 156. Have them work alone or in pairs to consider some of the positive and negative aspects of growing up gifted. Once they complete their charts, invite them to walk around the room and compare their responses to those of their classmates.

Follow this with a class-wide discussion of the ups and downs of being gifted—and be ready to hear some interesting banter. Don't be surprised if the children express a positive aspect of something negative. In the sample shown below, two fifth-grade boys, Teddy and Cody, note that being teased allows them to "come up with a good comeback."

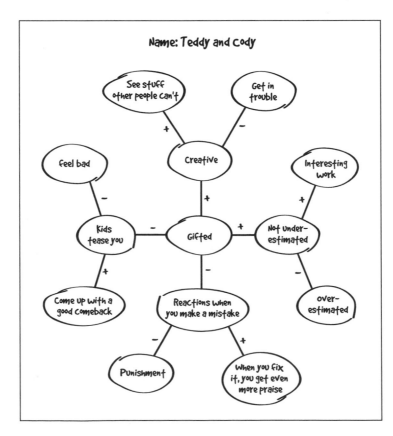

Activity: *Gifted Is . . . Gifted Means . . .*

Here's a simple but effective way for students to share how they feel about the "gifted" label. Give each student a copy of "Gifted Is . . . Gifted Means . . ." on page 157–158. If they need a few prompts to get started, you might offer one or more of the following:

- "Gifted is . . . hard to explain to other people."

- "Gifted means . . . having to do homework that you already know how to do."

- "Gifted is . . . a lot of fun, if you know what to do with it."

- "Gifted means . . . having friends who act more grown-up than they are."

Make sure that your students understand how to complete the second part of the handout: by imagining what *other people* in their lives would say.

The ensuing discussions can be a reflective overview of how and why different people have such varied views on what it means to be gifted.

Students may mention some of the less-than-pleasant names that gifted kids (and adults) are sometimes called: brainiac, nerd, teacher-pleaser, wonk, snob, know-it-all. They may point out that on television, gifted kids are often portrayed as "weird"— from Steve Urkel of *Family Matters* to Claudia of *Party of Five* to Malcolm of *Malcolm in the Middle.*

Ask your students to think about this: What is it about the word "gifted" that causes people to have such strong reactions? No one seems too concerned about the terms "athletic" or "artistic" or "talented," all of which mean that someone is gifted in a particular area.

Gifted Kids Speak Out

Here's how some of Jim's sixth-grade students responded to the "Gifted Is . . . Gifted Means . . ." activity.

To us, gifted is . . . / gifted means . . .

- being special, even if others don't think so

- being smart enough to think of a comeback for a bully who picks on you because you're smart

- thinking all the time

continued . . .

- being called "retarded" even though we are far from it
- being role models to younger siblings and nerds to your teenage siblings
- smarting off to teachers when you don't mean to
- being smarter than others but still being human
- a reason for people to make fun of you
- you are an ordinary kid with speedy learning skills
- being intense
- you are different (not in a bad way, necessarily)
- having classes that everyone says are hard but you think are easy
- me

To our parents, gifted means . . .
- having a special gift from God
- being just like them
- having to live up to their high expectations
- being outrageously smart

To our best friends, gifted means . . .
- being cool
- wishing they could do the things we do in our class

To our worst enemies, gifted means . . .
- being goody-goody freaks
- being stuck-up

To a teacher who "gets it," gifted means . . .
- getting respect
- having a talented brain that is hungry for knowledge
- knowing that smart kids are often ignored by schools

continued . . .

To a teacher who doesn't "get it," gifted means . . .

- "you just got a lucky score on a second-grade test"
- kids who get unfair privileges
- someone completely different from other kids
- not someone worth respecting

To our grandparents, gifted means . . .

- "a good thing on your record"
- good grades, which means more $$$
- smart kids who want books instead of money (wrong!)

To a TV producer, gifted means . . .

- an overexaggerated stereotype put together to win ratings
- someone easy to make fun of in a situation comedy

Evaluating One's Life Relative to Different Measures of Success

In today's era of high-stakes testing and performance-based standards, students are pressured to produce. Whether it's high test scores that will allow a school to call itself "effective," or three-dimensional projects that are hung in the school halls for visitors to admire, kids are bombarded with a false but pervasive bias: that one's worth is determined by one's scholastic achievements.

In a climate such as this, it's easy for gifted students to lose sight of the fact that not everything that can be measured matters, and not everything that matters can be measured. As teachers, let's encourage students to concentrate on what they *learned* rather than what they *earned*.

Facing Personal Challenges

by Frank Davies, fourth-grade teacher

We talk a lot in our class about having PCs—personal challenges—and we have spent time on discovering what our own PCs are. I strongly advise my students that facing their own PCs is far more important than learning curriculum (but don't tell my bosses at the South Australian Education Board!). Their PCs might be getting out of bed in the morning, or learning their multiplication tables, or it might be how to learn to follow your own dream. They know that they have my quality support in achieving their PCs. The other stuff is important as well, but what's the point of filling them with curriculum if their heart doesn't sing and they don't feel in control?

Activity: *Coffee for a Cause*

It was a rainy but warm night in May. The lava lamps were in place, the lattes were steaming hot and smelling great, and more than 200 parents, students, and community members were gathered at a local coffeehouse for an evening of student readings and musical performances.

Seventh grader Stevie began the night by reading his selection, "Poetry Is . . ."

Poetry Is . . .

What is poetry?
It is such a simple word, yet so hard to define.
Far from just rhyming
Poetry is a portal between destinations.
Poetry takes you away from normal life and into a rebirth,
Into imagination.
Poetry creates a division
Between those who are poets
And those who are not.
Poetry is a work of art that has a mind of its own.
Poetry describes what does not exist, yet always has.
Poetry opens your eyes to see what is invisible.
Poetry lets you hear the silence.

At the poem's end, people started clapping. Stevie stopped them, reminding his audience that "at a real coffeehouse, people do this" and snapping his fingers like a beatnik. Everyone laughed, then the snapping began.

More than 60 students shared their work that night. Little of it had been graded, and much of it had been completed outside of class time. Students merely chose something to share that made them proud—a story they'd written, a flute-and-piano duet, a scene from the eighth-grade play, *Hamlet*. A portion of the money raised that night from the sale of coffee and pastries (plus an end-of-the-evening passing of the hat) netted almost $400 for a charity of the students' choosing: a summer camp for children with severe burns that was sponsored by a local children's hospital.

No tests, no homework, no competition: just a chance for children to reveal their talents and benefit others.

Is there a coffeehouse in your school community? You, too, can offer Coffee for a Cause.

Activity: *Quotables*

Sometimes the fewest words convey the most meaning. Such is the case with quotations from people, famous or not, that leave impressions that are meaningful and poignant. For example, how would your students respond to the following?

■ "When you come to a fork in the road, take it."—Yogi Berra

■ "No person is your friend who demands your silence or denies your right to grow."—Alice Walker

■ "The respect of others' rights is peace."—Benito Juarez

■ "Birds sing after a storm, why shouldn't we?"—Rose Kennedy

■ "If you hear a voice within you say, 'You cannot paint,' then by all means paint, and that voice will be silenced."—Vincent van Gogh

■ "We learn more by looking for the answer and not finding it than we do from learning the answer itself."—Lloyd Alexander

There are countless books and Web sites that offer a variety of quotations for students to scan. Once suitable examples are found, the possibilities for projects are endless. A few ideas to try:

■ Have students select a quote and write an essay on its importance in their lives.

■ Ask students to locate a photo or draw a picture that brings to life the quote they have selected. Share these in small groups.

■ Have students work with the art teacher to learn simple calligraphy. Afterward, have them copy their quotes on a shield made from construction paper. The shield represents the students' "defense" against other people's angry, demeaning, teasing, or otherwise inappropriate words. Students can use the back of the shield to compose an essay on the importance of the quote in their lives and in their interactions with others. (If calligraphy instruction isn't available or convenient, students can print out their quotations in fancy computer fonts.)

Putting Success and Failure Into Perspective

by Scott H. Stuart, fifth-grade teacher

While walking down the school hallway yesterday, I bumped into Josh. Josh is in the gifted program, a better-than-average athlete, good-looking, and popular. He seldom appears anything but alert, attentive, and engaged in enjoying whatever happens to be going on (or trying to change things if they become monotonous). Yesterday, he looked as if not only his puppy, but everyone's in the universe, had been run over, poisoned, strangled, and finally had died.

"So," I asked him, "how's your Future Problem Solving writing scenario going?"

"Not so . . . Hey, how'd you know about that?" he replied.

"I work with the Future Problem Solvers at the middle school," I explained. "The look on your face resembles what I see on their faces after they've just had their scenario conference with Mrs. Ruttan."

"Yeah . . . I guess it's not coming along so well."

"Is this the first thing that has really, really been tough in school for you?"

"Yeah," Josh said, as he sniffed back the runny nose that accompanied the moisture collecting in the corners of his eyes.

We trudged along for a moment or two. Then I asked him, "How long did it take you to figure out how to use your left foot in soccer?"

Josh suddenly grinned. "It took a long time. I felt pretty stupid sometimes, too."

During a slow walk to Josh's classroom, I told Josh about how well previous years' students had done on their scenarios; shared that many kids over the years felt like the conferences were critical of *them*, not their work; talked about how much easier (or more tolerable) tough assignments like this one might get in the future; and finally admitted that I was facing a rather daunting writing task myself for my master's degree.

I'm glad to know that there are neat kids like Josh—capable of so much, yet needing a safe place to crash, burn, and rebuild from time to time.

Recognizing the Difference Between "Better at" and "Better than"

Few people would argue against providing special assistance to students diagnosed with a learning disability or a developmental handicap. Fewer still would say that there is something "undemocratic" about providing differentiated educational services that allow these children to realize their potential.

Unfortunately, this attitude does not always apply when special education options for gifted students are under discussion. While some people do acknowledge and espouse the need to provide extra intellectual stimulation for these high-end learners, many others see such provisions as wasteful expenditures on "kids who will make it anyway." Sometimes the term "elitist" arises, as critics contend that any separation of smart children from others will create one group of "haves" and several other groups of "have nots." Combating these biases—indeed, prejudices—against gifted children has been a constant battle for generations.

Addressing this issue directly with children, gifted or not, can result in valuable learning for all.

Which Would You Rather Be?

In a review of responses from 3,000 adolescents to the question, "In your high school, would you rather be the smartest, the most athletic or the best looking?" Stephen Schroeder-Davis, Ed.D., Professor of Education at St. Mary's University, Minneapolis campus, cited these trends:

- Student athletes are more respected by peers than student scholars.

- The "pure scholar" (the nonathletic academic achiever) is the least popular student in the typical school.

- Intelligent students report doing worse in school subjects than they are capable of doing to avoid being labeled a "nerd" by classmates.

- All students spend more time per week on virtually anything other than schoolwork, including socializing, sports, extracurricular activities, TV, jobs, and listening to music.

Stephen Schroeder-Davis, Ed.D., *Brains, Brawn or Beauty: A Content Analysis of Adolescent Attitudes Toward Superlatives* (St. Paul: University of St. Thomas, 1995).

Activity: Picture Books

For some unknown reason, teachers stop using picture books with students around fifth grade—just the age when children can really begin to appreciate their full meaning. But used well (and judiciously), picture books can provide colorful and important lessons about life.

For example, Patricia Polacco's heartfelt tribute to her fifth-grade teacher, *Thank You, Mr. Falker,* reminds us all that giftedness sometimes is disguised by a disability. It's only when a patient, helpful someone (like Mr. Falker) comes around and notices the gift that good things begin to happen.

As a child, Polacco could draw, and she yearned to read, but all she saw on the pages of books were "wiggling shapes." Her classmates scorned her as dumb, but Mr. Falker noticed her problem, got special help for her—and set her free. At the end of her book, Polacco writes:

> *I saw Mr. Falker again some thirty years later at a wedding. I walked up to him and introduced myself. At first he had difficulty placing me. Then I told him who I was, and how he had changed my life so many years ago.*
>
> *He hugged me and asked me what I did for a living. "Why, Mr. Falker," I answered, "I make books for children. . . . Thank you, Mr. Falker. Thank you."*

Then there's Taro Yashima's classic story, *Crow Boy,* about a humble and socially ostracized boy whose classmates finally begin to accept him after years of ridicule when his uncanny ability to imitate bird songs is recognized.

If you're in the mood for a little playtime on the classroom carpet, pull out a book like Leo Lionni's *Frederick,* the story of a mouse who spends his autumn collecting colors, sunshine, and warmth instead of nuts and berries—and is derided by his friends, who see him as a slacker. Only when winter drags on and Frederick brings out his "contributions" do the other mice understand the benefit of gathering such items to sustain them through the long winter nights.

Each book's main character deals with the "better at" and "better than" distinction. Each story is resolved in the main character's favor only when those around him or her begin to accept the character's gifts and talents. Each is ultimately about healing.

As a bonus activity, once the cookies and milk have been put away and you're staring at a bunch of tall eighth graders again, ask them to find a character in any literature they are currently reading (for example, Jonas in Lois Lowry's *The Giver*) who struggles with the idea of an identity that is being impacted by giftedness. Then discuss how stereotypes of gifted people affect one's life decisions and social relationships.

The picture books named above are only a few of many possibilities you might share with your students. Any children's librarian will be delighted to help you find more.

Activity: *Exploring Elitism*

In certain school activities, particularly athletics and music, it's both accepted and expected that strong performances will be rewarded. At rallies before big football games, students cheer wildly for the gifted quarterback. Roses are thrust on stage after a particularly stirring Beethoven opus is performed by a talented pianist, or a hard-to-reach high note is sustained by a student vocalist. Strong talents that make us stand up and take notice prove that the people of our nation, even our children, are neither ashamed nor intimidated by the presence of others' gifts . . . as long as they're not *intellectual* gifts.

For some reason that we have yet to understand fully, gifted athletes are served well in our schools with nary a hint of "elitism" attached to the special provisions provided for them. But a class for gifted students selected to participate in a special program matched to their intellectual abilities is viewed as suspect by many people— including many educators—who consider this separation of gifted students as being harmful to the democratic nature of our schools.

While there are no clear answers to this ongoing argument, it's certainly worth debating. Following are two activities to try with your students. The first is best done with older students, and the second is more appropriate for younger students.

For older students: Divide your class into two groups of equal size. Have one group research the viewpoints of those who promote separate gifted programs (like George Betts, Linda Silverman, and Julian Stanley), while the other group examines the writings and opinions of some of gifted education's main critics (like Alfie Kohn, Mara Sapon-Shevin, and Jeannie Oakes). Then have students address several specific questions. For example:

- In what ways is it better to separate gifted students in schools for at least part of the day? In what ways is it worse to do so?

- Who does the inclusion of gifted students in regular classes help? Who does it hinder? Which group's needs are more important to consider?

- What is the real meaning of the word "elitist"? In what ways can it be considered positive to be an elitist? In what ways is it negative?

- Are gifted programs elitist by the nature of their existence, or are gifted programs merely a positive expression of America's democratic ideal that every person should be allowed to reach for their highest potential? Defend your position with examples.

- What is the difference between "equal" and "the same"? How does this distinction have an impact on gifted child education—its rationale and its practice?

If your discussions lead where we think they might, you may want to record your debate for a future school board or faculty meeting where the schools' gifted programs are being highlighted for review.

For younger students: Create a bubble chart. (See page 130 for an example.) Write "Gifted Programs" in the middle bubble. Have students cite the positives and negatives of gifted programs in the surrounding bubbles. Follow with discussion.

You might ask your students, "What if we replace the words 'Gifted Programs' with the words 'Sports Programs' or 'Music Programs'? Does that make a difference?" Invite their thoughts and opinions.

Gifted Kids Speak Out

When asked, "Should schools have separate gifted programs?" these three students said "Yes"—and gave their reasons:

"Gifted programs give kids a chance to stay smart."
—Girl, 11

"The people who *can* do harder work or *can* go to special classes should be able to *get* what they deserve."
—Girl, 12

"A gifted program stimulates a gifted student's mind to learn about other gifted children and how they feel about being gifted."
—Girl, 12

Coping with the Frustration of Having Too Many Options

In a particularly poignant moment of insight, Charlie Brown came to a personal revelation about his life: "There is no heavier burden," he sighed, "than a great potential."

Many gifted students, from very young ages, are told something like this: "You are so lucky! You can become anything you want to be when you grow up because you're so smart!" This sounds like a compliment, but to many gifted students who suffer from multipotential—the ability to enter many careers due to diverse interests and multiple strengths—the pressure begins building from early on to choose a profession that befits someone "who is blessed with high intelligence."

The list of acceptable occupations generally looks something like this:

- doctor (a *real* doctor, not one of those Ph.D.-types)
- scientist (a Ph.D. will do here, but only if it's from a place like MIT or California Polytechnic or Cornell)
- lawyer (anything but a public defender)
- high-tech wizard (who starts a company and becomes a billionaire)
- professor (only if the above options fall through—the pay is too low)

But what if you, as a gifted student, have ambitions to be an actor, not an architect? A teacher, not a technical wizard? An advocate for the homeless rather than a Wall Street broker building economic empires? Where are the adults around you who should be saying, "I'll support you all the way"? These rare individuals are the solace sought by many gifted adolescents trying hard to determine what they want to be when they grow up. And as much as it might seem like a blessing to have so many more choices than others your age, it can actually grow to become an embarrassment of riches, where decisions are complicated by both internal and external factors that push against one another.

Multipotential, and the decisions to be made about one's far-off future, are the basis of the following two activities. We encourage you to share these letters with your students, then just open up the floor for general discussion.

On Becoming a Teacher

by R.G. McCune, 52

I was the only one in my family to graduate from college. My father was a mechanic and my mother stayed at home. When I was in high school, I belonged to the FTA—Future Teachers of America—during my senior year. I grew up in a small, rural county in West Virginia and there were no substitutes for absent teachers, so when someone was absent in the elementary schools, I was sent to substitute. I spent over 60 days of my senior year out in the schools and still managed to maintain all my own schoolwork.

When graduation came, someone asked me what I was going to do (this was the high school counselor), and I said I was going to college to train to be a teacher. She said, "How do you know that is what you want to do? Wouldn't you

continued . . .

> rather get a job that makes a lot of money? Besides, most men do not want to go into teaching."
>
> Fortunately, I didn't follow her advice and began college at 15 and finished up at age 19. Now, after all these many years, I have never regretted how I have spent my life.

Activity: *What Are You Going to Do with the Rest of Your Life?*

Give each student a copy of "A Valedictorian Speaks Out at His High School Graduation" on page 159. Explain that it was written by an 18-year-old named John. After everyone has read the letter, open the floor to a general discussion. You might also ask your students to write letters of their own—as if they, too, were 18, just graduating, and looking ahead to their future.

Here are few points you might want to raise and invite your students to comment on:

- More than 50 percent of college freshmen change their majors before graduation. The only reason to declare a major in high school is to apply for scholarships directed at certain areas, such as the arts or sciences.

- Some people are ready to announce at 18 what they want to do and be when they're 40. Others aren't. Either way, the option to switch gears should always be left open.

- John, the valedictorian, seems wise beyond his years. He realizes that not getting too serious about one's economic future while still a teenager is a good way to approach life. Financial responsibility will follow soon enough.

Activity: *Writing Your Dreams in Pencil*

Give each student a copy of "College: Week Two" on page 160. After everyone has read it, ask them to dissect the fears and feelings that Matt is experiencing as a freshman. Are his anxieties warranted? Or are they the typical adolescent desires to have it all and have it quickly? Ask them to imagine that they're Matt's friends or siblings. Have them write letters of their own to Matt, offering advice and solace.

Hand out copies of "College: Year Two" on page 161. After your students have read it, invite their thoughts and reactions. Point out that a year can make a big difference in someone's life, especially someone in his or her teens. In Matt's case, it meant a new school, a new major, and a new mind-set. He had learned, through tears and rough spots, that dreams must be written in pencil, for old desires need to be erased before new goals can be seen clearly and cleanly. Ask your students:

- Did it take courage for Matt to make the many changes he made, or was it mere frustration that led him down his new path?

- What about you? Have you ever had to set aside or change a goal? Have you ever watched someone else (a parent, a friend) do this?

- Are there any dreams you've written in pencil? Is there something in your life right now that you're undecided about? A choice you'd like to make over? A goal you need to rethink and redefine?

It won't be difficult to get into introspective discussions on these issues, because almost everyone has "been there" and can relate.

If your students wonder what happened next in Matt's life (because this is a true story—Matt is Jim Delisle's son), tell them that he graduated three years later and now lives in California, hoping someday to score big-time with a million-dollar screenplay. He's happy with his life and the choices he made.

Activity: Celebrity Majors Match-Up

This fun activity reinforces the message that it's good to keep one's options open—because you never know what the future will bring.

Give each student a copy of "Celebrity Majors Match-Up" on page 162. Chances are, they won't be able to match any of the celebrities with their college majors. (If they can, their matches will most likely be lucky guesses.) For this reason, don't wait too long before explaining that the point of this exercise isn't to score high, but to see how life can take new and unexpected directions. Then share the answers, allowing for brief discussion.

Celebrity Majors Match-Up Key:

- Oprah Winfrey: Speech and Drama, Tennessee State University
- Katie Couric: American Studies, University of Virginia
- Colin Powell: Geology, City College of New York
- Jesse Jackson: Sociology and Economics, North Carolina A & T State University
- Steven Spielberg: English Literature, California State University
- Regis Philbin: Sociology, University of Notre Dame
- Danny Glover: Economics, San Francisco State University

- J.K. Rowling: French and Classical Studies, Exeter College

- John Paul II: Literature and Philosophy, Jagiellonian University

- Arnold Schwarzenegger: Business and International Economics, University of Wisconsin

Overcoming the Barriers of Others' Expectations

"I don't know the key to success, but the key to failure is trying to please everybody."
—BILL COSBY

When you're gifted and others (parents, teachers, friends, etc.) know it, they have high expectations of your performance and behavior at school, at home, and in other areas of your life. Meanwhile, you have high expectations of yourself. The benefits of being bright are paired with the fear of being imperfect—of not measuring up to anyone's high standards, including your own.

With so many chances daily to fail or succeed, gifted children often come up short in their own minds. Their thinking goes something like this:

- "That B-plus might have been an A-minus if I'd studied for ten more minutes!"

- "If I don't make the Honor Roll this quarter, it'll be my first failure in two years!"

- "I've *got* to do well on these college essays. My parents and my school are counting on me!"

Surrounded by potential pitfalls, gifted children worry constantly about disappointing others. A peak performance is seen as a fluke, a precursor to an academic plateau. This fear, often unstated, may affect academic decisions. For example, a top student may choose not to take an advanced course, fearing that he or she might not get an A. The grade becomes more important than mental stimulation and intellectual rewards. Learning takes second place to earning the all-important A. As teachers, we need to help our students evaluate themselves and their achievements more realistically.

A Gifted Adult Reflects on Her Life

by Meg Hunter, 43

So I knew I was not normal, per se. I was *different,* and I still retain that gift. But because there were no provisions for students like me—at least in my community—I went unnurtured. But I nurtured myself, and thus, I learned. But there were so many, many parts of myself that could have been developed further and at a much younger age, had I been served in school. I was sensitive yet, at the same time, I was very tough—I *had* to be—for I was looked up to by friends at school and even by children at school who were not close to me. I was looked up to because I was *smart.* I was *funny.* I was *exceptional* in math and English and writing and art. I was a combination of Vincent van Gogh, Erma Bombeck, Mitch Miller, Mother Teresa, Bette Midler and Louisa May Alcott. I was a mixture and it *really, really* hurt. I was trapped within myself and I had no way to escape. I couldn't get away from all of it—the expectations, the praise, the adoration of others. And it did not stop at the elementary level; it carried through long past high school and it hunts me down to this very minute.

Activity: Fill in the Blanks

Open-ended statements that allow children to respond from the base of personal truth are a great way to gauge feelings and attitudes. Give each student a copy of "Fill in the Blanks" on page 163. Tell them that they may respond with a word or phrase, but longer answers now will require less explanation later.

If students feel comfortable doing so, ask them to swap lists with classmates they trust. Allow time for sharing and discussion. Then invite them to comment on particularly surprising or revealing responses. Conclude by asking students to create their own open-ended sentence stems and have other classmates complete them.

With younger students, have them team up with a classmate to illustrate one of the statements on "Fill in the Blanks" for which they wrote similar responses.

Activity: Bottom of the Top

It happens to each of us eventually: As smart as we think we are, we get into a situation that makes us feel dumb. As adults, we have the capacity to excuse ourselves to another venue, a more comfortable one that restores our sense of accomplishment and worth. Equilibrium returns, and we're happy. Children often don't have as much freedom to move from one setting to the next. They're required to tolerate an uncomfortable situation or reevaluate themselves by a new set of standards. Cases in point:

■ The first time a child enters a gifted program. Always used to being #1 in her particular classroom, she's now just one among many #1's, so the academic pecking order changes.

■ The first time a smart high school student enrolls in an arduous course with cutthroat competition among its students. "Is it worth competing with them" the student asks himself, "or should I settle for something less?"

■ The first time a gifted child participates in a summer enrichment program, a creative problem-solving program (example: Destination ImagiNation), or an academic competition at school. "Everyone seems so much smarter here," she wonders. "I'm not sure if I fit in."

The feeling and belief that you don't fit into an academic setting where everyone else is also smart (and, from your estimation, a lot smarter than you) is called the Bottom-of-the-Top Syndrome (BTS). In BTS, you realize that you had to have *some* brain power to get accepted into the mix initially, but after evaluating the others around you, you determine—often with no basis in fact—that you're the *least* intelligent of an intelligent bunch.

Share this BTS description with your students and ask them if they have ever been affected by it. Then ask how they responded to this experience. Here are three questions to start with:

■ Did you strive harder?

■ Did you give up entirely?

■ Did you talk yourself out of your negative feelings and just plow ahead in an effort to learn?

Such questions (and their answers) can go a long way toward achieving the ultimate goal of this activity: helping your students realize that almost everyone feels like the bottom of the top at some time, even if it's seldom discussed openly. Just knowing that you have company in your search for an academic comfort level is emotionally beneficial.

Understanding the Concept of Asynchronous Development

We've all seen it happen: A gifted 5-year-old has a picture in her mind of what she wants her hand-drawn house to look like. The trouble is, her mind has developed far in advance of her fingers' drawing capacities. The result? Tears at the table, crumpled-up pages of "bad houses," and an underlying feeling of stupidity in a bright young child who doesn't understand that some parts of the body (and mind) develop more quickly than others.

Asynchronous development is a concept that parents, teachers, and counselors of gifted children need to understand, and they need to share this understanding with the gifted children in their care—the same gifted children who experience asynchronous development from the inside out because they live it every day.

In 1991, a group of educators, counselors, and researchers involved with gifted children met in Columbus, Ohio, to explore new ways to define giftedness apart from IQ scores or high achievement. Led by Dr. Linda Kreger Silverman, one of the leading experts on the emotional development of gifted children, the Columbus Group began today's focus on looking at giftedness as more of an inner quality than one manifested in school work or high grades. They coined the term "asynchronous development" and came up with this definition:[3]

> *Giftedness is asynchronous development in which advanced cognitive abilities and heightened intensity combine to create experiences and awareness that are qualitatively different from the norm. This asynchrony increases with higher intellectual capacity. The uniqueness of the gift renders [children] particularly vulnerable and requires modifications in parenting, teaching, and counseling in order for them to develop optimally.*

Although not universally accepted as a way to look at gifted children, the asynchronous development idea rings true with many parents and educators. Children whose minds are developing at one rate while their bodies and emotions are developing at another need to accept that this uneven progression through childhood, though frustrating, is perfectly normal for them, even if atypical for most.

Activity: *The Ideal Me*

Sometimes, in order to see what's most important in your life, it helps to also consider some things that aren't so important.

Give your students copies of "The Unables" on page 164 and ask them to follow the instructions at the top of the form. Then start a discussion using some or all of these questions:

- What's the *most* frustrating "unable" on your list?

- Why do you think being able to do this thing is so important to you?

- Have you actually tried to do it? What happened when you couldn't do it? How did you feel?

- What's the *least* frustrating "unable" on your list?

- Why don't you care if you can do it or not? Why is it unimportant to you?

- Have you actually tried to do it? What happened when you couldn't do it? How did you feel?

- How many of your "unables" are within your control?

- Which "unables" will take more time and practice to master?

- Which "unables" do you simply have to wait to do until you're older? Is it hard to be patient? Why or why not?

Somewhere during the discussion, make the point (or wait for students to discover) that as much as they might like to "do it all," some things are beyond their personal control.

Activity: Pitching in at Preschool

This is less of an activity and more of an experience. It will help your students recall and appreciate what it's like to be *really* young—a time when life is full of "unables" and other things that are hard to do. It will broaden their understanding of asynchronous development.

Contact a teaching colleague who works in a preschool. Plan a time when you and your students can visit and spend 45 minutes to an hour with the children. The students will work in pairs—one of your students with one of your colleague's students. Prior to your visit, have each of your students choose one of the following and make appropriate plans:

- select a favorite picture book to read to the young child

- choose a dot-to-dot or coloring page to complete with the child

- select a simple board game, like *Chutes and Ladders,* to play with the child

- locate a Web site that has a suitable game or activity they can play together (find out first if the preschool has computers and Internet access)

- write the first half of several familiar adages or proverbs that the children will complete (examples: "When the cat's away . . ." "There's no fool . . .")

- plan a hands-on science experiment or demonstration

After your visit, ask your students about the fun they had and the frustrations they felt. Several will probably mention things like, "The little kids didn't understand my directions" or "They couldn't hold the pencil long enough to connect the dots." As they note these frustrations, chart the area of development each one relates to: physical, intellectual, or emotional. It should then be fairly easy to start a discussion of what asynchrony looks like in little kids, which is a natural bridge to discussions related to similar developmental lags that exist even in older students.

Follow up by having your students make thank-you cards to send to the preschoolers who helped them learn more about themselves.

Becoming an Advocate for Your Own Self-Interests

Even though the roles of "student" and "teacher" are clearly defined in most schools, there are times and places for role reversals. Some students know their needs and interests at least as well as their teachers do, and this is especially true with gifted students.

Teachers would be wise to understand that their gifted students can often provide insights into their own educational needs. You don't have to wait until you hear the words that make conscientious educators cringe ("I'm bored!") before modifying the curriculum for your most able learners. Also, don't let students put you on the defensive by claiming boredom. As we sometimes say to our own students, "Well, if you're bored, then maybe you're boring to be around!"

As teachers, we can help our students to become more than passive recipients of our teaching. With some enlightened self-exploration into their own educational agendas, your students will become partners with you in an enterprise that was never meant to be a one-way street: education.

Activity: *Focus on the Positives*

Sometimes students remember what they dislike about school more readily than they recall the positive events that occurred in the classroom or schoolyard. To encourage your students to look back on activities or lessons that were especially meaningful to them, set aside time each week for journal-writing. Have them respond to these questions:

- What is the most important lesson I learned this week that had to do with school?
- What is the most important lesson I learned this week that had to do with myself?
- Who was the most influential person in my life this week? Why?

Continue this journal-writing activity for a month or longer, depending on how your students respond. Have them start each week's writing by rereading their comments about the previous weeks.

You may want to do this activity yourself. It will keep you focused on the week's brightest spots.

Activity: *Taking Charge of Your Own Education*

If students need help convincing some of their teachers that a change in curriculum would be a change for the better, they also need help requesting specific modifications.

The "Ten Tips for Talking to Teachers" on pages 165–166 have guided thousands of students since they were first written more than 15 years ago. By following this simple advice (and working with responsive teachers), students can make substantial improvements in their lives at school. The "Ten Tips" describe realistic and respectful strategies students can use to approach almost any teacher about almost any education-related issue. It's a primer for starting to alter the curriculum. Best of all, students play a major role by acting as their own advocates.

Give each of your students a copy of the "Ten Tips." Let them know that you're open to talking with them about their specific educational wants and needs.

Understanding the Role of Socialization

More than 70 years ago, psychologist Leta Stetter Hollingworth wrote that "isolation is the refuge of genius, not its goal." What she meant then remains true today; gifted students don't seek to separate themselves socially from classmates, but sometimes it does happen. Usually it's for one or more of the following reasons:

- Gifted children, from a young age, often prefer complicated, rule-based games that others their age don't understand or care about.

- Gifted children are often concerned with world problems and other "big issues" that may not interest other kids their age.

- Gifted children's advanced vocabularies inadvertently isolate them from age peers who don't comprehend their words.

- Gifted children seek out others whose minds operate at the same fast pace as their own. Finding few, they may gravitate toward older children or adults, making them appear "snobby" to their classmates.

- Gifted children who feel distanced from their age peers may resort to solitary play or a world of video-game playmates, making them even less available for social interaction.

In an effort to fit in, some gifted children will "dumb themselves down" to appear more appealing to classmates. They may alter (lower) their vocabularies, get a poor grade on purpose, refuse to participate in "uncool" activities like the gifted program, or deliberately "lose" completed homework. As a teacher, you'll want to be alert to these behaviors and the purposes they are intended to serve.

Gifted Kids Speak Out

We asked gifted kids, "When you're lonely, what do you do?" Here's what some of them said:

"I shut everyone out until the loneliness goes away."
—Anna, 13

"When I'm lonely, I go around feeling sorry for myself and worrying about what everyone else is doing instead of realizing that the problem is mine, not theirs."
—Carrie, 13

"Loneliness is an empty feeling that forms in my stomach and heart. It can be like a hammer blow to your personality and can lead to depression. I escape from loneliness by distracting my mind. Anything will do, and if I currently have a friend, I will do something with him or her."
—Steve, 13

"When I am lonely, I try to get somebody to talk to me, and if they don't, I just try again."
—Ray, 14

"I usually just call someone or go on the Internet. If you're busy, you won't be lonely."
—Erin, 13

"If I am lonely, I like to read a book and meet new characters."
—Kevin, 13

"When I am lonely, I feel that something is missing from my heart, but it can be easily filled by my family and friends."
—Katie, 14

Activity: What's a Regular Kid?

> BUFFY: I wish we could be regular kids.
>
> ANGEL: Yeah. I'll never be a kid.
>
> BUFFY: Okay, then a regular kid and her
> cradle robbing, creature-of-the-night boyfriend.
> —BUFFY THE VAMPIRE SLAYER

It seems that every book, article, or news story about a young person who's done something amazing or shocking—starred in a movie, made a hit record, performed a heroic act, or committed a crime—includes at least one claim of being a "regular kid" after all.

Somehow it's comforting to know that Daniel Radcliffe, the star of *Harry Potter and the Sorcerer's Stone,* still has to do chores like a "regular kid." And that rapper Lil' Bow Wow (real name: Shad Moss), whose debut album went multiplatinum when he was just 14, misses being a "regular kid." And that Vino Vasudevan, the first 12-year-old to score a perfect 1,600 on the SATs, wants to remain a "regular kid."

What's so great about being a "regular kid"? Why do so many people insist that they're "regular" (or wish they were) when they're clearly not? And what does it mean to be "regular," anyway? Explore these questions with your students. You'll learn more about them—and they'll learn more about themselves.

Divide the chalkboard into two columns by drawing a vertical line down the center. At the top of the left-hand column, write:

A "GIFTED KID" IS SOMEONE WHO . . .

Ask your students to quickly complete the sentence. Write down their responses as fast as they offer them.

Next, at the top of the right-hand column, write:

A "REGULAR KID" IS SOMEONE WHO . . .

Ask students to complete this sentence. Write down their responses.

Afterward, have your students look at the two lists and think about what they imply. Start a discussion with questions like these:

- What does it mean to be a "gifted kid"?

- What does it mean to be a "regular kid"?

- How are "gifted kids" different from "regular kids"? How are they the same?

- Have you ever wanted to be a "regular kid"? Why or why not?

- Have you deliberately acted like a "regular kid"? If so, what did you do? Why did you do it? What happened as a result?

- Do you think you might have more friends if you were a "regular kid"?

Talk with your students about how we all sometimes make compromises to fit in and be accepted by others. For gifted kids, these compromises may include pretending they're not smart and hiding their real abilities. Ask them to think about one person with whom they can be themselves, without worrying about being "gifted" or "regular" or anything else. Suggest that this person is probably a real friend.

Activity: Going Along with the Crowd

Going along with the crowd may result in changing a view, attitude, opinion, or behavior that was once held dear. This can create some inner turmoil.

Invite students to tell about a time when they gave in to group norms. What did they do? How did they feel? Would they do it again? Then invite them to describe a time when they didn't give in. If they're slow in responding to either request, you might start things off by sharing examples from your own life.

Lead into more general questions about when it's okay to go along—and when it's best to stand your ground. Students may raise such determining factors as safety, morals, personal preferences, and/or fear of punishment. All are worth exploring further as you discuss topics both trivial and vital in one's development as a social being.

Activity: A World of Equals

In Kurt Vonnegut's short story, "Harrison Bergeron," the title character is a tall (*very* tall), intelligent (*very* intelligent) 14-year-old who lives in the year 2081. The United States Handicapper General has made it law that no one shall be different from anyone else—not smarter, not more athletic, not better looking. Those who naturally are any of these things are given artificial handicaps so they're more "equal" to their less-endowed peers. For example, a prima ballerina is forced to wear weights on her ankles so she can't jump any higher than the most average dancer. Everyone is the same . . . except Harrison, who refuses to play this game.

Vonnegut's story shows what happens when a spunky adolescent chooses to stand out as a singular entity rather than being one more lemming in the crowd. It doesn't have a happy ending (that's putting it mildly: Harrison is gunned down by agents of the Handicapper General on national television), but it will definitely prompt much discussion about what it means to be an individual, and the price that is sometimes paid for taking the social road less traveled. If you think it's appropriate, you might read "Harrison Bergeron" aloud to your class. You'll find it in *Welcome to the Monkey House*, a collection of Vonnegut's shorter works.

A Few Final Thoughts

> "A teacher affects eternity; he can never
> tell where his influence stops."
> —Henry Adams

We began this chapter with the words of a 15-year-old. On the following pages, you "met" other young people who had something to say about growing up gifted and the stamina it takes to keep both one's heart and one's mind intact.

The issues today's gifted youth face are not that much different from issues that intelligent people have struggled with since time began: self-understanding and acceptance, social meaningfulness, and the desire to learn and succeed in life. During the 12th century, a poet named Rumi wrote about two kinds of intelligence: one acquired in school, and one already inside the individual—"a freshness in the center of the chest." As we seek to understand the gifted kids in our care, let's not forget to look for and celebrate the freshness within them.

Notes

1. American Association for Gifted Children, *On Being Gifted* (New York: Walker and Co., 1978), p. 13.

2. A list of "Six Great Gripes of Gifted Kids" first appeared in the original edition of *The Gifted Kids' Survival Guide: For Ages 10 & Under* by Judy Galbraith, published in 1984.

3. Linda Kreger Silverman, "The Gifted Individual," in *Counseling the Gifted and Talented*, Linda Kreger Silverman, ed. (Denver: Love Publishing Co., 1993), p. 3.

Eight Great Gripes of Gifted Kids

1.
No one explains what being gifted is all about—it's kept a big secret.

2.
School is too easy and too boring.

3.
Parents, teachers, and friends expect us to be perfect all the time.

4.
Friends who really understand us are few and far between.

5.
Kids often tease us about being smart.

6.
We feel overwhelmed by the number of things we can do in life.

7.
We feel different and alienated.

8.
We worry about world problems and feel helpless to do anything about them.

Do you have other gripes that aren't on this list? Write them here:

_____

_____

_____

_____

_____

Everything Has Its Ups and Downs!

Name(s):_____

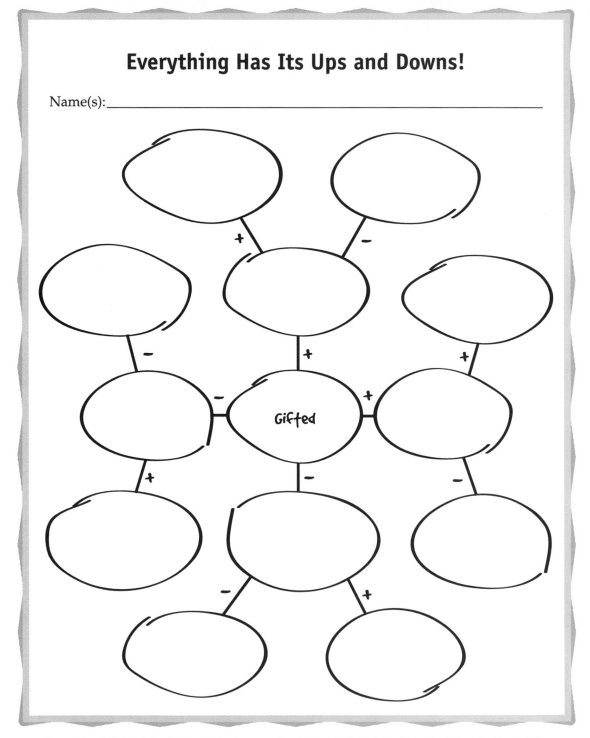

Gifted Is . . . Gifted Means . . .

To You

Complete each sentence with at least three *personal* responses. Write what *you* think gifted is and means.

Gifted is . . .

1. _____

_____

2. _____

_____

3. _____

_____

4. _____

_____

Gifted means . . .

1. _____

_____

2. _____

_____

3. _____

_____

4. _____

_____

continued . . .

Gifted Is . . . Gifted Means . . . (continued)

To Others

Think about how *other people* react to the term "gifted." How would each of the following complete the sentence "Gifted means . . ."?

Your parent(s): "Gifted means _____

_____."

Your best friend: "Gifted means _____

_____."

Your worst enemy: "Gifted means _____

_____."

A teacher who "gets it": "Gifted means _____

_____."

A teacher who doesn't "get it": "Gifted means_____

_____."

Your grandparent(s): "Gifted means_____

_____."

Your brother(s) or sister(s): "Gifted means _____

_____."

A TV producer of a show about gifted kids: "Gifted means _____

_____."

A Valedictorian Speaks Out at His High School Graduation

by John T. Ross

Like countless people have asked countless other graduates, a man asked me, "What are you going to do with the rest of your life?"

But as I stood there dumbfounded, eyebrows bent, mind perplexed, I realized I had no idea. And I realized, too, that it was good not to know and good not to have any idea.

It was good not to know where my money will be invested in ten years or where I will be working in five. Good not to know for whom I wanted to work or where and why. It was good not to know how big my house will be or what car I'll drive. Good not to know about retirement or IRAs or 401K plans.

As I stood there with that curious man, who was asking a question I couldn't answer, I realized that not knowing was good because if you aren't careful, you can grow up too fast, and die too early, thinking only of security, planning, jobs, and things. It's too easy to lose what matters.

To lose: the beautiful innocence of youth, the wild fun of running in the rain, going to amusement parks to eat cotton candy and ride rides, staying up late on purpose, going to ball games, fishing all day in dirty rivers and swimming, the purity of dancing, and singing loud off-key notes behind the comfort of a closed door.

To lose: Turning with friends to the wisdom of classic rock-and-roll to learn about life and women. Hanging out. Doing nothing. Making believe. Walking barefoot in the woods. Climbing trees with ball caps, sweatpants, and dirty T-shirts. Skipping rocks and spitting. Sitting, building sandcastles, asking questions about weird, crazy people, places, and things.

When you plan too much, you lose important things like watching cartoons and not caring that Wile E. Coyote comes back after every ill-timed attempt with boulders. Laughing at least 37 times every day. Loving everything and everybody because the world seems like one of those books that you save for a rainy day and a soft, high-backed chair by the window.

It was good not to know what I wanted to do, because when you're young and fresh and innocent, you can't go wrong. Someone once wrote, "When you're young, you're golden." So, wherever I go and whatever I do with the rest of my life, I'll always stay young and I'll always stay golden.

Thank you.

End note: John Ross loves staying up all night so he can listen to music, write, meet people, and find out what has been going on during the nights he slept through. John loves his family and his friends, and pretty much everyone else.

College: Week Two

Matt was raised in Ohio but had higher aspirations for college—literally. Ever since he was 12, he'd wanted to attend the University of Colorado in Boulder (CU), a state school at the foot of the Rockies. His reason for wanting to go there made perfect sense to a 12-year-old: He could ski every weekend of the winter.

At first, Matt's parents, Jim and Deb, didn't take his dream too seriously. They knew Matt too well. He often had goals that evaporated in several short weeks or months. His personal fads, interests, and hobbies came and went. Jim and Deb figured that his dream of a CU education would, too.

Except it didn't. At 17, Matt moved into a dorm at CU, 1,200 miles away from home. It's not an easy school to enter as an out-of-state student, but he'd done it. For him, it was a dream fulfilled . . . sort of. Only two weeks after arriving in Boulder, Matt sent this letter to his parents in Ohio.

Dear Mom and Dad:

At present, a desire to quell many of the anxieties, fears, and stresses that reside inside of me cause me to write this letter to you. During the past several days, I have found that I am continually contemplating the "what-ifs" of the future. Particularly unnerving for me has been my consideration of the "what-if-I-do-not-become-enrolled-in-medical school?" question, for at this point in my life, I cannot see myself performing any other occupation other than one that is medically related.

I know and understand that I am not alone in my fearfulness about the future, but still, that does not ease my worried mind. It seems that college and all that surrounds its demands are too overwhelming. I find myself studying continually, but still feeling that I am looking up a long ladder which I still have to climb even after closing my textbooks. However, as I walk to and from class and the library, I am able to see so many students enjoying themselves in the courtyards and fields contained on the university grounds. As I watch and listen to the smiles and laughter coming from them, I ask myself what I am doing wrong to deny myself such happiness and luxury.

I have found myself endlessly remembering how much I enjoyed childhood, especially my liking for school, and I want above all else to be a fourth- or sixth-grade student again. There is a very strong feeling inside of me that the past hurried along too quickly and that the future is all too near. Does such thinking suggest that I have grown up? I certainly hope not. Does such thinking raise questions of my maturity, or ability to adapt to change? I would hope to think that the majority of persons my age raise these same questions, inside of their minds, as they struggle to survive the darkness that haunts them each evening.

What can I do regarding all of these fears, anxieties and questions I have? Well, I was hoping that in writing to you, you could assure me that I am thinking "normally" and as most people under stress think.

Love,
Matt

College: Year Two

Matt finished out his year at CU—a rough one emotionally, but a solid one in terms of personal and academic growth. Meanwhile, he decided that he was neither a "Buffalo" (the common name for CU students and supporters, and the school's mascot), nor someone who particularly excelled in a large-campus environment. Even the ski season was lousy, thanks to El Niño. So, as a sophomore, Matt transferred to a small college in Boston, with a refocused vision of himself and a change of major: creative writing. Almost a year to the day after sending the first letter, he wrote this one to his parents in Ohio.

Dear Mom and Dad:

It is my belief that with each passing moment in time, there is one individual who basks in a spotlight given only for himself—one person echoing those famous words of Lou Gehrig. Somehow, though, somehow the many moments of my past week in Boston have not seen a change in that spotlight—it's been me repeating that I am the luckiest man in the world.

Tomorrow's greeting of the day will bring with it the beginning of a new school year, a time of change, hope, and wonder. As this evening's darkness beckons me to slumber, I rest knowing that there is no other place for me to be as happy, as optimistic, and as at ease as that of my current state, and the 'morrow's morning brings not solely a ray of sunshine for all to see, but a spotlight for me to walk in once again.

To each of you, my love and sincerity,
Matt

Celebrity Majors Match-Up

Who majored in what? Where? Try to match the following celebrities with their majors and colleges. Good luck!

Oprah Winfrey (television talk-show host, actress, producer, magazine publisher)

Katie Couric (television journalist, *Today* show co-host, children's book author)

Colin Powell (four-star general; former Chairman of the Joint Chiefs of Staff; Secretary of State under President George W. Bush)

Jesse Jackson (civil rights leader; founder of Operation PUSH and the Rainbow Coalition; winner of the Presidential Medal of Freedom)

Steven Spielberg (Academy Award–winning director, producer, and writer; his movies include *Jaws, Close Encounters of the Third Kind, Raiders of the Lost Ark, E.T. The Extra-Terrestrial, Jurassic Park, Schindler's List,* and *Saving Private Ryan*)

Regis Philbin (television personality; host of his own talk show and the game show *Who Wants to Be a Millionaire*)

Danny Glover (actor whose movies include the Lethal Weapon series)

J.K. Rowling (author of the Harry Potter books)

John Paul II (Pope John Paul II, leader of the Catholic Church)

Arnold Schwarzenegger (former bodybuilder; actor whose movies include the Terminator series)

Business and International Economics, University of Wisconsin

French and Classical Studies, Exeter College

Sociology, University of Notre Dame

Sociology and Economics, North Carolina A & T State University

Economics, San Francisco State University

Speech and Drama, Tennessee State University

American Studies, University of Virginia

English Literature, California State University

Geology, City College of New York

Literature and Philosophy, Jagiellonian University

Fill in the Blanks

Name: _____

When I get an A . . . _____

_____

When I don't get an A . . . _____

_____

When I bring my report card home . . . _____

_____

If I forget to do my homework . . . _____

_____

My parents expect me to . . . _____

_____

Most of my teachers expect me to . . . _____

_____

Most of my friends expect me to . . . _____

_____

No one expects me to . . . _____

_____

The Unables

Read the following list of "unables." Cross out anything you *are* able to do.

Add other things to the list that you'd like to be able to do, or think you'll be able to do someday but can't right now.

Then rank all the un-crossed-out items in order, from *most* frustrating ("I'd love to do it but I can't yet") to *least* frustrating ("It's really not important to me if I can do this or not").

Right now, at this point in my life, I'm unable to:

____ swim

____ understand some adult conversations

____ draw well

____ do something I want to do because I'm "too young"

____ be taken seriously by older kids

____ get straight A's in everything

____ speak a foreign language

____ play basketball (or another sport) with the bigger kids

____ attend college because of my age

____ _____

____ _____

____ _____

____ _____

Ten Tips for Talking to Teachers

Are you having a problem with a class or an assignment? Can you see room for improvement in how a subject is taught? Do you have a better idea for a special project or term paper? Don't just tell your friends. Talk to the teacher!

Many students don't know how to go about doing this. The following suggestions are meant to make it easier for everyone—students *and* teachers.

1.

Make an appointment to meet and talk. This shows the teacher that you're serious and you have some understanding of his or her busy schedule. Tell the teacher about how much time you'll need, be flexible, and don't be late.

2.

If you know other students who feel the way you do, consider approaching the teacher together. There's strength in numbers. If a teacher hears the same thing from four or five people, he or she is more likely to do something about it.

3.

Think through what you want to say before you go into your meeting with the teacher. Write down your questions or concerns. Make a list of the items you want to cover. You may even want to copy your list for the teacher so both of you can consult it during your meeting. (Or consider giving it to the teacher ahead of time.)

4.

Choose your words carefully. Example: Instead of saying, "I hate doing reports; they're boring and a waste of time," try, "Is there some other way I could satisfy this requirement? Could I do a video instead?" Strike the word "boring" from your vocabulary. It's a word that's not helpful for teachers (and it might *even* make them mad).

5.

Don't expect the teacher to do all of the work or propose all of the answers. Be prepared to make suggestions, offer solutions, even recommend resources. The teacher will appreciate that you took the initiative.

continued . . .

6.

Be diplomatic, tactful, and respectful. Teachers have feelings, too. And they're more likely to be responsive if you remember that the purpose of your meeting is conversation, not confrontation.

7.

Focus on what you need, not on what you think the teacher is doing wrong. The more the teacher learns about you, the more he or she will be able to help. The more defensive the teacher feels, the less he or she will want to help.

8.

Don't forget to listen. Strange but true, many students need practice in this essential skill. The purpose of your meeting isn't just to hear yourself talk.

9.

Bring your sense of humor. Not necessarily the joke-telling sense of humor, but the one that lets you laugh at yourself and your own misunderstandings and mistakes.

10.

If your meeting isn't successful, get help from another adult. "Successful" doesn't necessarily mean that you emerged victorious. Even if the teacher denies your request, your meeting can still be judged successful. If you had a real conversation—if you communicated openly, listened carefully, and respected each other's point of view—then congratulate yourself on a great meeting. If the air crackled with tension, the meeting fell apart, and you felt disrespected (or acted disrespectful), then it's time to bring in another adult. Suggestions: a guidance counselor, the gifted program coordinator, or another teacher you know and trust who seems likely to support you and advocate for you. Once you've found help, approach your teacher and try again.

CHAPTER 6

Underachiever or Selective Consumer?

"I have yet to find an underachiever who is truly lazy and unmotivated."

—HARVEY MANDEL

Few situations are more frustrating for teachers than working with children who don't perform as well academically as we know they could and we think they should. Their potential is obvious. Why won't they just do their work?

Often, we get so frustrated that we label these children "underachievers." Once this label has been applied, an army of strategies is employed, most involving contracts, verbal agreements, and losses of privileges for students who stubbornly refuse to live up to our expectations. We bargain. We cajole. We punish. We nag and scold:

- ▉ "You're a smart kid—if only you'd apply yourself."

- ▉ "I don't care if the homework is boring. An assignment is an assignment! Everyone else has to do it. Why shouldn't you?"

- ▉ "If you'd argue less about your work and just plain do it, you wouldn't be having these problems."

Change, we insist, is up to the student. It's his choice, his responsibility, his burden. (Most students labeled underachievers are boys, hence the "his.") So much for the theory that education is a positive partnership involving school, home, and students!

This chapter distinguishes between the identification and treatment of two types of low performance by gifted students: underachievement and nonproduction, which we prefer to call "selective consumerism." We review the literature and research on what has historically been called "underachievement." Then we suggest strategies for reversing patterns of underachieving and selective consumer behaviors through curricular and counseling interventions.

Matt's Story

When Jim met Matt, Jim was a first-year teacher and Matt was a fifth-grade student. To Matt, school was irrelevant, and he told Jim so every day by writing that very word—in red crayon—across the top of any worksheet he found either distasteful or unrelated to the needs he perceived he had. More often than not, Matt then formed a paper airplane out of his worksheet and sent it nonstop to Jim's desk. Thanks to this behavior, among others, Matt spent much time in the hall, at the principal's office, or (horror of horrors) off-task.

Then, one day, a miracle occurred: Matt got sprayed by a skunk in his backyard—a common event in northern New England, where this story took place. Actually, Matt's spraying was a harbinger of good things to come. Skunks emerge from hibernation in early spring to seek mates. Also, maple sap starts to flow as the days get warmer but the nights remain cold. Matt was a maple-sugar farmer, and his unfortunate and smelly meeting took place when, in the process of tapping a tree, he interrupted a couple of amorous skunks.

Matt and Jim talked (downwind, at Matt's suggestion) and decided that maple-sugar farming would become part of Matt's curriculum. Thus, his math assignments went from rote drills to making change and converting quarts to pints. His reading and writing assignments involved completing invoices and preparing posters and flyers to advertise his product (he made $65.50 after expenses). His social studies assignment was a photo essay of his skills at maple-sugar farming. Matt even spoke at a Rotary Club luncheon, where he listened to old war stories and contributed a tasteless joke or two of his own to the colorful discussion.

Was Matt an underachiever who suddenly came to appreciate school under the guidance of his skilled first-year teacher? It's tempting to think so, but the answer is probably no. More likely, Matt was "selective" about his education, not "turned off" to education in general. His learning never stopped, even during difficult times. He needed a reason to learn, a purpose, and he was not finding that purpose in the regular curriculum. Rather, like Dorothy in *The Wizard of Oz*, Matt found the magic of learning in his own backyard—not, in his case, a Kansas cornfield, but a New Hampshire sugar-maple grove.

Defining Underachievement

Both early researchers and more recent authors have defined underachievement in terms of a discrepancy between a child's school performance and some ability index, such as an IQ score.[1] Such "discrepancy" definitions, though clean-cut and precise, are actually quite limiting. When underachievement is seen from the vantage point of test scores vs. daily performance, it becomes associated exclusively with academic, school-based endeavors. Yet, as Maple-Sugar Matt clearly has shown us, underachievement in particular subjects is often more a symptom of another concern (in Matt's case, an inappropriate curriculum) than it is a problem in and of itself.

Defining underachievement is important because the term itself is a buzz word among educators. The mere mention of "underachievement" generates many images (all of them negative) about the child in question. We picture the underachiever as belligerent, difficult to work with, smart but not motivated, or a "poor-me" type who could get good grades with some effort but just doesn't want to. These mental images can transform quickly into mental blocks, as we may begin to resent the apparent unwillingness of the student to perform on cue and may accuse the student of creating problems that could be resolved with a little extra effort.

The bottom line is this: Where underachievement is concerned, the name of the game is blame. Everyone involved (including the student) tries to attribute its presence to being someone else's fault, and therefore someone else's problem.

A New Approach

If the discrepancy formula is too narrow a definition for underachievement, how else might it be described? In fact, there are several useful ways to consider underachievement without getting overly precise about defining it.

First, however, a caveat: To some educators, this might not be acceptable. After all, there is safety in numbers. For those who feel secure only when a specific, numerical line of demarcation exists, the suggestions offered here won't suffice. But given the choice between exact numbers that may have little or no validity and more amorphous indicators that get at the heart of the problem, which should we choose? We'd like to think that most educators will be open to considering the following new approach to "defining" underachievement.

Underachievement Is First and Foremost a Behavior and, As Such, It Can Change Over Time

Too often, underachievement is seen as a problem of attitude ("He's just being stubborn; he can do the work") or personality ("If she weren't so lazy, she could pass that course"). However, neither attitude nor personality can be modified as directly as behaviors can. To speak of "underachieving behaviors" is to pinpoint those parts of children's lives they are most able to alter: actions.

Underachievement Is Content- and Situation-Specific

Gifted children who do not succeed in school are often successful in outside activities—sports, social events, after-school jobs, talent or hobby interests. Also, even children who do poorly in *most* school subjects often display a talent or interest in at least *one* school subject.

When we label a child an underachiever, we disregard any positive outcomes or behaviors that child displays. Since it is more useful to label the student's behaviors rather than labeling the student, we should identify a child as "underachieving in math and language arts" rather than as an "underachieving student."

Underachievement Is in the Eye of the Beholder

For some students (and educators), as long as a passing grade is attained, underachievement does not exist. "After all," this group would say, "a D isn't failure!" To others, a grade of B+ constitutes underachievement if the student in question was "expected" to get an A.

When it comes to academic grades, we all have different thresholds of pain. A grade of B might elate one student and devastate a classmate of equal ability. Recognizing that the definition of underachievement varies with each person is the first step in understanding this complex phenomenon.

Underachievement is Tied Intimately to Self-Image Development

> *"Almost everybody walks around with a vast burden of imaginary limitations inside his head. While the burden remains, personal success is as difficult to achieve as the conquest of Everest with a sack of rocks tied to your back."*
> —J.H. Brennan

A child who learns to see himself or herself in terms of failure eventually begins to place self-imposed limits on what is possible. Thus, any academic successes are written off as lucky accidents, while low grades or achievement serve to reinforce one's negative perceptions about oneself.

This self-deprecating attitude often results in such comments (spoken or unspoken) as, "Why should I even try? I'm just going to fail anyway," or "Even if I do succeed, people will say it's because I cheated," or "Nothing I do is ever good enough, so why bother?" The end product is a low self-image, in which the student sees himself or herself as weak in academics. Under this assumption, a child's initiative to change or to accept a challenge is limited.

Putting Failure into Perspective

- The greatest quarterbacks complete only 60 percent of their passes.
- The best basketball players make only about 50 percent of their shots.
- Most major-league baseball players get on base about 25 percent of the time.
- Oil companies dig an average of ten wells before they find oil, even with the help of expert geologists.
- A successful actor is turned down 29 out of 30 times when auditioning for TV commercials.
- Winners in the stock market make money on only two out of every five investments.
- John Grisham's first novel, *A Time to Kill,* was rejected by 28 publishers.
- William Golding's *Lord of the Flies* was rejected 21 times.
- The first edition of *Chicken Soup for the Soul* was rejected by more than 30 publishers.

Underachievement Implies That Adults Disapprove of a Child's Behavior

Underachievement is a problem for children because it is recognized as such by adults. Students who are labeled "underachievers" suffer the pangs of knowing that they are disappointing significant others—parents and teachers. Thus burdened, these children learn to assess their abilities relative to what they have not accomplished instead of what they are capable of doing.

Similar to the frustration felt when attempting to deepen a hole in wet sand, the underachiever sees each victory squelched by the collapse of other unmet goals. So, when a trusted adult in this child's life praises the so-called underachiever for a successful grade or project, the child may dismiss this compliment as meaningless. "After all," the child might think, "it probably won't happen again."

Sadly, the overall disapproval felt when things don't go well overrides the occasional success, which the child notes as an exception—nothing more.

Underachievement Is a Learned Set of Behaviors

Underachievement can be learned by gifted students for whom "school" and "education" exist in separate spheres.

In three national studies of education, published decades apart, criticism was leveled at curricula that are designed strictly by grade-level norms with little regard for individual rates of learning.

In 1970, a congressional mandate required the Commissioner of Education to determine the extent of programs for gifted and talented students. Published in 1972, the Commissioner's report—known as the *Marland Report*—noted that:[2]

- ■ "The boredom that results from discrepancies between the child's knowledge and the school's offerings leads to underachievement and behavior disorders affecting self and others."

In 1983, the National Commission on Excellence in Education published *A Nation at Risk,* the first of many national critiques of the practice of education in America. Speaking specifically to the education of gifted students, the commission concluded that:[3]

- ■ "Over half the population of gifted students do not match their tested ability with comparable achievement in school."

- ■ "Only 31 percent of high school graduates complete intermediate algebra; 13 percent complete French I; and calculus classes, though available in 60 percent of U.S. high schools, are completed by only 6 percent of the students."

- ■ "Textbooks are too easy for able students, and rigorous texts remain unavailable because of the 'thin market' for sales that is perceived by publishers."

In 1993, *National Excellence: A Case for Developing America's Talent* presented similar bad news about the state of our nation's education as it serves gifted children, including:[4]

- ■ Economically disadvantaged and minority students are offered the fewest opportunities for academic advancement and are the most at risk for underachievement.

- Students are not asked to work hard or master a body of challenging skills. Adequacy prevails over excellence.

- Exceptional talent is viewed suspiciously in America. It is seen as a valuable resource, but it is noted by many as a troublesome expression of eccentricity.

Although National Excellence was as much a political document as an educational manifesto (for example, the word "gifted" was replaced by "talented"), it did refocus attention not only on underachieving behaviors, but also on the underachieving curriculum.

Underachievement Is Taught

The year before *A Nation at Risk* was published, an 11-year-old boy wrote a poem that's still appropriate today:[5]

> Teachers told me I was rude,
> Bumptious, overbearing, shrewd.
> Some of the things they said were crude
> I couldn't understand.
> And so I built myself a wall,
> Strong, solid, ten feet tall.
> With bricks you couldn't see at all.
> So I couldn't understand.

How ironic: Gifted children, who often receive curriculum and instruction that is unchallenging and lacking in rigor and creative appeal, have come to be seen as the source of their own difficulties. In fact, the real problem lies in a lackluster set of academic offerings which leave students pleading for more. Perhaps in the final analysis, underachievement is *learned* because it is *taught* so well, year after year.

We know this hurts, and we realize, too, that if you are reading this book, you're probably not one of those offending educators who teaches a "one-size-fits-all" curriculum. Still, with so many highly able students turned off to learning, it's obvious that some teachers neither believe in nor practice curriculum differentiation that benefits gifted students.

Underachievers vs. Selective Consumers

"Don't mistake activity for achievement."
—John Wooden

The problem of underachievement begins with its definition. There is no consensus on what underachievement actually is, where it starts, and how or when the metamorphosis to achievement occurs.

Another stumbling block is this: Any child who is not working up to potential, however that potential is defined, can be dubbed an underachiever. Too seldom do the people who attach that label actually consider the source of the problem. They see the result—the lack of achievement—and rush to label the student as something she or he may not be.

In many cases, the child in question is not an underachiever but is, instead, a selective consumer, adept at taking the best from what school and teachers have to offer and leaving the rest behind.

Two case studies can help us understand the distinctions between an underachiever and a selective consumer.

Case Study: Stephanie

Stephanie is a fifth grader whose report card comments read like a list of missed opportunities: "Stephanie is bright, but seems insecure about her ability to do well"; "Stephanie's perfectionism prevents her from pursuing new topics or projects."

In class, Stephanie seldom causes trouble; in fact, you hardly know she's there. She pursues her work with caution, and when her teacher hands her an assignment, Stephanie's out-loud comment is, "This is too hard for a stupid-head like me." Often, she is her own worst enemy. When she receives a high grade on a project, she attributes it to "being lucky," and when she doesn't do well, she internalizes the failure and calls herself "dumb."

Socially, Stephanie fits in with one or two friends she's had since first grade, but most students don't know her well. It's not that she's totally withdrawn, but she is *very* quiet.

Stephanie would like to do better in school but claims she can't. She insists she's not as smart as everyone says, and she can prove it by showing you all her low grades and poor papers.

To the casual observer, Stephanie is a nice, quiet girl who just lacks confidence. To the careful observer, Stephanie is a sad girl who seems to have little hope of ever being anything more than she is right now: self-critical, self-deprecating, and unable to chart her own course, socially or academically.

Case Study: Mark

Mark is a student most teachers hear about before they ever meet him. His reputation precedes him because Mark is the source of constant teacher-lounge banter: "You've got to approach him just so, or else he'll walk all over you"; "He's a smart kid, and he knows it—*that's* his biggest problem"; "He can do great work one day and no work the next."

In class, Mark's performance and behavior are sporadic. On some days, he's the most animated discussant in a review of current world events. On other days, he just sits there, completing seatwork when he feels like it and turning in homework when the mood strikes him.

Mark dislikes "busy work" and teachers who assign it. Although he can and does succeed on projects that pique his interest, he often concentrates solely on this work to the exclusion of other tasks. This, of course, makes it difficult for teachers to assign grades. They know that Mark understands the concepts of his lessons, but if he refuses to turn in all of his required work, how can they possibly reward him with high grades? It wouldn't be fair.

Socially, Mark has few problems, and some students may even see him as a leader—a rebel with a cause, an agent with a mission: to take the best from school and leave the rest behind.

Almost everyone is frustrated with Mark's sporadic performance, except for one person: Mark. He does know he's smart and he realizes, too, that if he "played the game by the rules" he could be a straight-A student. Somehow, though, getting high grades isn't necessarily one of Mark's personal goals. He's into learning, but it doesn't naturally follow that school is the place where lots of learning occurs.

To the casual observer, Mark is rebelling for the sake of rebelling. If he isn't willing to change his attitude, then "he can just sit there and get Fs." To the careful observer, Mark is a selective consumer of education. He knows what he knows, and he doesn't want to have to keep proving it through homework and "dumb" assignments that do little more than fill time. Mark could improve his school performance dramatically and almost overnight. He knows what the hoops are, but he's just not willing to jump through them.

Conclusions

If you compared the report-card *grades* of Stephanie and Mark, the similarities would outweigh the distinctions. If you compared their report card *comments,* you'd find that teachers have very different impressions of these two "underachievers."

In fact, Mark is not an underachiever, despite grades that indicate otherwise. He is a selective consumer: a student very much in touch with both himself and the world of learning but unwilling to do much of his assigned work because he sees little purpose in doing so.

Stephanie does display underachieving behaviors. She is a lost soul in the academic miasma called school. She desperately wants to do better—and feel better—but is at a loss about how to begin.

A Child's Fate

by Abel Lopez

This poem was composed by Abel Lopez at a workshop where he learned about the difference between being an underachiever and a selective consumer (his word: "nonproductive"). Abel now teaches gifted children at an elementary school in Texas.

> What happened on that dreadful day
> Is something I just realized here today.
>
> A nonproductive child just sat and stared
> At a teacher who just did not care.
>
> Although considered gifted, smart, and all that stuff,
> This teacher thought it was all a bluff.
>
> The nonproductive child sat in awe
> Because the teacher only saw
> A poor student without the right clothes
> A poor student who didn't know.
>
> The nonproductive child knew what was going on
> The self-fulfilling prophecy was quickly turned on.
>
> She just didn't know, she just didn't care
> The nonproductive child was not treated fair

continued . . .

("Abel, I have spoken to the counselor and WE have agreed that you will be better off if we move you out of the accelerated classes and put you in the remedial courses . . .")

That nonproductive child sits here today
And realizes what happened on that one dreadful day.
If that teacher knew then what exists today
There may never have been that dreadful day.

Differences At-a-Glance

Here's a fairly simple way to present the similarities and distinctions between students like Stephanie and Mark. As is true with any such side-by-side comparison, each trait or behavior listed is etched in soap, not stone. Although a particular student may seem to fit one pattern more than another, some of the items listed under that pattern will probably not apply. This chart is provided more as guidance than gospel and should, therefore, be regarded more as a relative than as an absolute. Nonetheless, the overall idea that some so-called underachievers are actually selective consumers seems legitimate and is worth exploring further.

Underachievers . . .	Selective Consumers . . .
. . . do not understand causes or cures	. . . can explain both the problem and possible solutions
. . . are dependent and reactive	. . . are independent and proactive
. . . tend to withdraw	. . . tend to rebel
. . . respect or fear authority figures	. . . see teachers as adversaries; can be contentious
. . . need both structure and imposed limits	. . . require little structure; need "breathing room"
. . . exhibit uniformly weak performance	. . . exhibit performance that varies relative to the teacher and/or content

Underachievers . . .	Selective Consumers . . .
. . . generally require family intervention	. . . can usually be dealt with within school resources
. . . may change over the long term	. . . may change "overnight"
. . . are often perfectionistic; nothing they do is ever good enough	. . . are frequently satisfied with their accomplishments
. . . have a poor academic self-image	. . . see themselves as academically able

What are some characteristics that underachievers and selective consumers may have in common? There are at least four:

1. Their socialization with classmates may be impaired.

2. They prefer a "family" vs. a "factory" classroom atmosphere.

3. They need to change both their behaviors and their attitudes.

4. They may need guidance or counseling to achieve academic success.

Much Research, Few Conclusions

When Jane B. Raph and Abraham Tannenbaum reviewed 30 years of research studies on underachievement (1931–1961), they analyzed more than 90 empirical studies—and could not find any one unified explanation of underachievement.[6] In 1974, and 1977, C. Asbury and Avner Ziv concluded that no specific psychosocial factors seem consistently associated with underachievement.[7]

More current research on underachievement indicates that both its definition and its treatment remain complex. Sally M. Reis and D. Betsy McCoach mention the need to "individualize programs for achieving gifted students."[8] They also emphasize the need to focus on factors within the family, school and home if underachievement is to be reversed—a finding consistent with work done by other researchers.[9]

When all is said and done about the causes and treatment of underachievement, it seems that we know as little now about reversing it as we did when Raph and Tannenbaum threw up their arms in frustration in 1961.

How can decades of research show so little direction toward understanding a phenomenon that everyone agrees exists? We believe this is due to two issues previously described here: the unfocused definitions of underachievement, and the lack of recognition of the distinctions between the underachiever and the selective consumer.

In their extensive review of underachievement as a multifaceted set of behaviors, Gary Davis and Sylvia Rimm allude to this distinction between the underachiever and the selective consumer, though they do not use those exact terms.[10] Rather, they create composites of specific (but fictional) children such as "Manipulative Mary," "Rebellious Rebecca," "Taunted Terrence," and "Dramatic Dick." What distinguishes the varieties of underachievement within these children is their unique levels of dependence and dominance.

Seen from another vantage point, these children could represent the characteristics of underachievers vs. those of selective consumers. Davis and Rimm go on to explain the circumstances and environments that prompt the emergence of the "Depressed Donnas" and "Dramatic Dicks" of the world, including school climate, inflexible and competitive classrooms, negative expectations, and an unrewarding curriculum.

In her review of 15 years of research studies on underachievement, Barbara Clark arrives at 16 characteristics of children with underachieving behaviors:[11]

1. They have low self-concept and give negative evaluations about themselves. These feelings of inferiority are demonstrated by distrust, lack of concern and/or hostility toward others.

2. They are socially more immature than achievers, lacking self-discipline and refusing to do tasks they deem unpleasant. They are highly distractible.

3. They harbor feelings of rejection, believing that no one likes them and that parents are dissatisfied with them.

4. They have feelings of helplessness and may externalize their conflicts and problems.

5. They do not see the connection between effort and achievement outcomes.

6. They are rebellious, have feelings of being victimized and have poor personal adjustment.

7. They have few strong hobbies or interests.

8. They are unpopular with peers and have fewer friends.

9. They are hostile toward adult authority figures and distrust adults, generally.

10. They are resistant to influence from teachers or parents.

11. They have lower aspirations for their future, lacking future plans or career goals.

12. They may withdraw in classroom situations and be less persistent or assertive in these situations.

13. They lack study skills and have weak motivation for academic tasks.

14. They dislike school and teachers and choose companions who share similar feelings.

15. They often leave schoolwork incomplete and nap during study time.

16. They perform at higher levels on tasks requiring synthesizing rather than detailed computational or convergent responses or those tasks requiring precise, analytic processing.

Some of these characteristics show a resemblance to the items previously listed on pages 177–178—with one important exception. Clark's list does not differentiate between behaviors (for example, items 6, 9, 12, and 15) and attitudes (for example, items 1, 3, 5, and 11).

What Next?

At this point in our knowledge (or lack thereof) about underachievement, it seems important to take a few steps back before trying to take any more steps forward. That is, before we begin to offer solutions to reverse the patterns of underachievement, educators need to reexamine—again—what they mean by that term.

It is our suggestion, based on both our clinical experiences as teachers and counselors and our review of pertinent research, that underachievement be subdivided as described in the chart on pages 177–178. Once it is acknowledged that some so-called underachievers have nearly total control of their academic lives but merely choose not to perform, while others cannot change their behaviors because of a lack of personal power or inner resources, then the general strategies that are used to address the specific behaviors will become more on-target and focused.

When approaching any problem, there are two general lines of attack: the "shotgun" approach, where strategies are applied willy-nilly in hopes that something will hit its target, and the "spotlight" approach, where a sharp, precise beam is focused on a specific situation or problem. In issues as complex as these, time and effort spent on locating the target will result ultimately in more effective and efficient treatment strategies.

As a final comparison between an underachiever and a selective consumer, let us offer two analogies. The child who chooses not to perform up to others' expectations—the selective consumer—reminds us of the adage, "You can lead a horse to water, but you can't make him drink." With just a little editorial license, this new proverb describes such a case: "You can lead a child to knowledge, but you can't make him think."

On the other hand, the child with underachieving behaviors, who has little control over or understanding of his or her depressed performance, is reminiscent of Narcissus, the Greek mythological character, who, upon seeing his reflection in a pond, pined away for the lovely creature he saw. In his case, Narcissus was longing for something that he already had, so his was not a problem of attainment but of realization.

And just as Narcissus was eventually transformed into a beautiful flower, so might the child with underachieving behaviors come into full bloom, given the proper mix of support and nurturance.

Strategies to Reverse the Behaviors and Attitudes of Selective Consumers and Underachievers

"What is it that causes so many gifted children to lose this spark? What can be done to rekindle it?"
—JAMES T. WEBB, ELIZABETH MECKSTROTH, AND STEPHANIE TOLAN

Since both selective consumerism and underachievement are noted especially in academic situations, it makes sense to look toward the roles played by schools in the treatment of these problems. This is not meant to either deny or downplay the important influences of the family, but rather to focus attention on the situations and structure most amenable to change by educators: school.

Although many strategies work better with selective consumers than they do with underachievers (and vice versa), there are some common denominators that apply to both groups. Joanne R. Whitmore, in what is considered by many to be the most comprehensive treatment of underachievement ever published, has classified these strategies into three clusters:[12]

1. Supportive strategies. These "affirm the worth of the child in the classroom and convey the promise of greater potential and success yet to be discovered and enjoyed."

2. Intrinsic strategies. These are "designed to develop intrinsic achievement motivation through the child's discovery of rewards available . . . as a result of efforts to learn, achieve, and contribute to the group."

3. Remedial strategies. These are "employed to improve the student's academic performance in an area of learning in which (s)he has evidenced difficulty learning, has experienced a sense of failure, and has become unmotivated to engage in learning tasks."

These three families of strategies all focus around one central theme: putting the child back in charge of his or her own education. Only when students feel academically capable and internally motivated to learn will school success occur. And since success is more likely to breed additional success, the child who learns early on that he or she has a good degree of power in determining learning outcomes will be more ready to absorb knowledge independent of adult supervision once the structured parameters of school are in the past.

Gifted Kids Speak Out

Here's how intelligent young men from urban environments defined their will to achieve—and the roles others played in encouraging them.

An Internal Will

"It sounds off the wall, but it's an internal will. For example, if I am curious about something and I want to learn about it, like my science fair topic—cold fusion. I didn't care if the material I needed was radioactive or not. I said to the professor, 'Send it to me in a lead bottle UPS. I'll pay the shipping!' Nothing is going to stop me. I am going to do this experiment. If I get this inner drive pointed toward academics, I'll do well. That's basically it. It's like a driving force. If I find some reason to motivate myself to push for something, I'll do it."
—Matteo, 11th grade

The Role of Family

"I remember when I was younger, my parents used to sit me down, often after dinner, with no interruptions at all. I'd go off to my room or off to watch TV, and my father would call me back to the kitchen and have me sit down and listen to him tell me how it was way back when they were growing up in Puerto Rico. They really instilled the idea that I have to do well in school. They're always telling me that. They didn't have the opportunities for education, and ever since I was a young kid, I've had that drilled into my brain. Even today, they say, 'Keep working hard.'"
—Rafael, 12th grade

The Role of a First-Grade Teacher

"Mrs. Scarfa was my first-grade teacher. My parents have told me I loved her. She gave me one theory that I still walk around with, and I think it's my major driving force. When people tell me that things are impossible, there is no such thing as 'can't.' That word is not in the English dictionary. Mrs. Scarfa told me that you can do anything and everything you want just as long as you have the drive and the power to do it. That's one thing I still carry around. Nothing stops me from doing what I want. There is no 'can't.'"
—Matteo, 11th grade

continued . . .

The Role of a High School Teacher

"Mrs. Lowell taught with a lot of enthusiasm. She told us on the first day of class that we were never leaving the room. 'This is not a democracy!' she said. 'Whatever you need from the nurse, I have right here. You gotta get sick, there is the trash can. You want a drink of water? I have bottled water.' She had bottled water! 'People come in from the rain some days and your hair is all wet. I have a blow dryer.' She really did, and she let people use it. She had people keep their jackets in her teacher's closet. She was a real good teacher. I loved her from the first day. . . . She was at every football game. You know who your true fans are . . . I connected with her from the start."
—**Wallace, 11th grade**

The Role of a Coach

"He is a father figure to a lot of us. If something goes wrong, he'll talk to us about a lot of things, like the gang stuff that's going on around here. He doesn't want to see us make major mistakes. He takes the time to listen and he tries to understand. If there is an individual problem, he'll talk to the swimmers individually. With things in general that are going on in school, we'll all sit together, and he'll talk to all of us."
—**Lucio, 11th grade**

From Thomas B. Hebert, "Defining Belief in Self: Intelligent Young Men in an Urban High School," in *Gifted Child Quarterly* 44:2 (2000), pp. 91–114.

Case Study: Mark

Let's see how the three types of strategies Whitmore described might work with Mark, the selective consumer.

Some people might surmise that Mark doesn't need much in the line of supportive strategies ("Surely his cockiness is a sign of a strong self-image"). But, just as looks can be deceiving, so can bravado. Mark's rebellious attitude toward authority may be a well-disguised "front" to cover for the inadequacies he fears he might have.

Mark probably does need support—who doesn't?—to show him that it's okay to show a vulnerability; a need for others to like and accept him for himself, not for someone he is trying to be. Therefore, a supportive teacher would acknowledge and thank Mark whenever he showed a glimmer of cooperation or whenever his independence was demonstrated in a positive or helpful way.

Intrinsically, Mark already knows that he is the "real teacher" in the sense of controlling when and if he learns, and he needs to be rewarded for these insights. At the same time, Mark and his teacher need to come up with some type of "pact" that leads to the following accord: As long as Mark learns what he needs to learn (by the teacher's standards) via his own methods, the teacher won't interfere. However, if Mark's methods fall short, or he is at a loss as to how to proceed, then his teacher will intervene on Mark's behalf—by mutual consent.

Mark may have few areas in need of remediation, but if they do exist, they should be approached in an up-front manner by his teacher: "I know you don't like to write note cards before doing a report, but I need to see one set from you just so I know you have that skill. Then I'm off your back." This gives Mark a chance to demonstrate a skill he says he has, and it satisfies his teacher's need to know how close Mark's perception is to reality.

Case Study: Stephanie

Could Whitmore's strategies also work with an underachiever like Stephanie? Let's find out.

One minute, one hour, one day at a time, Stephanie needs to hear that she is a valuable person, regardless of the grades she attains. Supportive comments such as, "It's so great to have you in class, Stephanie. When you smile, it lights up the whole room!" need to be interspersed with accolades for Stephanie's attempts (not necessarily successes) at academics: "I saw you practicing spelling with Julie. Thank you for helping her out." In subtle and obvious ways (for example, words and smiles), in both one-on-one and in group settings, Stephanie needs to be reminded that she is able, valuable, and responsible.

Intrinsically, Stephanie's need is to feel that she is an active participant *in* rather than a passive recipient *of* her education. When she does a good job on a project or paper, the teacher should ask Stephanie how and why she thinks she succeeded. If Stephanie claims it was due to luck or fate, a few words of rebuttal will help: "I bet you studied—even a little," or, "The way you put this report together shows me that you have fine organizational skills." The more specific the comments, the better, as it is harder to deny direct statements than it is to dismiss as trivial a general "Good job, Stephanie!"

If there is any remediation to be done, Stephanie needs to know that it's okay to be better at some things than others. The catch phrase to apply to Stephanie should be, "Less than perfection is more than acceptable." Should she need help with handwriting, research skills, or any other area related to school success, Stephanie needs to be told that even she—a gifted child—isn't expected to know everything.

Stephanie cares about and respects school a great deal. It's the prime source of her attitudes toward herself and learning. Knowing this, the concerned teacher will take great care in acknowledging Stephanie's efforts and will support her both directly (through words) and indirectly (through gestures) so that Stephanie's attempts to succeed are noted as the brave efforts they are.

Strategies At-a-Glance

Specific distinctions between supportive, intrinsic, and remedial strategies for addressing the behavior of underachievers and selective consumers are found below and on the following page.

Notice that the teacher is a supportive partner in the learning process in both cases. When working with students who underachieve, the teacher is more directive and in control. When working with selective consumers, the teacher adopts a more relaxed, "how-can-I-help-you-learn-the-best?" attitude. Either way, the teacher is fully in charge of the events transpiring in the classroom and the conditions under which learning is most likely to occur for specific, individual students.

The approaches used to attain success give new meaning to the phrase, "The end justifies the means." In this case, it does. Students who may appear at first glance to be similar because of the commonality of their poor academic performance are, in fact, very different from each other. Thus, the strategies used, the demeanor displayed, and the degree of autonomy provided by the teacher may (and should) differ considerably from student to student.

	For Selective Consumers	**For Underachievers**
Supportive Strategies	Eliminating (or at least significantly reducing) work already mastered	Holding daily class meetings to discuss student concerns and progress
	Allowing independent study on topics of personal interest	Directive atmosphere shows the student that the teacher is in charge and is competent
	Nonauthoritarian atmosphere	Daily/weekly/monthly written contracts of work to be completed
	Permitting students to prove competence via multiple methods	Free time scheduled each day to show importance of relaxation and free choice

	For Selective Consumers	For Underachievers
	Teaching through problem-solving techniques over rote drill	Using instructional methods that are concrete and predictable
Intrinsic Strategies	Students help determine class rules	Students are aware of specific rewards for attempting and/or doing their work
	Assigning specific responsibilities for classroom maintenance or management	Allowing students to evaluate work prior to the teacher assigning a grade
	Teacher practices reflective listening—comments to students serve to clarify statements, not evaluate them	Frequent and positive contact with family regarding child's progress
	Students set daily/weekly/monthly goals with approval of teacher	Verbal praise for any self-initiating behaviors
Remedial Strategies	Self-selected, weekly goals for improvement determined between student and teacher	Programmed instruction materials, where students grade their own papers immediately on completion
	Private instruction in areas of weakness	Peer tutoring of younger students in areas of strength
	Use of humor and personal example to approach areas of academic weakness	Small-group instruction in common areas of weakness (e.g., spelling, sequencing, phonics)
	Familiarizing students with learning-styles research and its personal implications for classroom performance	Encouraging students to work on projects which don't involve a grade

The idea of individualizing curriculum and instruction for different students is hardly revolutionary. Even the most staunch traditionalists would agree that since children learn at different rates, some degree of consideration may be given to the possibility that what works for one pupil won't work with another.

Taught to Underachieve

"In second grade, I was asked to cut out the rising and setting times of the sun from the newspaper. After the first few times I refused to do it—once I understood the concept, I saw no point to it. That year the teacher announced to the class that I was passing by the skin of my teeth. I remember sitting there thinking that teeth don't have skin."
—Meg, a teacher and doctoral candidate in her 40s

"The teachers would always say, 'He isn't doing the work we give him now, why should we give him new work?' It was like being made to count the grains of sand in a bucket. . . . It's easy to do 1 + 1, then 5 + 8 . . . 18 + 5 isn't really any different; it's still 'sand'—the repetition of the same pattern. It would be different if they gave you new things. It could be like counting a bucket of diamonds. Hold them up to the light and you get different shapes, and glitters and shines."
—Lee, age 16, from a juvenile detention center

From Marylou Kelly Streznewski, *Gifted Grown Ups* (New York: John Wiley & Sons, 1999), pp. 76 and 172.

A Modest Proposal

The work of Jane B. Raph and Abraham Tannenbaum was cited earlier in this chapter. One can almost read the disappointment in the words Tannenbaum used to summarize their three decades of research on underachievement: "Added together, the studies yield a tangle of conclusions that are more puzzling than revealing."[13] There is no way that a phenomenon such as underachievement—and its reversal—could remain that elusive for so long except for one reason: the term itself was (and is) too ill-defined.

In their review of research on underachieving gifted students, Cynthia Dowdall and Nicholas Colangelo conclude that "the inescapable result [is that the variability] in definitions is of a magnitude that makes the concept of underachieving gifted (students) almost meaningless."[14]

With a single exception—Whitmore's analysis of underachievers based on years of classroom intervention and research—it is our belief that it might be best to throw out what we think we know and start over with a *tabula rasa* on which we might draw conclusions based on new research, new beginnings, and a new set of guidelines regarding underachievement. Specifically, we propose the following:

1. That clear distinction be made between underachievers and selective consumers, as explained in this chapter.

2. That studies look at student behaviors over a span of time, not merely over one school term or one testing situation.

3. That underachievement be defined specifically and painstakingly by individual researchers, so that those who use this research will not generalize a study's findings to other groups of similarly labeled (yet very different) students.

4. That you, as a caring educator, come to understand and appreciate the central role you play in the academic and emotional lives of gifted children who are not performing at levels that all agree they are capable of reaching.

By recognizing the vast and important distinctions between underachievers and selective consumers, and by altering our approaches to working with these children, we will have a better chance of achieving success with smart kids who love to learn, even if their grades and behaviors might have us believe otherwise.

Passion vs. Achievement

by Jason, 14

To some teachers, *passions* are as important as *achievements*. Thank heavens! Some of us just don't seem to be able to make high grades like we should be able to—for whatever reasons—but we still have passions.
   Usually, this "failure" is met with two responses:

1. "He's not really gifted or he would be making better grades," or

2. "He's just not trying hard enough."

   Me? I just hope that gifted people can be happy. If you have an IQ of 160 and if learning every bit of knowledge and going to college at age 12 and making

continued . . .

straight A's is your passion, then go for it! But if you are like me and find that being with people, playing video games, reading about stuff that is interesting, having fun, and laughing a lot is your passion, then I think we should be allowed to do that without feeling guilty that we are letting society down. Bunches of gifted people don't seem to have much fun unless, as I said before, their view of fun has to do solely with books and laboratory mice. Fine for them, just not for me.

A Few Final Thoughts

We wish we could have provided you with a nice, tight definition of underachievement to end this chapter. Unfortunately, that's not possible. Underachievement and selective consumerism are constructs that take on personal interpretations—always. Like other collective nouns—justice, beauty, respect—their definitions cannot be fully appreciated on paper. Like beauty, they are in the eye of the beholder; like justice, they seem to vary depending on the surrounding circumstances; and like respect, you know it when it's there, though explaining exactly what makes it so remains elusive.

Still, having difficulty defining beauty doesn't diminish our enjoyment of seeing it in a painting, a person, or a relationship. And not being able to accurately pinpoint what we mean by justice doesn't keep us from critiquing the latest Supreme Court decision.

So must it be with the underachiever and selective consumer. For even if we can't define them to our own satisfaction, that doesn't diminish our responsibility to Matt, whose passion to make maple sugar is surpassed only by his ability to do so, or to any other student who "does not go to school well" and is, therefore, labeled as something that no one wants to be.

Notes

1. Jane B. Raph, Mirriam L. Goldberg, and A. Harry Passow, *Bright Underachievers* (New York: Teachers College Press, 1966); Gary A. Davis and Sylvia B. Rimm, *Education of the Gifted and Talented,* 4th ed. (Needham Heights, MA: Allyn & Bacon, 1998).

2. S.P. Marland, *Education of the Gifted and Talented: Report to the Subcommittee on Education, Committee on Labor and Public Welfare* (Washington, DC: U.S. Government Printing Office, 1972), p. 25.

3. National Commission on Excellence in Education, *A Nation at Risk: The Imperative for Educational Reform* (Washington, DC: U.S. Government Printing Office, 1983), pp. 8, 18–19, and 28.

4. U.S. Department of Education, Office of Educational Research and Improvement, *National Excellence: A Case for Developing America's Talent* (Washington, DC: U.S. Government Printing Office, 1993), pp. 1, 11, and 13.

5. Jim Delisle, "The Gifted Underachiever: Learning to Underachieve," *The Roeper Review* 4:4 (1982), pp. 16–18.

6. Jane B. Raph and Abraham J. Tannenbaum, *Underachievement: Review of Literature* (New York: Teachers College, Columbia University, 1961).

7. C. Asbury, "Selected Factors Influencing Over and Underachievement in Young School-Age Children," *Review of Education Research* 44 (1974), pp. 409–428; Avner Ziv, *Counseling the Intellectually Gifted Child* (Toronto: The Governing Council of the University of Toronto, 1977).

8. Sally M. Reis and D. Betsy McCoach, "The Underachievement of Gifted Students: What Do We Know and Where Do We Go?" *Gifted Child Quarterly* 44:3 (2000), pp. 152–170.

9. See, for example, Jean A. Baker, Robert Bridger, and Karen Evans, "Models of Underachievement among Gifted Preadolescents: The Role of Personal, Family, and School Factors," *Gifted Child Quarterly* 42:1 (1998), pp. 5–15.

10. Gary A. Davis and Sylvia B. Rimm, *Education of the Gifted and Talented,* 4th ed. (Needham Heights, MA: Allyn & Bacon, 1998).

11. Barbara Clark, *Growing Up Gifted: Developing the Potential of Children at Home and at School,* 5th ed. (Upper Saddle River, NJ: Merrill/Prentice-Hall, 1997), p. 492.

12. Joane R. Whitmore, *Giftedness, Conflict and Underachievement* (Boston: Allyn & Bacon, 1980), pp. 256, 265, and 271.

13. Abraham J. Tannenbaum, *Gifted Children: Psychological and Educational Perspectives* (New York: MacMillan, 1983), p. 210.

14. Cynthia Dowdall and Nicholas Colangelo, "Underachieving Gifted Students: Review and Implications," in *Gifted Child Quarterly* 26:4 (1982), p. 179.

CHAPTER 7

Understanding Gifted Kids from the Outside In

Success means . . .

"Reaching a manifest destiny."
—JASON, 13

"Not having to worry about my manifest destiny."
—JESSIE, 13

(From a graffiti board in a GT Resource Room)

In Chapter 1, we introduce the "Eight Great Gripes of Gifted Kids." The "Student Questionnaire" on pages 40–45 asks kids to identify how often they experience each problem. We briefly discuss the gripes in Chapter 3, page 67, noting that these challenges to gifted children's well-being come from without—from the individual's conflict with the family, school environment, peers, or society in general. Chapter 5 includes an activity on pages 129–130 that focuses on all eight gripes. In this chapter, we consider the gripes individually and provide discussions and activities for each one.

The Eight Great Gripes of Gifted Kids

1. No one explains what being gifted is all about—it's kept a big secret.

2. School is too easy and too boring.

3. Parents, teachers, and friends expect us to be perfect all the time.

4. Friends who really understand us are few and far between.

5. Kids often tease us about being smart.

6. We feel overwhelmed by the number of things we can do in life.

7. We feel different and alienated.

8. We worry about world problems and feel helpless to do anything about them.

Group Discussions of the Eight Great Gripes

Gifted kids need to talk about the challenges, issues, and problems in their lives—and they need to talk with people who will listen, empathize, and understand. There's no better place to do this than in a small group of their peers, led by a teacher or counselor with knowledge of and experience in gifted education. In this setting, gifted kids can be themselves, without worrying about appearing "too smart."

Preparation

If you haven't already asked your students to complete the "Student Questionnaire" on pages 40–45, we suggest that you do so before beginning any of the discussions that follow. It helps to know ahead of time how your students feel about the "Great Gripes," and this questionnaire will tell you.

You may also want to review the "Creating a Supportive Environment" section in Chapter 4: Being a Gifted Teacher (pages 97–122) and use the first four strategies described there:

- "Clarify Your Role as Teacher and Your Students' Roles as Learners" (page 102)

- "Clarify Expectations—Yours and Theirs" (pages 103–104)

- "Set Ground Rules" (pages 104–108)

- "Decide What to Reward and How" (pages 108–110)

These will help to set the stage for a positive group experience for everyone.

Because these discussions touch on personal topics, and talking about personal things takes a certain amount of risk and trust, you may want to go beyond the basic ground rules. Give every student in the group a copy of the "Group Guidelines" on page 216.* Read them aloud or ask group members to read them. Ask if anyone has questions about any of the guidelines. Tell the students that everyone is expected to follow these guidelines—including you.

You might introduce the "Great Gripes" discussions by saying something like this: "Remember the 'Student Questionnaire' I asked you to fill out *[last week, last month, at the start of the year]*? The questionnaire had a section that asked about the conflict in your lives and how often you have certain feelings or problems, like feeling that gift-edness is a big secret, or that people expect you to be perfect all the time. In fact, gifted

---

* These guidelines are adapted from Jean Sunde Peterson, Ph.D., *Talk with Teens About Feelings, Family, Relationships, and the Future* (Minneapolis: Free Spirit Publishing Inc., 1995), p. 19. Used with permission.

kids everywhere have those same feelings or problems. Over the next several *[days, weeks]*, we're going to talk about each one and figure out ways to handle it."

We recommend that if you discuss one "great gripe," you discuss them all. We envision this as a series of eight discussions in the order presented here. If students need reminders of what the "great gripes" are, have copies available of the "Eight Great Gripes of Gifted Kids" handout on page 155.

Discussion of Great Gripe #1:
No one explains what being gifted is all about—it's kept a big secret.

Purpose

To review definitions of giftedness and explain how students qualify for gifted programs.

Preparation

Gather definitions of giftedness including those from your program, other sources, and readings. Prepare a handout on which you have written your program's definition, along with the current federal definition (at this writing, it's the one from the *No Child Left Behind Act of 2001*; see page 15), the *Marland Report* definition (since it's so commonly used; see pages 15–16), and any other definitions you think are worth discussing—for example, your own personal definition.

Be prepared to explain any tests involved with your selection process, as well as the Stanford-Binet Intelligence Scale, properties of the normal ("bell-shaped") curve, and the measuring of standard deviations. Also be prepared to deal with questions concerning the reliability and validity of these tests.

You may find it helpful to review the information in Chapter 1: What Is Giftedness? and Chapter 2: Identifying Gifted Kids.

Procedure

Ask students to arrange their chairs in a circle (or to sit on the floor). Have each person define giftedness, intelligence, or talent. Keep going until no one can think of another definition or characteristic to add. Do this quickly; just have the students name one definition or element after the other, off the tops of their heads. Then distribute the handout you prepared that includes various definitions of giftedness.

Discussion Questions

1. What do you think giftedness means?

2. Is that the only definition there is?

3. How are the definitions on this handout different?

4. Why do you suppose there are so many definitions?

5. Why is giftedness so hard to define?

6. Are gifted people "better" people? How are they different from, and how are they the same as, other people?

7. Do people here today understand how or why they were chosen for this program?

8. Do you have any questions about this program or what's expected of you?

9. What expectations do you have of me, your teacher?

Discussion Guidelines

The group may not reach a consensus on the meaning of giftedness in one discussion. (Adults certainly haven't, so we can hardly expect students to!) Aim to demystify the word, and to clarify why students are in the class or program. Emphasize that we're still learning a lot about exceptional ability and talent. The "gifted" label isn't meant to type-cast people as much as it is to recommend certain kinds of instruction in certain fields.

You'll want to summarize that gifted people are not "better" people, but that other people may be angry about the superiority which the label suggests. Gifted students may be superior academically or in specific areas of talent, but there are many other valuable qualities in human beings, and intellectual or creative abilities are only some of them. How any student develops his or her abilities is what's important, and people at all levels of ability make significant contributions to our world.

For fun, and if time allows, you may want to share "More Possible Meanings for the Acronym IQ" on page 49 with the group.

Finally, tell students that the "gift" they have is theirs, to nurture and share as they can. They don't owe society for having been born with a high potential. They don't owe the world anything more than any other citizen does.

Gifted Kids Speak Out

When we asked gifted students, "What are the best and worst parts of being a gifted child?" here's what they said:

"Best: "I feel proud to be in TAG. I think self-esteem, and learning how to keep it, are really important for being pleased about who you are just the way you are. That's not to say that you can't or shouldn't try to be even better. But you

continued . . .

need to believe in your own basic worth in order to take advantage of the positives of giftedness."
—Scott, 11

"Worst: One of the worst parts about being gifted is boredom in school. We have a lot of slow learners in our class, and my teacher has to explain (and explain, and explain) things. This is very frustrating to those of us who get it the first time."
—Janelle, 10

"Best: Our GT program is really fun and challenging, and our teacher is very encouraging. It's one of my favorite things about school, and I feel lucky to have been chosen for the class."
—Manuel, 10

"Worst: A negative of being gifted is that there's nothing higher than a 4.0 grade point average. I don't get excited about my perfect report card (all A's and 1's), yet all my friends would be ecstatic to even get all B's. I wish there was something higher for me to strive for."
—Annie, 13

Discussion of Great Gripe #2: School is too easy and too boring.

Purpose

To understand what feelings underlie boredom; to clarify what is boring to help students acknowledge their own responsibility for being bored.

Preparation

Gather several large photographs showing close-ups of human faces—people of various ages, from various ethnic and cultural backgrounds. Photography books, magazines, books of portraits, etc., are all good resources. Ideally, you'll have enough that you can give each student a different photograph.

Procedure

This exercise is composed of two parts. First, you'll introduce the topic of boredom, find out how prevalent it is among your students, discuss what they think the causes of boredom are, and hear their feelings about boredom. Then you'll ask them to write about a face in a photograph. This task will take at least 15 minutes, and you'll follow with a summary discussion. Depending on your schedule, you may need to spread the discussion of Great Gripe #2 over two days.

Part One

Have students take their usual seats or find a comfortable spot. Tell them you'll be discussing the subject of boredom.

Discussion Questions

1. Does anyone in here ever feel bored?

2. What is that feeling like?

3. Are there other feelings that seem to go along with boredom? What are they? Can you describe or name them? (*Common responses are anger, disappointment, frustration, and resentment.*)

4. When do you feel most bored? Can you predict which things—which events, subjects, people, obligations, or tasks—will bore you most? Has this type of thing always bored you?

5. What can you do about being bored?

Discussion Guidelines

Try to get students to look at all the feelings that go along with the phrase "I'm bored." Kids often say they're bored when they really mean something else, such as "I'm afraid to make the effort," or "I'm lonely," or "I really don't know how to focus or get involved," or "I'm angry they're making me do this again," or "I'm mad about something unrelated." By probing and rephrasing, you should be able to elicit some of these feelings. If students are angry about schoolwork, they're also probably frustrated and depressed that people don't recognize the work is boring, or don't trust them to work on something more meaningful.

Knowing specifically what is boring is useful self-knowledge. Not everyone will be interested in everything. Try to get students to list very specifically what bores them. Is it chemistry? School dances? Cars? Television? Math? Basketball? Questions about feelings? Politics? Being told what to do? Being 13 years old? If "the whole system" bores them, this may point to a larger problem involving anger and self-esteem.

Write down the various actions students say they can take when they're bored, but hold your comments until you've finished Part Two.

Part Two

Have students choose a photograph of a face, study it, and write about the face. Tell them they'll have 15 minutes to do this. Explain that their "essay" doesn't need a beginning, middle, or end, it won't be judged on literary merit, and you don't care about their grammar. Ask them to focus; to stay engaged; to keep looking for something interesting in the face; to keep finding something there to observe and describe.

This exercise is about seeing, and realizing there is always something more there, if one looks long enough. For this reason, it needs to last long enough to stretch students' usual period of concentration. Fifteen minutes may or may not be long enough. When students start looking around as though they're bored, press them to keep looking and keep writing, even when they think they've said it all.

Discussion Questions

1. What kinds of things did you write about?

2. As you spent time looking at the person's face, did you discover anything about it that surprised you—that you didn't see in the beginning?

3. How many people found it hard to keep writing? Did you reach a point when there seemed to be nothing new to say?

4. For those of you who kept writing, how did you keep yourself involved? What did you do to keep going?

Discussion Guidelines

Find out and discuss what kinds of observations, descriptions, and stories the students wrote. Were the essays imaginative? Factual? Personal in nature? Emphasize how many different approaches students took with the same exercise. If they all say they were bored, try the exercise again, giving them more clues on how to stay involved. Examples: "Highlight what you see visually." "Fantasize about the person. What is the person thinking or feeling? What kind of life has the person had?"

If students were able to push themselves beyond initial observation and discover something new, reward them. Ask them to relate their discovery and describe the feeling it gave them.

The wrap-up for this discussion is, of course, that we are all somewhat responsible for our own boredom. Sometimes our boredom is in direct proportion to the amount of effort or energy we invest in a subject. Typically, we choose not to invest much of ourselves in a subject that is difficult, threatening, or simply unappealing, thus automatically lessening the return we might get from it.

A constantly bored student may be a fantastically brilliant, accelerated-type learner, but be skeptical! He may also be a floater, not able to risk self-disclosure, failure, or personal energy. What's more, kids today are used to being passively entertained, whereas all the best strategies for combating boredom require action.

Stress concrete steps to take when students are bored. Refer to their own solutions: Encourage them to find out more about "uninteresting topics" and to take risks by trying new approaches to old problems. Generally, solutions boil down to "Change what you can change, avoid what you really need to avoid, and make it interesting when you can." Reinforce the notion that they have more power over their boredom than they think.

Creative Tips for Battling Boredom

by Felice Kaufmann, Ph.D.

Felice Kaufmann, Ph.D., is an independent consultant in gifted child education. She came up with this list of unusual ways to combat boredom at school. Share them with your students—and see if they have any equally creative ideas of their own.

■ Alternate the school supplies you use. Use different colored notebook paper every day. Write with a different pen. Plan a monthly trip to buy new school supplies instead of buying the whole year's worth all at once. It may sound simplistic, but for some people, the novelty of different pens, paper, and the like really helps!

■ Use "idea traps"—like self-sticking notes or small notepads—to record and collect the good ideas you have when you're supposed to be thinking of something else. Challenge yourself to keep up with what's going on in class while thinking your own thoughts. This is called "multitasking"—and for some people, it's a preferred way of learning!

■ While listening to the teacher or doing your work, use another part of your brain to turn your classroom into a movie set. Think about how the room would look from different camera angles. Create a soundtrack. Imagine different scenery and costumes. For example, picture your class taking place on the moon and visualize your classmates wearing spacesuits. Who knows—you could turn out to be the next Steven Spielberg!

continued . . .

■ Ask fun questions to yourself about whatever topic is being discussed, like: How could a clown use this information? How could my favorite movie star use this information? How could I use this information in spring, summer, winter, or fall? At midnight versus 8 A.M.? How might I use it ten years from now? How would I explain this to my dog? See how many different questions you can come up with in five minutes.

■ Make lists of *everything*. Gifts you want to buy for yourself or someone else. Ideas for your science fair project. Places you want to go now and in the future. Slogans for your presidential campaign. Your favorite meals or songs. Keep all your lists in one folder or notebook. Each week review your lists and decide which ideas you want to pursue now and which you want to set aside for a later date.

■ Ask your teacher to let you sit in a different chair when you get bored. Tell him or her that the change in environment will help you stay alert.

■ Play the game of opposites. If you're learning about multiplication, how is it similar to, and different from, its opposite, division? How is a comedy like and unlike a drama? How are girls like and unlike boys?

■ Suspend rules of logic. Wonder about how a noun feels about being a noun, or whether a tree would rather be a bird, or whether the number three would rather be the number five.

Some of these may sound crazy, but the whole point is to keep your imagination going and to keep you connected to the material that is being taught.

Discussion of Great Gripe #3: Parents, teachers, and friends expect us to be perfect all the time.

Purpose

To discuss sources of perfectionism (self, parents, teachers, "society"), feelings associated with perfectionism, and ways to handle perfectionism; to help students understand the difference between perfectionism and the pursuit of excellence.

Preparation

Review the "Perfectionism" section in Chapter 3: Emotional Dimensions of Giftedness (pages 64–66). Make copies of "Perfectionism vs. the Pursuit of Excellence" on page 217.

Procedure

Arrange students in a circle, introduce the topic, and have students help generate the agenda. Begin by listing two or three agenda items yourself, then request others. Once the discussion gets going, you may want to let other students moderate the discussion (one at a time, of course). This gives them a chance to practice leadership skills and also helps the group to focus on itself, rather than looking to you for answers.

Possible Agenda Items

- sources of perfectionism
- feelings associated with failure
- what to do about expectations—ours and theirs
- a healthy alternative to perfectionism

Discussion Questions

1. Who says you have to be perfect? How do they say it? If the message isn't verbal, how does it come out? Why do you suppose they expect or want you to be perfect?

2. Is it possible to be perfect? In anything? In everything? Some of the time? All of the time?

3. What are your standards or goals? Are they realistic or idealistic? Which should they be?

4. What happens when you're less than perfect? How do you feel when you get answers wrong or receive less than an A?

5. How many people feel anxious about being "good enough"? How many people worry about their grades?

6. Who should set your performance standards?

7. What answers can you give to people who expect too much?

8. How else can you protect yourself against unrealistically high expectations—your own and other people's?

9. Does anyone think there might be an alternative to perfectionism—a positive, healthy way to approach achievement and success?

Discussion Guidelines

In the beginning of the discussion, kids will simply need to ventilate about how everyone else expects unreasonable things from them, values them only when they perform well, or "punishes" them in some manner for poor performance. Let students air their views, but also try to get them to articulate how these expectations are conveyed (have them "reality-test" their perceptions). Some of the messages they hear may be ambiguous, some may be unmistakably clear—and some may be entirely in their heads. Periodically summarize for them the sources of their perfectionism and ask how frequently they hear the messages urging them to be perfect.

Get students to explore their intrinsic needs for success and perfection. Introduce the idea that their own expectations may influence how they perceive other people's expectations, and that their own internal goals and needs can be more powerful and more fulfilling in the long run.

Some of the clues to perfectionism lie in the emotions that accompany "failure" (lack of perfection). What are the consequences of poor performance? Loss of identity? ("She must not be as smart as we thought," or "Perhaps he's not gifted after all.") Heavy guilt and anxiety suggest a deep need to satisfy parents and teachers, and concern about being valued as a person rather than being valued for high performance. Disappointment and anger suggest a need to satisfy one's own internal standards, and perhaps the inability to admit to certain limitations. ("I can't be gifted if I don't get all A's.") Have students try to name the emotions they feel upon "failing," and ask them to analyze the source of that feeling.

One's defense in the face of perfectionism depends on its source. If parents are the taskmasters, then students need to understand their parents' feelings (a misunderstanding of what perfectionism really is and means? wanting only the best for their children? love and concern? self-aggrandizement?) and find appropriate answers to it. Talk about ways in which students might approach their parents on this topic. What might they say? How might they express their own feelings about their performance and achievements? How might they differentiate between their personal goals and their parents' goals for them? If societal or educators' views are the source, then appropriate responses to them need to be found. Is a particular teacher the problem? (Are *you* the problem?) If the source of conflict is partially or predominantly internal, the student needs to learn how to become his or her own "best friend" or supporter rather than taskmaster. Encouragement, support, and careful goal-setting can help here.

If time allows, you might read aloud the section on "Perfectionism" on pages 64–66. Read the list of characteristics in the "Perfectionism-At-a-Glance" box on pages 65–66, and invite students to consider which ones describe them.

After students have responded to question 9, distribute the "Perfectionism vs. the Pursuit of Excellence" handout. Ask students to read it, reflect on it, and share their views about what it has to say. Tell them that you made this a handout because you want them to keep it and refer to it often.

Discussion of Great Gripe #4: Friends who really understand us are few and far between.

Purpose

To tell stories about friendship; to contrast loneliness with aloneness and popularity with friendship; to share common questions about friendship, and possible answers; to introduce ideas for making and keeping friends that students can try.

Preparation

Make copies of "Questions and Answers About Friends and Friendship" on pages 218–219 and "Twelve Tips for Making and Keeping Friends" on pages 220–221.

Procedure

Tell the students that for the first part of this discussion, you're going to divide the group into three teams. Explain that each team will spend 10 to 15 minutes sharing stories about friendship. Then you'll reconvene to discuss the differences between friendship and popularity, and between aloneness and loneliness.

Before breaking the large group into small groups, give the students these instructions:

Each person in your group is to think of an episode, real or imaginary, involving a friend.

This can be either a positive or negative episode. You can describe the ideal friend or the worst possible friend. The episode can express what you long for in a friendship, what you fear about friendship, what you don't understand, or what you regret.

When you have your episode in mind, tell it to the group.

While someone is talking, the other group members are to listen without interrupting until the speaker is finished.

When the speaker is finished, the group may comment on or ask questions about the story.

While the students are working in their small groups, circulate among them and listen to their stories. Ask questions like these:

1. Why did you choose to tell that particular story?

2. How many other people have had an experience like that, or imagined that kind of incident?

3. Why do you suppose the friend behaved that way (so rottenly, so generously)?

4. How do you (the speaker) feel now, when you think back on that episode?

5. What kind of friend does that make you want to be?

Once you've reconvened the large group, ask a couple of students if they would share their episodes. Ask them if they have any additional comments; ask them if they learned about some common feelings and experiences.

Next, write these two pairs of words on the board as large headings above blank columns:

Loneliness/Aloneness   Popularity/Friendship

Tell the students that you want to discuss the differences between loneliness and aloneness, and between popularity and friendship. During the discussion, list the attributes of each beneath its appropriate heading.

After students have voted on the most important qualities for a friend to have (discussion question 8), hand out copies of "Questions and Answers About Friendship." Tell the students that these are questions that many gifted kids have. You might want to go through the handout one question at a time. What do your students think of the questions? Do they sound familiar? What do they think of the answers?

Finally, say that you have a list of ideas you'd like to share with them. Hand out copies of "Twelve Tips for Making and Keeping Friends." Invite students to try one or more of these ideas before the group meets again. Maybe they can report back to the group next time on what worked and didn't work for them.

Depending on your schedule, you may need to spread the discussion of Great Gripe #4 over two days.

Discussion Questions

1. How do you feel when you're alone? When you're lonely? What's the same? What's different?

2. Does anyone like being alone? Or lonely?

3. Is it possible to be alone without being lonely?

4. How can you tell when other people are lonely?

5. Name some examples of famous people in history or fiction, TV programs, movies, or whatever whom you suspect are or were lonely. Explain why you chose them.

6. What personal qualities make a good friend? What qualities make a good friendship?

7. What personal qualities make someone popular? Are the qualities the same as those you look for in a good friend? Which characteristics overlap and which are unique?

8. What are the most important qualities for a friend to have? Let's vote . . .

Discussion Guidelines

Telling tales of friendships past and future is a positive way to ease into some pretty intense feelings. If students need coaxing to open up, be ready with an anecdote of your own to start the group rolling. Or bring a few passages from literature (fiction or biography) to serve as examples. One of our personal favorites is the "Loneliness" chapter from E.B. White's classic story, *Charlotte's Web*, but you'll have to decide what's appropriate for your group.

Summarize what the groups discover in terms of common human needs. In friendships and groups, we seek such things as acceptance, identity, loyalty, support, companionship, advice, solace, and power. Relate how their episodes underscore any of these human needs.

Some of the sting can be taken out of aloneness if students realize its benefits. Solitude can be a wonderfully creative state; it provides time and space for reflection and integration. Artists, inventors, musicians, writers, and presidents learn to tolerate solitude, and many people crave it. Aloneness should not be feared as an unnatural state, for solitude is not a problem; loneliness is.

Remind students that one doesn't necessarily need a lot of friends. One or two close friends may be enough. Great popularity usually falls to outgoing people who possess qualities others admire and wish to emulate, yet who remain within the range of "normal" or familiar. Popular leaders represent the more dominant values of the group. Popular girls look and dress in ways most conforming to group tastes; popular guys use language adopted by the dominant clique. When popularity depends on conformity to norms, this often excludes the highly gifted student.

But sometimes highly popular people are also lonely. They may have the acquaintanceship of many and the friendship of few. Friendship should provide a refuge from having to perform, and it should respect differences as well as similarities.

Close by summarizing ways to handle aloneness and loneliness. Recap students' observations regarding good friends. What are those good friends capable of doing? How do they do it? How can we all make better friends? How can we, as a group, help each other out?

Looking Back on Friendship

by Jeremy Shorr, age 20

During my first two years of school at Ohio University, I have had several people tell me how much they wish they were "gifted." They inform me how everything must have always been easy for me. They tell me how the problems a "normal" person has while growing up must have seemed trivial to me. They let me know that I should always consider myself lucky. Looking back on my earlier years of education, I do consider myself lucky, but I didn't always feel that way.

Growing up gifted yields many rewards and advantages, but the road to those rewards is not easy. Contrary to how some people may feel, we do go through the same thoughts and emotions that every other school-age person does. Being gifted does not mean being without feelings.

During elementary school, several people tried to push me in the direction of new groups of friends who were gifted. That was a problem, though, because I didn't want to be pushed in their direction. Although it is very important for the gifted student to have peers he can make intelligent conversation with, it is equally important for that student to be allowed to be a kid. My friends were the kids considered to be "popular"—and many people from outside this group had a problem with my being inside it. Many of my friends would tease other kids for being geeks. I tried to stay away from participating in these kinds of things, but I can't say that I never did them. This is what made people angry: They couldn't understand how I could stay friends with people who didn't always accept everyone. But these friends were there for me when I needed them. They took care of me if I needed help, and most of all I just liked spending time with them.

In fourth grade, I joined the gifted program. The students in this class often shared my opinions and always shared my craving for new knowledge. After only a short period of time, these kids became my friends, too.

You might think that this would solve all my problems, but actually, it made things worse. My old friends gave me a hard time for hanging out with these new ones. Everywhere I turned, people seemed to want me to choose one group of friends or the other—but not both. I knew there had to be another solution.

That solution came in time. I realized that there was nothing wrong with having more than one group of friends. My new friends offered an intellectual outlet that I had needed. They showed me that there was nothing wrong with

continued . . .

being gifted. My old friends were the ones close to my heart. They were always there for me, they would always protect me if it were within their power, and they always assured me that everything would be OK. In time, I even convinced my older friends that there was nothing wrong with these other gifted kids.

In retrospect, I do consider myself lucky. I had lots of friends who cared about me. It seems so simple now, but when I was growing up, it couldn't have been more confusing.

Discussion of Great Gripe #5:
Kids often tease us about being smart.

Purpose

To learn how to respond to teasing in a nonthreatened, nonthreatening way.

Procedure

As a group, discuss what teasing is all about, what forms it comes in, and its effects on both the teaser and the person being teased. Next, brainstorm responses to teasing. Conclude by discussing positive ways to respond to differences.

Discussion Questions

1. Do any of you ever get teased? What are you teased about? What words or things are said?

2. When people tease you, how do you feel? Is what they say about you accurate and true? Do you have to listen to it and accept it?

3. Do some kinds of teasing feel okay, and other kinds make you extremely furious or upset? What's the difference? Can you give me some examples?

4. Why do you suppose people tease others? What do you suppose is going on inside them, and with their feelings about themselves?

5. Have you ever teased anyone? Someone who was younger, or different? Do you remember why you teased him or her? How did it make you feel?

6. When someone teases you, either a little or a lot, what do you usually do? What would you like to do? What would you ultimately like to have happen about this teasing? (*Discuss whichever one or ones apply.*)

- I just want the teaser to leave me alone.

- I'd actually like to be friends with the teaser.

- I want the teaser to shut up and respect me.

- I'd like to get even—teach the teaser a lesson.

- I don't mind the teasing. It helps ease the tension, and it's meant in fun.

As a group, try brainstorming some possible answers for each "outcome" or solution listed above. For instance, students might choose to ignore certain remarks if they want to be left alone; think of something witty or sensibly cool if they want to earn some respect; and invent something equally humiliating if they need revenge. List possible responses on the board. Talk about how they sound and what they might accomplish.

The kids could get carried away here playing around with nasty retorts. A little of this might be appropriate, particularly for some shy kids who need practice standing up for themselves. But keep asking/reminding students that what they probably want is to be included, at least respected, or just left alone. Inflammatory remarks don't tend to buy you those outcomes. The best defense usually is to not let the teasing "get to" you, but to make light of it or to respond assertively if it continues.

Some suggested responses to teasing are:

- Big deal. Who cares about that?

- I don't have a problem with that. Do you?

- Personally, I'm glad I'm different.

- Frankly, that's my best part! (Or my best quality.)

- Why, thank you! I didn't think you had noticed!

- Are you still hung up about that?

- You know, I really couldn't care less what you think.

- Hey, you're above that.

- I was just starting to like you! Why use names like that?

- I have a right to be a klutz! Geez, give a guy a chance!

- Give me a break! Who said I was perfect?

Discussion Guidelines

People who are different get teased. If His Holiness the Dalai Lama walked into the room tomorrow, someone might make fun of his lack of hair, his monk's robes, his speech, his movements. Unfortunately, humiliating other people about their differences makes us feel "one up" on them.

Kids who are different are going to be teased, so gifted kids will probably qualify on several counts. Tell students that some teasing may be inevitable, but that doesn't make the substance of the remarks necessarily true. Gifted students' differences don't necessarily make them "weird," "a snot," "a ninety-pound weakling," "a nerd," or "Miss Perfect." It just means they're different, and certain people feel powerful when ridiculing them about it. When the teasing contains a grain of truth in it, sometimes the best tactic is to agree to and exaggerate it, as some of the examples above did. ("I have a right to be a klutz!" "Who said I was perfect?")

Teasing at its worst is not a particularly pleasant trait. But it is human, and we have all dished it out at some time as well as been the brunt of it. Some forms of teasing are also more tolerable than others, and we enjoy people we can kid around with and who understand that our jokes are meant in fun. For gifted kids, however, the issues may be too sensitive to withstand remarks even meant in fun. As the gifted kid relaxes about her or his differences and learns to see the light side of things, the teasing will lessen. As a teacher, you can provide healthy examples by laughing at your own mistakes or idiosyncrasies, but stopping short of playing the clown.

Conclude the discussion by asking students to generate some ground rules about teasing they'd like to have for the classroom.

Discussion of Great Gripe #6: We feel overwhelmed by the number of things we can do in life.

Purpose

To examine specific choices facing students; to discuss the problems of pursuing one endeavor or interest.

Preparation

Review "Coping with the Frustration of Having Too Many Options" on pages 140–144.

Procedure

Have students write their own obituaries. Start them off with these instructions:

You have 20 minutes to write your own obituary. Presume that you have had a long and full life and opportunities to accomplish much of what you'd like to do.

Your obituary should contain facts (such as your schooling, your occupation, residence, whether you married or had children) as well as major accomplishments.

Be sure to include personal characteristics, such as "A shy and private woman, she is best remembered for her terrific creativity, and her love of chocolate and cats."

Discussion Questions

Ask for a few volunteers to read their obituaries aloud to the group. Ask each volunteer one or more of the following questions:

1. What did you think about as you wrote this?

2. How did you arrive at these projections?

3. Did you have to make choices (between career options or accomplishments), or did you include everything you'd like to do?

4. How did you make these choices? How did you determine what was important?

5. Is it hard to make choices? Why or why not?

6. How possible do you suppose it is to have the life you've described?

7. What do you suppose you'd have to do to have this life?

Discussion Guidelines

Explain to students that the purpose of the exercise is to help them focus on what is most important to them in life. Looking at this "after the fact," from the perspective of the obituary, does this quite neatly. For here, one has to contemplate the answers to questions like these:

■ How do I want to be remembered?

■ What are my ambitions?

■ What do I expect to accomplish?

■ What is most meaningful to me—awards, job titles, books published, community or social service, money acquired, family?

■ Will I be remembered for my generosity to nonprofit causes, leadership in my community, or dedication to duck hunting?

■ Will I have some notable defeats as well as successes? ("She lost her second bid for the senate but won the race for governor." "After a mountain climbing accident, he didn't perform for another ten years; when he did, it was to a sell-out crowd.")

■ Will I have a family?

■ Will I have several careers?

■ Will I have several major interests?

■ Will I lead a life of obscurity or notoriety?

During the discussion, try to have students articulate why they made the projections they did and what choices they saw for themselves. Did they have to decide whether their final interest would lie in playing the piano or conducting the orchestra? Between choreography or dancing? Between teaching or raising children? Between medical research or practice? What kinds of personal values came into play with their decision-making?

Depending on the students' age, you may want to discuss what kinds of investments (time, energy, money) need to be made to pursue particular careers and the types of training involved. Although the career counselor at your school can help older students with these specifics, you might start kids thinking about their human and financial limitations. Emphasize also, however, that lifetimes are long, and opportunities to change course are ample.

Conclude by saying that, in general, having too many options before you is preferable to having too few. Having little or no choice in one's life is confining and stressful. Flexibility and multipotential are two of the best "problems" in life to have. The difficulty with too many options seems to stem from one or more of these feelings:

- you have to choose too soon what you want to do

- it's hard to isolate or concentrate on one option—they all seem related and equally valid

- you can't decide which option will be better in the long run

- you want to do it all—you don't want to give up or let go of one part of it

Discuss these options with the students and see what ramifications come with taking each option. What happens if you decide on a career too early? Too late? What happens if you try to do it all? What happens if you choose the wrong option? You can relieve their anxiety by telling them that they have time to make up their minds; that they can change their minds; that they may not be able to "do it all" all at once, but they may be able to do a lot of it spread out over their entire life. Reinforce the notion that choices have to be made—life will force you to make them. Yet choosing among alternatives is basically healthy. It helps you channel energy into an area long enough to succeed in it.

For an interesting variation on this exercise, ask students to write an obituary for someone else in the class. Make sure that everyone has a partner. As long as known enemies are not paired, students may learn something constructive about how other people perceive them.

Discussion of Great Gripe #7: We feel different and alienated.

Purpose

To help students feel more comfortable with being different.

Preparation

Locate a former student from the gifted program, or an adult in the community who has been identified as gifted, and invite the person to speak to the class. Ask him or her to address particular questions pertaining to peers, problems with isolation, connecting with a profession or avocation, and fitting in socially. You'll want your guest to talk about the rest of his or her life as well, but make sure the person understands that you're looking for an adult role model who can talk about the pains of isolation and growing up "so differently" from other kids. Have students prepare for this speaker by writing down questions in advance.

Suggested Questions for the Speaker

1. Can you talk about your current profession, or avocation, or interests?

2. How did you figure out what you wanted to do in life? When did you become involved with . . . ?

3. Can you talk about some of your experiences growing up? What was it like for you at your school(s)?

4. Were you in any special program(s)? Did you receive any special instruction?

5. How were you different from other kids? How were you similar to them?

6. Who were your friends? Were friendships a problem for you?

7. How did you get along with your siblings and parents?

8. It's been said by some gifted students that being gifted is something that doesn't "pay off" until you're grown up. As a kid, you're only penalized for it. Is that true in your case? How can we help kids realize the benefits of being different at a young age?

9. What other advice for gifted kids do you have?

Facilitate group discussion between your guest speaker and kids after the speaker's prepared discussion is over. Perhaps the speaker could brainstorm, with you and the students, ways we could all better appreciate differences among people.

Gifted Kids Speak Out

"I was involved in a gifted and talented program in third through fourth grades. I loved every second of the actual class. But my main problem with this type of class is that while mentally/academically I was ready, emotionally I wasn't. Too often, in these classes, too much emphasis is placed on how smart we are. The academic talents are nurtured, yet the social ones are taken for granted. Yet, all the math problems in the world can't make a friendship. Other kids made fun of us as nerds or called us stuck-up. It was not true, it was just that we weren't sure how to relate to some of our peers. We were informed that we were smarter by our teachers, but to a child, that is just plain 'different.' We needed help understanding ourselves."
—**Erin, 19**

"Gifted kids tend to hide their intelligence, as well as their talents, for a very simple reason: Conformity."
—**Claudia, 16**

Discussion of Great Gripe #8: We worry about world problems and feel helpless to do anything about them.

Purpose

To discuss students' feeling about world problems and generate possible ways to respond to these problems.

Procedure

Use a general group discussion as a way to invite students to voice their concerns and questions and decide the limits of their responsibility. Then brainstorm as a group possible courses of action on one or two of the most common shared concerns.

Introduce the topic by saying:

Today we're going to talk about how affected we feel by certain world problems. It's been said that advanced technology, like television and satellite communications, is bringing the world closer together; that the world is becoming a "global village." Although this may be good in some ways, it certainly makes us more aware of how stressful life can be. Violence from around the world comes into our living rooms via

TV, radio, newspapers, and the Internet. On the other hand, by exposing conflicts to many world nations simultaneously, the media may be helping to contain violence.

After discussing questions 1–6, say:

Now that we've talked about the kinds of problems that worry us, and some specific questions we have about these problems, let's take one of these concerns and brainstorm what you, individually or in a group, could do about it.

Write the problem on the board and list the ideas students brainstorm.

Discussion Questions

1. Are there any world problems you feel especially concerned about?

2. How have you learned about this? From your parents? From school? From the media? What do these sources have to say about it?

3. Is this a confusing issue for you? Do you understand why it's a problem (why people in the Middle East are fighting; why people are demonstrating against oil drilling in certain places such as the Arctic National Wildlife Refuge; why terrorism is directed at the United States)?

4. Would you like to get more information on this subject? Where or how do you suppose you could get it?

5. Do people at home or in this room have strong feelings about this topic? What are they?

6. Are there any other social problems, perhaps closer to home (in your neighborhood or city), that concern you? *(Repeat questions 2–5 for this and other concerns.)*

Discussion Guidelines

In leading this discussion, be prepared for two kinds of problems. One is the student who is so overly sensitive to world problems, particularly suffering and violence, that she can't separate herself from them and feels overly responsible for them. It's very hard to accept millions of people starving in a faraway country, or the threat of nuclear holocaust emanating from certain nations around the world. But a student shouldn't feel the suffering of others to the extent that it immobilizes her, or feel such extreme anxiety for the future when the future is yet to be.

Rather than working to increase the sensitivity of this student, relieve her of her guilt feelings and help her to put the situation in a place separate from herself. Invite her to learn more about the issues (both the positive and negative aspects) and to take constructive social action. But remind her also that she is healthy and safe; that she has time to grow up and deal with these problems as an adult; and that she is not expected to take them on single-handedly right now, at this point in her life. Empirical evidence shows the world will probably continue to turn, despite the most terrible events.

The second kind of problem concerns the opposite type of student, one who is apathetic and lacks sensitivity toward people suffering in remote places in circumstances he can't relate to. This student is probably uncomfortable discussing world problems. He doesn't want them to concern him, and therefore believes that they don't. Or he believes the government or some superpower is controlling things, which means—for better or worse—that it's out of his hands and he can't do anything about it.

For this student, you may want to emphasize how important individual efforts can be. Ask students whether they can think of a time when the collective efforts of many people changed the course of history (or life in their city, town, neighborhood, school, or family). Emphasize how basically similar all human beings are in terms of needs and wants, regardless of their nationality or status. Ask students to join in a discussion about what the proper level of responsibility for others is—how important it is to care about other people even when their troubles don't involve us directly.

Depending on the kinds of opinions expressed and the types of students in your classroom, you may want to turn the discussion into a spontaneous debate. Or ask students to debate the issues and their chosen course of action at a later date.

For many students, the horrific events of September 11, 2001, brought world problems very close to home. Like many of us on that day and for many days afterward, they may have been glued to the television, watching scenes and images they'll never forget. Some may have known people who died in the World Trade Center, the Pentagon, or the plane that crashed in Pennsylvania. Subsequent events—the anthrax scare, heightened airport security, the war in Afghanistan (which suddenly didn't seem so far away), and the escalating crises in the Middle East made us all feel more vulnerable than we ever had before. Don't be surprised if 9/11 is a major focus of your discussion. If there was ever a day when Americans (and people around the world) felt utterly helpless, that was the day.

Another kind of issue that may come up during discussion is that of accepting or rejecting adults' belief systems. Students are in the process of developing their own beliefs and values—about abortion, marriage, politics, religion, terrorism, and nuclear armament. They may be particularly eager to talk about how their views differ from those of their parents, or how influenced they have been by a socially conscious parent.

In conclusion, help students understand that there is much to sorrow for in the world, but much to rejoice over as well. We all need to "work for a better world," and every effort counts. Clarify whatever misconceptions of theirs you discover. (In one discussion of nuclear war, it was discovered that students thought there were hundreds of "buttons" all over the world that anyone could push to blow up the planet at any time.) Bring unrealistic fears back down to the ground. Encourage students to take action on social issues because it is morally good, and working for change can make one feel more positive. But dissuade them from feeling overly responsible (particularly as the "gifted youth of tomorrow") for saving the world.

You may want to work through the year building your list of possible actions to take in assuming social responsibility. Options such as letter writing, newsletter or article writing, neighborhood organizations, fact-finding tours, individual recycling habits, demonstrations, forming committees, joining national organizations, sending private donations, and volunteer work can highlight how many individual and collective activities can be pursued.

Group Guidelines

1. Anything that is said in the group stays in the group. We agree to keep things confidential.

2. We respect what other group members say. We agree not to use put-downs of any kind, verbal or nonverbal.

3. We respect everyone's need to be heard.

4. We listen to each other. When someone is speaking, we look at him or her and pay attention.

5. We realize that feelings are not "bad" or "good." They just are. Therefore, we don't say things like "You shouldn't feel that way."

6. We are willing to take risks, to explore new ideas, and to explain our feelings as well as we can. However, we agree that someone who doesn't want to talk doesn't have to talk.

7. We are willing to let others know us. We agree that talking and listening are ways for people to get to know each other.

8. We realize that sometimes people feel misunderstood, or they feel that someone has hurt them accidentally or on purpose. We agree that the best way to handle those times is by talking and listening.

9. We agree to be honest and to do our best to speak from the heart.

10. We don't talk about group members who aren't present. We especially don't criticize group members who aren't here to defend themselves.

11. When we do need to talk about other people—such as teachers and peers—we don't refer to them by name unless it is absolutely necessary. For example, we may want to ask the group to help us solve a problem we are having with a particular person.

12. We agree to attend group meetings regularly. If for some reason we can't attend a meeting, we will try to let the teacher know ahead of time.

Perfectionism vs. the Pursuit of Excellence

There is a healthy alternative to perfectionism. It's called the Pursuit of Excellence. Here are three ways in which the two differ:

1. Perfectionism means thinking *less* of yourself because you earned a B+ instead of an A. **The Pursuit of Excellence** means thinking *more* of yourself for trying something new.

2. Perfectionism means being hard on yourself because you aren't equally talented in all sports. **The Pursuit of Excellence** means choosing some things you know you'll be good at—and others you know will be good for you or just plain fun.

3. Perfectionism means beating yourself up because you lost the student council election. **The Pursuit of Excellence** means congratulating yourself because you were nominated, and deciding to run again next year—if that's what you want.

How can you become a Pursuer of Excellence? By:
- determining the sources of your perfectionism
- reassessing your feelings about failure and success
- standing your ground against people who pressure you to be perfect
- learning ways to be easier on yourself so you're free to take risks and try new things

What other ideas do you have for pursuing excellence? For avoiding the perfectionism trap?

_____

_____

_____

_____

_____

Questions and Answers About Friends and Friendship

Q: *Some of my friends seem to resent me, or they're prejudiced against me because I'm gifted. Why is that?*

A: Usually, people have prejudices when they don't understand something or someone. They may feel inferior if they don't have enough good things going on in their own lives. So putting you down may make them feel better about themselves (at least for the moment). Just be yourself, and they may come around—or you may need to start hanging out with other people.

Q: *Does everyone have trouble making friends, or is it just me?*

A: Relax; it's not just you. Some people seem to make friends effortlessly—they're in the right place at the right time with the right social skills. Other people find it difficult to connect because of shyness, circumstances, or whatever. But everyone—whether adept or awkward—has to work at forming and sustaining meaningful friendships.

Q: *I don't have any trouble making friends, so why is there all this talk about gifted people being social misfits?*

A: It's true that many gifted children and teens make friends easily, but for others it's not so easy. They might perceive themselves as "social misfits," which sabotages their self-confidence. Also, some people assume that because gifted kids are brighter and more intellectually advanced than their peers, they will automatically have problems relating to so-called "normal" kids.

Q: *Does it matter if my friends are two, three, or even four years older or younger than I am?*

A: No! Adults have friendships with people of all ages, so why shouldn't you? What matters is to cultivate friends you can count on and relate to. Sharing the same birth year isn't as important as sharing interests, goals, and values.

continued . . .

Questions and Answers About Friends and Friendship continued . . .

Q: *Is it normal to have just a few close friends?*

A: Yes! Gifted children and teens tend to be more adult-like in their relationships, favoring a few intense relationships over several more casual ones. What's important is to have at least one or two friends that you can rely on. When it comes to relationships, quality matters more than quantity.

Q: *Do I have to conform to be accepted?*

A: It's not a bad thing to go along with the crowd—as long as the crowd is right for you. It's only when you compromise your own values, beliefs, and goals that conformity becomes a problem and can even be dangerous. On the other hand, if you always insist on doing things your way, be prepared for a lonely life.

Q: *I've just met someone I'd like to be friends with, and he asked me what "gifted" means. What can I say that won't alienate him or sound arrogant?*

A: You might begin by asking him what he thinks it means. If he's serious about wanting to know, this could lead to an interesting discussion about your individual points of view. Remember, there are no right or wrong answers about giftedness, and even the experts can't agree on a single definition. By now, you probably have your own ideas about giftedness. Share as much or as little as you want.

Q: *How can I cope with "leech" friends—people who rely on me for homework and test answers?*

A: First, ask yourself, "Are they really my friends?" People who like you only for what they can get from you don't qualify as "friends." So that's something you'll have to decide. Second, if you feel like helping (with homework, not with test answers), and if you have the time, then go ahead and do it. Otherwise, simply explain that you have your own work to do and you're not available this time around. Maybe the "leeches" will take the hint—or maybe not.

Twelve Tips for Making and Keeping Friends

1.

Reach out. Don't always wait for someone else to make the first move. A simple "hi" and a smile go a long way. It may sound corny, but you'll be amazed at the response you'll receive when you extend a friendly greeting.

2.

Get involved. Join clubs that interest you; take special classes inside or outside of school. Seek out neighborhood and community organizations and other opportunities to give service to others.

3.

Let people know that you're interested in them. Don't just talk about yourself; ask questions about them and their interests. Make this a habit and you'll have mastered the art of conversation. It's amazing how many people haven't yet grasped this basic social skill.

4.

Be a good listener. This means looking at people while they're talking to you and genuinely paying attention to what they're saying. (A long litany of "uh-huhs" is a dead giveaway that your mind is somewhere else.)

5.

Risk telling people about yourself. When it feels right, let your interests and talents be known. For example, if you love science fiction and you'd like to know others who feel the same way, spread the word. If you're an expert on the history of science fiction, you might want to share your knowledge. BUT . . .

6.

Don't be a show-off. Not everyone you meet will share your interests and abilities. (On the other hand, you shouldn't have to hide them—which you won't, once you find people who like and appreciate you.)

continued . . .

Twelve Tips for Making and Keeping Friends continued . . .

7.

Be honest. Tell the truth about yourself and your convictions. When asked for your opinion, be sincere. Friends appreciate forthrightness in each other. BUT . . .

8.

When necessary, temper your honesty with diplomacy. The truth doesn't have to hurt. It's better to say "Your new haircut is interesting" than to exclaim "You actually paid money for THAT?" There are times when frankness is inappropriate and unnecessary.

9.

Don't just use your friends as sounding boards for your problems and complaints. Include them in the good times, too.

10.

Do your share of the work. That's right, *work*. Any relationship takes effort. Don't always depend on your friends to make the plans and carry the weight.

11.

Be accepting. Not all of your friends have to think and act like you do. (Wouldn't it be boring if they did?)

12.

Learn to recognize the so-called friends you can do without. Some gifted kids get so lonely that they put up with anyone—including friends who aren't really friends at all. Follow tips 1–11 and this shouldn't happen to you.

CHAPTER 8

Making It Safe to Be Smart: Creating the Gifted-Friendly Classroom

"A gifted teacher opens your mind to help you with your life."

—BOY, 10

Mrs. Sanders was a remarkable first-grade teacher. She had 28 students in her class, including three who did not speak English and several more whose backgrounds, interests, and abilities made cluster grouping difficult. There are many qualities about Mrs. Sanders worth mentioning here—her varied teaching strategies, her effective use of praise—but most special was what she did at the end of each day.

As the children were preparing to go home—"walkers" on the right, "riders" on the left—Mrs. Sanders made a point to take each child and either squeeze a shoulder, rub a head, or make a funny face to encourage any frowners in the group to smile. Each gesture was accompanied by a verbal statement, such as "Good answer in math today, Mary!" or "Nice high-tops, Jeff!" Each child, each day. A different gesture, a different expression.

Why did she do this each day, with every student? Her answer was simple, straightforward, and indicative of a teacher for whom 110 percent is typical:

I have no idea what happens when the students leave school. Some ride on the bus and get ridiculed; others go home to an empty house; still more rush around from ballet to soccer to who-knows-what. I have no idea, and I have very little control. But I do have control over how each student will remember his or her last moment of the day with me, and that memory will be a fond one.

Mrs. Sanders did admit that on some days, with some children, it was tough coming up with a positive statement. (Once she was overheard saying, "This was a good day for you, Eric. You didn't bite me so hard.") "But they're worth it," she said. "I dig until I find something good."

Even the smallest act can make a big difference. You probably know this from your own experience. Now imagine how effective frequent, deliberate, consistent efforts to reach out, support, and encourage children can be.

This chapter presents activities that will help you create the kind of classroom where students feel welcome and wanted. As you read through them, you may find yourself wondering, "Aren't these ideas good for *most* students? What makes them especially good for gifted students?" In fact, many of the activities *are* good for most (if not all) students. Gifted students may respond to some of them at a depth that other students do not. Still, we challenge you to encourage all of your students to dig deep within themselves and produce work that reveals something about their minds, hearts, and/or personalities.

Self-Esteem and School Achievement: A Natural Link

Gifted children are, first and foremost, children. Their feelings, needs, and wishes are more like those of other children than they are different. This being so, the comments that follow may lead you to ask, "But isn't the development of self-esteem good for *all* children?" The answer, of course, is yes.

Still, there are at least three reasons why this section is here, in a book about the social and emotional needs of gifted children.

1. Gifted children, often more aware of reactions of others toward them, may begin to develop their self-esteem at a very early age.

2. Since many gifted students tie their success in school to their worth as a person, early attention to self-esteem enhancement is essential.

3. The belief that perfection is an attainable and expected goal limits some gifted children from giving themselves credit—and experiencing a personal sense of worth—for many of their lesser achievements.

If you read educational or psychological literature, it's tough to find a writer who does not link self-esteem with school achievement. This is as true in articles in the *Journal of Educational Psychology* as it is in *Family Circle.* No writer (at least none of whom we are aware) states publicly, "Who cares if you think you're worthless? You can still learn, can't you?" Everyone, from everyday people to eminent scholars, seems to agree that attitude affects performance.

Remembering Mr. Walls

by Frank Davies, fourth-grade teacher

Ken Walls was an amazing person. Very unpretentious and not gushy with praise. But his underlying belief was that he treated students with respect and dignity. He encouraged us to follow our interests and would be very flexible in going with individuals' choices. He never shouted or put us down. I knew that he believed in me, and I saw him make some amazing changes in other students, too.

We were about 14 to 15 at the time—a bunch of little so-and-sos. Our class was basically remedial and we were just waiting to finish school. Yet, when we were in Mr. Walls's class for that couple of hours a week, my fellow students and I became responsible and responsive, and we took pride in our work.

Ken Walls didn't come down to our level, he invited us up to his. He asked our opinions and yet he was also very strict, as there were very clear boundaries in place in his classroom. But the bottom line was, he liked us and we liked him.

Which Comes First?

If there is any disagreement about self-esteem and school achievement, it comes in the form of a chicken-egg conundrum: Which comes first? Does a solid sense of self encourage a person to want to learn more, or does successful learning make an individual gain a more positive sense of self?

An important question, perhaps, and an intriguing one, but we're afraid our response is, "Who cares?" We already know that self-esteem and school achievement occur in tandem, so the question of which precedes which is as meaningless as trying to remember which half of a happily married couple first said "I love you" to the other. If the marriage is working, the point is moot.

A Daunting Task

Franklin Delano Roosevelt once said, "The ablest man I ever met is the man you think you are." Quite an optimistic comment, especially coming from a man whose dyslexia was so severe that he could not even read his own speeches. Still, he persevered, and the entire world was his ultimate beneficiary.

It's a daunting task, being an educator, bearing the responsibility for shaping both academics and attitudes. Accountability, as defined in today's schools, often measures the easy stuff: the math facts memorized, the commas placed correctly, the historical events accurately sequenced. But the true measure of an educator's teaching performance is not so readily determined.

No computer-scanned bubble sheet measures how our students feel about learning, or their biases toward self and others. These indexes, the true value of learning and education, elude detection and measurement, sometimes for years. And even if we could measure attitudes and biases (there are self-esteem scales available to do just that), we might pick up general trends, but not specific thoughts. For instance, answering "I like to take challenges" on a score sheet is one thing, but signing up for an honors chemistry course where receiving a B is likely is quite something else.

So, those brave educators wishing to enhance both students' self-esteem and their achievements must be content with knowing the immediate impact of their actions. Some changes will be noticeable, while others will be stubbornly absent (at least in the short term). But as Mrs. Sanders knows quite well, ripples expand as they leave the central core.

Building Self-Esteem: One Teacher's Approach

A teacher we know very well worked for several years as a resource teacher of gifted students in a rural school district. She worked in four different buildings, seeing about 30 first- through sixth-graders at a time (4 schools x 30 students = 120 students per week). A difficult task, even for an expert juggler.

Meeting with each group of students only once per week created some gaps. Projects that were expected to be completed in the interim sometimes got "forgotten." Resource books, outlines, and note cards stayed buried under math texts and more pressing homework assignments. On a more personal note, some students' lives went topsy-turvy from one week to the next. Pets died or ran away, best friends moved, new babies arrived, school awards were won. A lot occurred between one Monday and the next that affected the students' attitude and performance.

In an effort to learn more about her students, the teacher introduced "New and Goods," a time period (15 minutes or so) that began each resource-room class. During New and Goods, students met in a group to review the past week. Each child (and the teacher, too) was given the chance to share something new and good that had occurred since their previous meeting. Talking was encouraged, though not required, but most children took advantage and spoke of something real, something personal, something only theirs. Occasionally, as the groups became more intimate and trusting, a child would ask to share a "new and sad" or a "new and bad." This was allowed. The purpose of New and Goods was to communicate; the content of what got shared was an individual choice.

As the year moved on and the pace became more hectic, class schedules became less predictable. Still, New and Goods began each resource-room meeting. The children demanded it. Having been given the chance to express themselves freely and without criticism (a key point), they were not about to forgo this special time. Projects could wait. First, they wanted to talk about themselves and learn about each other.

New and Goods is just one example of an activity that promotes both self-esteem and achievement. It requires no materials, no budget, and no preplanning; in other words, it's a teacher's dream. What it does require is a belief that listening to what children say is important, and a willingness to take the time to do so within the confines of a classroom schedule.

If you're in a regular classroom setting where you, as a teacher, see your students every day, New and Goods may not seem as necessary. Right?

Wrong! Just as middle-school educators have discovered success with the incorporation of "advisory groups" into the daily or weekly calendar, it's vital to get to know our students from the inside out. (In typical advisory groups, one teacher is responsible for 10 to 15 students, who often stay together as a group for two to three years. Discussions and fun activities are planned for these 20-minute sessions.) Without this time for more personal interaction, kids may feel lost in a sea of faces. Advisory groups, or classroom-based activities meant to encourage self-exploration and knowledge, are more necessary than ever in this age of rampant testing and prescribed curriculum.

From the Field

"These . . . meetings have several advantages. They help us identify and resolve problems, develop a closer working relationship with the family, and show parents that the school is an institution that cares about children. After seven years, we have found that these meetings usually produce positive changes in academic achievement and behavior."

—Penelope de Mello e Souza

"Counselors Set Steps for Smooth Transitions," *Middle Ground* 4:3 (February 2001), p. 23.

Invitational Education

If New and Goods makes sense to you, then you'll probably value the idea of Invitational Education. As defined by its authors, William Purkey and John Novak, invitational education is a "self-concept approach to the educative process and professional functioning."[1] It relies on four basic principles:

1. People are able, valuable, and responsible and should be treated accordingly.

2. Teaching should be a cooperative venture.

3. People possess untapped potential.

4. This potential can become realized in an environment that respects individual differences and preferences.

When teachers communicate to students their belief that the students are capable, the students are more likely to act in ways that prove their competence. Conversely, if teachers tell students—verbally or through nonspoken cues—that they are "as dumb as they come," it's likely that the students will behave in ways that confirm this impression.

An important contention underlying Purkey and Novak's theory is that most teachers are in the business of building character, not tearing it down. It is the rare educator who sets out for school on Monday morning thinking, "I wonder whose ego I can crush today." Such teachers do exist—every profession has its buffoons and its meanies—but it's unusual to find an educator who practices deliberate self-esteem destruction.

Those teachers, counselors, administrators, and other school personnel who do destroy others' love of or desire to learn often do so unconsciously—or, as Purkey and Novak phrase it, "unintentionally." These unintentional disinviters would argue vigorously that their aims are to improve student performance and attitude. What goes awry is this: The "messages" they send that are intended to instill pride in or a love of learning are interpreted by individual students as negative and critical.

Some examples of unintentional disinvitation—provided by students themselves—will help clarify this point.

I never seem to be able to live up to the expectations of my teachers or my family. Everyone keeps telling me how smart and gifted I am, and if I don't meet their expectations, it brings my pride to an all-time low. When this happens, I figure that I can't possibly be as smart as they think I am.

—**Melissa, 13**

I think teachers can, at the very least, keep their expectations normal while recognizing the giftedness of a student. I have one teacher who has ULTRA-high expectations of my performance . . . even in gym class! She uses my results as the benchmark for other peoples' grades (which doesn't exactly help me in the popularity area). And then, if I make a mistake, she announces it to everyone, which is very embarrassing. It's as though I can't be human.

—Ray, 13

My social studies teacher is driving me nuts. She targets me as "the perfect one" in class by always asking me (whether I've raised my hand or not) what I think about issues . . . as though I'm always supposed to have some outstanding insight. Whenever I hand in a paper, she always makes a point of saying how neat my handwriting is or something, right in front of everyone. This is embarrassing, and people think I'm a teacher's pet even though I don't want to be. This creates an atmosphere where there's a disincentive to do well. I know she doesn't mean to humiliate me, but really, I'm not the only person in class who has a brain and can do well.

—April, 14

Most likely, those teachers who make public declarations of how "perfect" gifted children are do so to reward high-achieving students and prod others to imitate their academic or social behaviors. We know that at least *some* of these gifted students are embarrassed by this unsolicited attention. Besides, when you're put on a pedestal, the only direction to go is down.

Invitations Defined

Intentional Inviter: This teacher understands the importance of acknowledging a child's unique existence, and strives to actively support a child's efforts, however small, to improve. *Example:* "If I allow children to post their favorite work on the bulletin board, and to let them use my Teacher's Guide to grade their own homework, they will know that I trust them to do the right thing."

Intentional Disinviter: This teacher actively seeks out ways in which children fail in academic or social settings, and never lets them forget they have found

continued . . .

these "chinks in the armor." *Example* (said in front of class): "You know, just because you're 'gifted' doesn't mean you're entitled to anything special. And looking at that C you got on your science project last month, I even question if that 'gifted' label is accurate."

Unintentional Inviter: This teacher sends positive, inspiring messages to students, through words and actions, but doesn't recognize their importance in a child's life. *Example:* "As your English teacher, I can't possibly write comments on every one of your papers—I wouldn't have a life for myself! But I promise to write each of you at least one letter this quarter where I comment on how good your work is. I hope this is okay, and I wish I could do more."

Unintentional Disinviter: This teacher implements strategies or makes comments that make some students go "ouch!" even though the teacher claims there are no negative results from these words or actions. *Example:* "Okay, let's all trade quizzes and we'll correct them together. At the end, when I call out the student's name, just shout out the grade and I'll place it here in my grade book."

Positive or Negative?

Messages sent, messages received: Sometimes the lines of communication get crossed, and when they do, the end result is often no communication at all.

Donald MacKinnon, a scholar in the field of creativity, once wrote, "The same fire that melts the butter, hardens the egg."[2] He was reviewing the elements of creative environments and discovered that few creative people agree on the ideal setting that prompts original thought. Some people love loud music, open spaces, and a beer by their elbow. Others demand quiet, a closet with a light, and herbal tea. The same is true for message sending and receiving: Their impacts are as individual as fingerprints or snowflakes.

The chart on pages 230–231 shows how a singular message may have multiple meanings and interpretations. As illustrated by the variety of contexts in which messages are sent and received—social, academic, and other settings—it's easy to see the pervasive nature of the thousands of invitations that we give and get within even a single day. Nonverbal clues—the raised eyebrow, the broad grin, the pat on the back—are as common as spoken statements. Often, they are just as open to interpretation.

Message Sent	Message Received: Positive	Message Received: Negative
Social Messages		
"Great haircut!"	I guess I look pretty good.	I must have looked awful yesterday.
"I would have invited you to my party, but you live so far away. I didn't want you to feel obligated to come."	How considerate! I was spared having to turn down an invitation.	That's only an excuse. If they really wanted me there, I would've been invited anyway.
"Interesting meal: I never would have thought of glazing the chicken with orange juice."	I got their taste buds talking. How exciting!	Everyone hates it. So much for recipe experiments.
Academic Messages		
"There was only one A on yesterday's test. Can anyone guess who got it?"	I'll feel so proud if it's me; I really studied hard.	I'll die if it's me! How embarrassing to be picked out as "Mr. Smarty Pants" in front of your friends.
"What's your opinion, Sally? We can always count on you for the wildest ideas."	The teacher really appreciates my creative ideas.	My teacher thinks I'm weird. She even expects me to act that way when I give my opinion.
"Whoever finishes this assignment first will be my special helper for the day."	I'd love to help out. I'll work as fast as I can!	So, I'm only "special" when I'm fast? Forget it, I'm not into speed! Besides, I'll never finish ahead of everyone else.

Message Sent	Message Received: Positive	Message Received: Negative
Other Messages		
"Of course I trust you, but I never lend my car to anyone. Really, it's not just you."	I can't argue with him if that's his policy for everyone. He'd say no to anyone who wanted to borrow his car.	He doesn't trust me.
"It's okay to be alone sometimes."	My parents understand that solitude is important to me.	If I'm not always on some sports team, my parents will think I'm strange.
"I'll bet you'll be even more successful in life than your sister."	My family really wants me to do well.	I'll never catch up to my sister, so why try at all? I hate being compared to her!

Gifted children are especially apt at picking up the multiple meanings of both blatant and subtle messages, as their sensitivity to others' impressions of them is often quite strong. However, this precocity in perception is not always accompanied by a similarly advanced ability in interpretation. The result can be a misreading of invitations sent by teachers or parents so that the gifted child notes the negative over the positive. For example, a child who is told that report card grades of A's and Bs are signs of good work may hear the message as a warning to do better, rather than as an acknowledgment of strong efforts.

These negative misinterpretations are most apt to occur in gifted children who are perfectionists or those whose self-esteem is low. In fact, if individuals believe something about themselves, they are likely to accept as true only those statements that validate their established beliefs or attitudes. Thus, a child who thinks, "I am stupid," will readily accept those messages—intentional or not—that go along with this belief. Likewise, a child with strong self-esteem will be more likely to interpret messages in a more positive way.

Four messages people send to gifted children that can have unintended negative effects are:

1. "You did a great job on this project, but . . ." When we couple a compliment with a suggestion to improve, what is usually remembered the most is what comes after the "but," diminishing the impact of the intended compliment.

2. "I don't care about your grades as long as you try your best." No adults we know try their best at everything they do. As we all have discovered, there are some things in life that just take precedence over others. This "try-your-best" statement is a sure way to breed perfectionism as well as limit a child's ability to set priorities.

3. "This'll be easy for a smart kid like you." "And what if it isn't?" the child might think. "That means I must really be some big loser, if even a task that is simple to others seems complex to me." When you interpret this message like this, there's no way to feel but low.

4. "You're not working up to your potential." This implies that someone else knows the range of another's potential and is somehow keeping it a secret from that person. This statement is a sure way to make someone's efforts seem less than worthwhile. Further, it implies that "potential" has an end point when, in fact, it is an ever-changing set of goals based on personal interests and strengths.

The importance of invitations, and their correct interpretation, has been proved through reams of research and years of human interaction. As adults, we often recall the times in our own childhood when we were either invited or disinvited, and these memories, if powerful enough, can affect our behavior even decades later. A teacher in Gary, Indiana, related the following incident:

> When I was in third grade, I raised my hand to answer a question, and the teacher called on me. I gave the wrong answer. To this day, I remember how she reacted. She said, "Oh, Catherine, you're just like an old hen. You cackle and cackle but never produce an egg." I'll remember how hurt I felt then—and now—for the rest of my life.

Invitational Education in Action

If you've read this far, you probably realize the importance of invitational education. But saying "I believe" and taking appropriate actions are two very different things. What follows are specific ways to construct an inviting environment—for yourself and for those you teach.

To us, there are at least five areas in which educators can provide "invitations" to gifted pupils:

1. within the curriculum

2. in grading procedures and student evaluation

3. within the classroom environment

4. in establishing disciplinary procedures

5. through self-satisfying behaviors that energize you as an educator

Invitational Education Within the Curriculum

Strategy: Provide Posttests as Pretests

It is more common than rare that gifted students know portions of the regular curriculum before instruction begins. If teachers allow able students to take the textbook-provided posttest at the *beginning* of a particular unit of study, then curriculum can be adapted to meet the current level of student achievement. This not only prevents many "I'm bored" comments, but it also gives students credit for their past accomplishments and present competence.

This is easier said than done, and in the short term, it will require more work on your part. You'll need to design some alternative assignments for gifted students (at least initially), and this is an extra effort. However, as time goes on and students become more savvy about the procedures, they can be given the responsibility of designing a replacement curriculum from which they would draw both enjoyment and academic satisfaction.

Also, don't forget to use the services of your school's gifted specialist to help design alternate assignments or locate supplemental books or materials. Librarians can be enormously helpful as well. That's why they're there!

Scientific Poetry

This poem, written by an 11-year-old boy named Robert, was completed as part of a 20-part compendium of "scientific poetry." Robert wrote the poems during class time, after his fifth-grade teacher confirmed that he already had an understanding of the unit on fractions that was about to begin.

Fall Leaves

I see a leaf
It is yellow with red and orange mixed in.

continued . . .

My mind says,
"The yellow is caused by the oxidation of leftover sugars.
The red and orange are caused by the emergence
of recessive pigments."
I see a leaf.
It is yellow with red and orange mixed in.
My heart says:
"The yellow is a bit of leftover sun from summer.
The red and orange is the leaf spiraling down
into the lower spectrum as it is going to sleep."
I see a leaf.

Strategy: Coordinate Student Schedules

Many gifted programs operate in a "pull-out" format, where students leave the regular class for a period of time each day or week. Whether you are the "sending" teacher (in the regular classroom) or the "receiving" teacher (in the resource room), be aware of the scheduling dilemmas that are part and parcel of pull-out programs. Try to coordinate tests, special events, and the introduction of important topics so students don't get caught in a bind as they try to serve two (or more) masters in their different classrooms.

Please don't become one of those teachers who gifted students know "just don't get it." Don't:

■ Schedule a party or field trip on the day of the pull-out class.

■ "Forget" to give gifted students the homework required when they return from their pull-out class, and then give them zeros for not turning in homework that they didn't know they had.

■ Say to the students who return to your class following their gifted pull-out time, "Thanks for returning to *our* world. Are you sure you're not too good for us?"

■ Introduce a major new topic or project on precisely the day that the gifted kids aren't there, then expect them to understand it anyway because "they're supposed to be gifted, aren't they?"

These are all questionable strategies that have been used by some teachers to knowingly or unknowingly subvert gifted pull-out programs and the gifted kids in them.

Gifted students who get pulled from your classroom deserve the same degree of personal and educational respect afforded to students who leave your room for speech therapy, a special class for students with learning differences, and so on. Anything less is discriminatory and inhumane.

Strategy: Provide "Instead of" Enrichment, Not "In Addition to" Enrichment

Often, gifted students are told that they can work on special projects or in learning centers only after they have finished their assigned work. This is all well and good, except for those times when the assigned work is little more than a task requiring a rote drill of an already mastered concept. "Instead of" vs. "in addition to" enrichment is seen in these two examples:

- **The "instead of" teacher says,** "Desmond, since you scored 95 percent on both your math and spelling pretests, why don't you use your time to work on another activity instead?"

- **The "in addition to" teacher says,** "Desmond, once you've written your spelling words ten times each and completed these three pages of math seatwork, you may work on your independent project."

"Instead of" enrichment, also known as curriculum streaming, allows teachers to buy time within the school day for students whose past efforts have proved their competence in basic skill areas. Termed "curriculum compacting" by Joseph Renzulli, Sally Reis, and Linda Smith and "telescoping" by Abraham Tannenbaum, this provision benefits students whose knowledge base of particular curriculum areas precludes the need for extensive instruction.

Strategy: Provide Incentives

Many teachers are frustrated by the seemingly haphazard attempts gifted students make when completing simple tasks. For example, when a top math student makes ten computation mistakes on a review worksheet, the student is often chided for making "careless errors." The student balks at redoing the assignment with complaints of "I already know this stuff!" The teacher agrees and says, "I *know* you can do the work—just be more careful." Thus begins a cycle of frustration for everyone concerned.

Think how much of an incentive it would be for students if they were told, "There are 50 math problems on this page. Anyone who completes the first 25 examples with no more than two errors does not have to finish the remaining problems."

This comment invites achievement in a way that rewards students who take the time to think about what they are doing, and it offers a "quality discount program" that prods attention to the task at hand. (Also, and not so incidentally, it cuts down on the teacher's grading time while ensuring that students have mastered basic concepts.)

Letting Students Go Wild

by Kelly, 22

When I was sometimes asked to write an essay or poem—no topic selected by the teacher—I'd go wild. It wasn't often we were trusted with our own minds to wander where we chose. The time I grew most, intellectually, was during the spring of eleventh grade, when my Honors English class was studying Thoreau. Our class was asked to keep journals. The only limit on our writing was that it was to be about nature. Nature! That's anything! To me it was anything. To Thoreau it was anything. And to my teacher . . . it was anything.

My advice to you is to let your kids (whatever their age) go wild with their own brains. Whether on paper, computer, or canvas, don't always tell them what to do! Let them use their own ingenuity. Tell them to call forth from their innermost selves the truth that is alive in all of us. Let them define beauty, knowledge, nature, and meaning in their own individual ways. This is why we were all made different! The only way to learn something really worthwhile, I am convinced, is to look inside and try to find out what's alive in there. Most people have never dared to consult themselves, before others, in making their own opinions.

Invitational Education in Grading Procedures and Student Evaluation

Strategy: Get the Red Out

The ubiquitous red pen that is used to grade students' projects and papers is perceived as an instrument of torture by many children, especially those who are either perfectionists or extremely averse to criticism. Able children make the connection early: "The more red marks, the worse my grade."

Solutions? Use any color but red to grade students' papers, or use red ink only to point out pupils' accomplishments or *correct* answers.

Strategy: Let Students Grade Their Own Papers

Every text has a teacher's edition; every workbook has an answer guide. Hand these over to those students who finish their tasks early and allow them to grade their own work.

Not only does this allow students a chance to determine the extent of their knowledge, but it also cuts down on your grading time, so everyone wins. Also, and most important, allowing students to grade their own assignments implies that you trust them to be honest about their errors. And, ironically, when most students are given the chance to cheat, they won't. There's no need to be dishonest when the person in charge respects your right to make errors (and to learn from them).

Strategy: Help Students Set Reachable Goals

Many gifted children select topics of study that are bigger than they are. "I want to study dinosaurs," they say, or "I'd like to learn about chemistry," or "I'm worried about crime in my neighborhood, and I want to do something about it." Great topics, but each is hardly manageable in a six-week independent study.

The first step to success is setting limits in terms of the depth and breadth of the project focus. One approach, called curriculum "webbing," is illustrated on page 238. By constructing such webs (a colleague calls them "spider plans"), students get to see the many facets of a topic that, at first, may have appeared one-dimensional. Then they may pinpoint their specific areas of interest within the broader scope of their initial topic idea and work on a scaled-down version of the original theme.

Limiting one's scope is not the same as lowering one's standards. If a web is well thought out, the student can return to it if the new, trimmed-down project seems too lean. It's easier to build on a firm foundation than on patches of scattered thoughts.

Strategy: Post Less-Than-Perfect Papers

Walk into many classrooms, and you'll notice collections of perfect papers placed on bulletin boards for all to see. Every spelling paper an A, every coloring page drawn within the lines, each 3-D relief map of the USA complete with all 50 states and a couple of oceans.

But what message does this send to students whose work, while good, is not perfect? And what about the child who may never (or seldom) have a perfect paper but continues to show improvement over time? Doesn't this youngster deserve to get the accolades of others by seeing his or her work on display?

Tell your students that they have the chance, and the choice, to post projects that make them proud. Remind them that these need not be perfect, and start the ball

Web Diagram for an Independent
Study on Crime Prevention

1. Find out how often police patrol the park.

2. Ask about more lights in park.

3. Ask for more adult supervisors during the days.

1. Find out how to start a neighborhood watch program.

2. Have a neighborhood meeting. Invite police to talk about ways to prevent vandalism.

3. Have a block party so neighbors get to know each other.

1. See if neighborhood organization or city has money for dead-bolt locks, lights on garages, etc.

2. Invite police to check houses and give burglar-proofing tips.

3. Encourage neighbors to tell each other when they're going out of town.

1. Get more trash cans for neighborhood.

2. Start Adopt-a-Sidewalk and Adopt-an-Alley programs.

3. Hand out litter bags for people to put in their cars.

1. Report all graffiti to police right away. Special phone number?

2. Find out if city government has people who clean up or paint over graffiti.

3. Learn what other neighborhoods have done.

rolling by posting something of your own that is good, but not great, work. (Remember that graduate paper you got a B-minus on? Now's the chance to show it off.)

Posting less-than-perfect work neither lowers standards nor rewards mediocrity. Instead, it acknowledges an essential truth: Less than perfection is more than acceptable.

One last word in these litigious times: Some states have enacted laws or policies forbidding the posting of any graded student work on which the student's name appears, citing it as unconstitutional on the grounds of freedom of privacy being violated. Be this right or wrong, it may be a reality in your state. Check with the your school's principal to be sure that displaying student work does not constitute a legal violation.

Strategy: The BUG Roll

Few would argue the benefits of having some type of Honor Roll in schools. Call it the "Principal's Club" or the "Academic Aces" or whatever other euphemism you choose: It makes sense to reward those students who excel in the business of schooling.

But what about a student like Ben? A smart kid—and everyone knows it—Ben has had grades that fluctuate as wildly as April temperatures in Chicago. Then there's Monchelle, a quiet girl who's not convinced that her mind is as sharp as everyone says. She can do well, but since her grades are seldom top-notch, there's nary a mention of her successes.

Enter the BUG Roll. BUG—an acronym for Bringing Up Grades—gives credit and public recognition to students who improve at least one letter grade between report cards, without letting any other grades fall back. So, if Ben goes from all Cs during his first quarter to a combination of Cs and Bs in the second quarter, he makes the BUG Roll. So would Monchelle, if those B-minuses she was toying with one quarter rose to become B-pluses by next term's end. Neither student is in top form academically, but their progress toward improvement is noteworthy and deserves some public recognition.

If you work at the middle-school level, the BUG Roll moniker will seem too childish for emerging adolescents. So change the name to "On a Roll," a homophone for "Honor Roll" that gets the same point across: "Your efforts are appreciated."

Some schools have added a few modifications to the BUG Roll/On a Roll, such as students needing to attain a minimum average of C to earn list status (going from Fs to Ds doesn't cut it). Other educators require that students go up at least one grade in two subjects in order to earn this recognition.

We believe that any improvement in academic performance is noteworthy and, therefore, we don't support these modifications. However, we also understand that the climate of each school is different, and we would rather see a modified BUG Roll than no BUG Roll at all.

Use the BUG Roll. It can make a difference in the lives of gifted students (and others) who realize that academic success sometimes comes in small steps, not giant leaps. You'll find a reproducible BUG Roll on page 264.

Spotlight On External Rewards

Despite Mae West's assertion, too much of a good thing is not always a good thing. Take the case of the preceding two suggestions: the posting of less-than-perfect work and the BUG Roll.

In some ways, educators who use them (and similar methods) are resorting to bribery to get children to perform academically. "Do a good job and we'll let everyone know it" may be how some students interpret either action, especially those who are smart enough to recognize that they deserve to be valued not for their work but for themselves.

This is the main point raised by Alfie Kohn, whose classic book, *Punished by Rewards,* lambastes America's fascination with praise and rewards for work that may, in fact, be meaningless to the child. In a chapter titled "The Trouble with Carrots," Kohn points out four reasons why external rewards have no long-term, positive impact:[3]

1. Rewards punish. "If you're a good boy, you can have ten extra minutes of recess" is "functionally identical"[4] to a threat, as the student realizes what will be lost—free time—if certain steps aren't followed.

2. Rewards rupture relationships. Implementing a "Genius of the Week" program, where one student is selected as the top boy or girl for the week in a classroom, actually pits students against each other in unhealthy ways, and creates a power structure where the teacher lauds his or her biases over students.

3. Rewards ignore reasons. Did anyone ever ask Ben why his grades are low? (Perhaps the curriculum is meaningless to him; hence, so are his grades.) Or question Monchelle about her relatively low grade achievement? (Maybe she's afraid that if she gets straight A's once, she'll be expected to do it time and again.) In an externally-based reward structure, the main core of a problem may never be addressed.

4. Rewards discourage risk-taking. According to Kohn, "When we are working for a reward, we do exactly what is necessary to get it, and no more."[5] As a corollary, people who work for the reward are less likely to take chances or experiment with ideas that do not lead directly to the desired result. The objective becomes earning the reward, not learning or testing new thoughts. Risk-taking, and the resultant growth, is scaled back considerably.

continued . . .

Kohn's work is both elegant and controversial—and, some would add, unrealistic. After all, how long would you go to work if you never received a paycheck, even if you loved what you did? Still, his ideas merit attention, especially when considering that gifted children might interpret an externally-based reward structure as little more than a thinly-disguised bribe to perform work that, intrinsically, does not matter to them.

It is up to you to reach a balance between encouraging students to do work because of the outside benefits or recognition it brings, and allowing them to pursue projects solely because of their passion for a particular subject or topic. And you have your work cut out for you, as this balance often differs from student to student.

Strategy: Determine Evaluation Criteria

"When I was growing up, I always wanted to be somebody,
but now I see that I should have been more specific."
—LILY TOMLIN

It doesn't take a brilliant mind to figure out that if you don't know where you're going, you'll probably end up someplace else. Life in the classroom is like a trip down the interstate. A road map that clearly marks your intended destination will get you there a bit more quickly and smoothly than just following your nose.

This advice rings true for, among other things, the completion of student projects. Too often, as students embark on adventures in learning, they have only a vague idea as to their goal. "I want to learn about outer space" is about as precise a statement as "I think I'll visit Kansas." While the former is significantly bigger than the latter, both are large enough to get lost in unless you add some specificity to your plans.

To guide students through learning excursions that will lead them to places they intended to go in the first place, try using an "Independent Study Guide" like the one on page 242. This outline is designed to encourage students to consider a project's scope, starting points, possible pitfalls and "escape routes," and evaluation criteria from the beginning.

Of course, some parts of the plan may change as the student learns more about the topic (didn't you ever diverge from your scheduled itinerary?), but it's always easier to switch from a known direction than to set out without one and hope for the best. Not all students may need this formal a plan to study a topic, but for those who do, a curriculum road map can save time and energy for both the students and the teachers.

Independent Study Guide

1. Your subject area, broadly defined. (*Examples:* Dinosaurs; chemistry. Create a web diagram for your subject area.)

2. Your subject area, narrowly defined. (Select one or more topics from your web diagram. Write a sentence or two about what you'd like to learn.)

3. Resources you could use. (Describe what they are and where you can find them. *Examples:* Printed resources; human resources; Internet resources; other resources.)

4. Personal evaluation. (How will you know you've achieved your goals for this project?)

5. First steps. (List the first five things you will do to begin your project. As you complete this list, add more items. *Example:* Locate two books and three Web sites on my topic.)

6. Possible problems and solutions. (Write at least three things that could go wrong with your project. Think of ways to overcome these problems and write those, too.)

7. Sharing your work. (What form will your project take? A report? Movie? Demonstration? Explain what type of project you will do and who will see your results.)

8. Timeline. (Write the dates when you expect to complete each stage of your project.)

9. Project approval. (Have your teacher sign off on your plan.)

Strategy: Praise and Critique Separately

Remember your last job performance evaluation? All "excellents" or "goods," we suspect—except for maybe that one item about turning in paperwork on time or arriving at school before the students get there. One flaw (maybe two) on an otherwise perfect record. So, what do you remember? Generally, human nature prevails, and we recall the negatives.

Our students have similar reactions. When we tell them, "Your essay was good, *but* you could improve your grammar," or "I like your picture, *but* elephants aren't really blue," they may feel as if they just got kicked in the "but." What they remember is what *should have* been done rather than what *was* accomplished.

When praise is coupled with criticism, it is usually the latter that is retained. Even though both types of comments might be appropriate and important, it's best to mention them at two separate times. "Your essay was well-written" or "I like the colors in your picture" is all you need to say for the moment. Suggestions to change or improve can come later.

Invitational Education Within the Classroom Environment

Strategy: *Keep Private Things Private*

Many teachers are guilty of unintentionally embarrassing their students by classroom actions that should be stopped. For example:

- Do you place a student's name on the board when he or she misbehaves or speaks out of turn?

- Do you have students grade each other's spelling tests, then have them recite the grades out loud for you to record in your grade book?

- Do you announce, "There was only one A on the social-studies paper. Can anyone guess who got it?"

Each of these teacher behaviors takes something that belongs to the student and puts it out front for public display.

In the first case, the name-on-the-board strategy is a not-so-subtle attempt to intimidate the student into compliance. The problem is, any stranger (or parent, or principal) who walks into your room knows who "the bad kid" is—something that no one but you needs to know. As an alternative, have any students who act out write their own names on a notepad on your desk. You'll still know who did what and needs to suffer the consequences, but no one else will be the wiser—which is how it should be.

The two other examples both involve the public display of something intended to be private: a student's level of academic performance. Having kids grade each others' papers and relay the grades to you orally saves time, but what about the child who gets a D, or the superstar speller who got an A for the 38th time this year? Both might be criticized or ostracized by others outside of your earshot. And what about the "only one A" comment? Again, good intentions gone awry. The child being lauded now might be the child being pummeled later at the bus stop for being the teacher's favorite.

It's always a good idea to ask ourselves, "Am I treating my students the way I would have wanted to be treated as a child?" and then act accordingly.

A few final words on the practice of having students grade other students' papers: In 2000, a federal appeals court declared it illegal, saying that it violated the *Family Educational Rights and Privacy Act of 1974* (FERPA). In 2002, the U.S. Supreme Court reversed the decision of the appeals court and ruled unanimously that peer grading does *not* violate FERPA. Legal or not, we don't recommend it.

Strategy: Establish a Planning Council

In most classrooms, the teacher determines the decor. Prints, posters, bulletin boards, and desk arrangements are all in place as the school year begins, and if changes are made throughout the year, it is due to the teacher's initiative. But students spend as much time in the classroom as teachers do. Why not give them a say in how it looks and feels?

Enter the Planning Council (PC). Chaired by the teacher (or a designee), the PC comprises students who are members of the class in question. It is their job to recommend changes in the classroom environment and to implement these suggestions, either by themselves or by "subcontracting" the job to an interested group of students. Of course, the teacher may request that an "environmental impact study" be done prior to any major changes. For example, will putting the desks in clusters instead of rows create unnecessary talking or congested traffic patterns?

By establishing a PC, you're telling your students in a very real way that *this* classroom is *their* classroom, too. (As the year progresses, PC membership may change to involve as many students as possible.) Successfully implemented, the PC turns the classroom atmosphere from one of factory to one of family. As noted in Chapter 6, this is the atmosphere that underachievers and selective consumers prefer. It's safe to assume that other students will feel the same.

Strategy: Take the Classroom Temperature

Moods affect performance, no question about it. But moods are sometimes subtle and secretive, and it is easy to suppress anger behind a calm demeanor or to veil disappointment with a smile. Often, the very students who need the most care and attention are the ones most adept at disguising their moods.

Counselor George Betts and psychologist Maureen Neihart recommend that educators invite students to take their "emotional temperatures." They suggest a rating scale from 1 (low; I don't feel good about life right now) to 10 (high; I feel good about life right now and want to tell everyone how exciting it is).

You could use this 1 to 10 scale. Or, in keeping with the "temperature" metaphor, you might have your students construct cardboard thermometers with sliding markers. (Make one for yourself, too!) Then have everyone monitor and record their moods throughout the day. For example, a student might have this type of day:

9:00 A.M. 72° (very comfortable). Feeling good after a bus ride seated next to my best friend.

10:50 A.M. 32° (cold and uncomfortable). Picked last (again) for the recess kickball team.

12:30 P.M. 95° (very hot and uncomfortable). Everyone lost free time because a few kids were fooling around at lunch. No fair!

1:20 P.M. 78° (feeling a little better). Ms. Fong let us talk about our feelings about the lunchroom problem.

2:45 P.M. 72° (comfortable again). A good end to the day—a B on a test and a surprise popcorn treat!

A simpler (but similar) suggestion is to let students use a color wheel—the kind found in many board games—to express their moods. Red indicates anger, blue means sadness, green shows joy, and so on.

A mood indicator, whether a thermometer or a color wheel, allows students to monitor their changing emotions throughout each day. It helps them pinpoint and acknowledge the events that get them angry or calm them down. When teachers also participate, this lets students know that we, too, are affected by different moods as the school day unfolds. Imagine—a teacher, and human!

Strategy: Design Classrooms That Respect Learning Styles and Preferences

Just as people differ about the environment most conducive to creativity, they also vary in their styles and preferences for completing academic tasks. Some students love group projects, where each person participates actively in a cooperative learning venture. Others prefer solitude—a study carrel in a corner, where the outside world *remains* outside. Still others learn most efficiently by reading, lecture, or drill, while their classmates prefer educational games, films, or class discussions.

Educational literature is filled with research evidence (backed by common sense) that even gifted students learn in varied ways. Two notable examples are the learning-styles work of Anthony Gregorc and the multiple-intelligences work of Howard Gardner. From them (and other experts) and our own experience as teachers, we've discovered that some kids learn best by listening, others by seeing, and others by actively doing. There is, however, no consensus on which teaching style or setting works best for everyone (or almost everyone).

One thing is certain, though: A classroom designed to allow for both private and group learning through a variety of techniques invites learning more than does a setting in which lecture alone is used to convey lessons. So vary the "menu." It will enhance and enliven any learning environment.

Strategy: See Each Student as an Individual

Quickly add this column of numbers—out loud or in your head:

```
1000
  40
1000
  30
1000
  20
1000
  10
```

If you arrived at 5,000, congratulations . . . for being wrong. This is the most common answer given by both kids and adults, even though the correct answer is 4,100. Go back and check carefully; you'll see that we're right.

What's going on here is *patterning*. As you add, the thousands keep increasing—until the end, when they don't. But since you expect the pattern to stay the same, you give an answer that's logical, consistent . . . and wrong.

Try this activity with your students. Place this list of numbers on an overhead transparency, revealing the numbers one at a time. When the resounding sound of "Five thousand!" emanates from your apt pupils' mouths, let them know this: Lots of people look at gifted individuals and see them as a collective 5,000—easy to interpret, more similar than different from each other, stereotyped as A students who have few friends. Then let them know that you understand how wrong this notion is, and you intend to look at each of them as an individual 4,100; a unique entity who is a little more complex than may first meet the eye.

You might hang two big, bright posters on opposite classroom walls—one with "4,100" on it, the other with "5,000." Tell your students that they have the responsibility to remind you (and each other) when the tendency to treat one like all (5,000) is apparent.

Strategy: Help Students Get to Know Each Other

In any classroom, students will form new friendships. Kids who have been friends in previous years will likely continue their close relationships. And some students will form cliques designed to keep others out.

As a teacher, you can encourage *all* students to be more open to and accepting of each other. One way is by setting aside time for fun activities in which students learn about their classmates and share information about themselves. Of course, by guiding, participating, and observing, you'll learn more about your students, too—an added bonus. Following are five activities that have worked for us.

Activity: *Visual Enigmas*

Almost everyone we know is intrigued by optical illusions—those eye puzzles that cause you to think in new ways about something that looks simple on the surface but is really quite complex. For example, what do you see in these pictures?

If you see a knight on a horse in the first set of abstract shapes, join the club. It's not there, of course, but in our mind's quest for solving problems, we create an image that reminds us of something we know. The question mark in the other illustration is quite obvious to many, but the black bird—a phoenix—is less so. Again, neither is there, except in our mind's eye, and if our culture did not use the "?" symbol, we probably wouldn't see the question mark at all.

Kids love mind-bogglers like these. You can find many books of optical illusions at your local library; one of our personal favorites is *Can You Believe Your Eyes?* by J. Richard Block and Harold Yucker (New York: Brunner-Routledge, 1992). They're great for filling those extra moments at the end of a unit, a period, or a day. They can also help your students get to know more about each other's lives. Just don't call them "optical illusions." Instead, use the more sophisticated term "visual enigmas," and present them like this.

Give each student a copy of "Visual Enigmas" on page 265. See if your students can decipher any of these complex words (most cannot), and explain to them that each of them—*enigma, quandary, conundrum*—is almost synonymous with the word at the bottom of the page: *mystery*.

After sharing this handout, do what we do: Make up your own visual enigmas using your full name (see the example below), followed by brief descriptions of things about you that interested people may want to know. Then have each of your students take a turn at unraveling the mystery that is him or her, using either a first name or a first and last name (kept separate). Hang the completed enigmas on a window wall and watch as students try to unravel the mysteries of their classmates' lives, discovering important things that make each of them unique.

1. I like to travel to places where people do not speak English.

2. I think the Three Stooges are way funnier than Jim Carrey.

3. I enjoy listening to alternative music that people my age are not supposed to like.

4. The quality I respect most in a person is integrity.

Activity: Welcome to Our School

Every school building has the overlords (students in the school's highest grade) and the underlings (kids in the lowest grade). For example, if you work in a school designed for fourth through sixth graders, the head honchos are generally those sixth graders who learned the ropes of the school long ago—back in fourth grade. This activity brings the oldest and youngest groups just a little bit closer.

Near the end of the school year, have students who will be in the building's highest grade the following year get together to write a student handbook for the incoming youngest students. The goal: to make school a less scary place for students who will soon experience it as a brand-new place. Topics might include:

- the physical layout of the building ("where stuff is")

- how to get along with your teachers

- how to deal with older kids

- homework policies

- where to go and who to turn to for help

Once the handbook has been written, edited, and illustrated, make enough copies to give each incoming student a copy at the start of the new school year. (Or post it on the school's Web site, or provide it as an enclosure in an information packet sent to new students before the school year begins.) Then, during the first few days of school, have representatives from the school's highest grade visit each new classroom to review and explain the handbook, and to let the incoming students know that "if anyone gives you any trouble, come see us."

When the students at one intermediate school created a handbook, here's what they wrote. The final booklet was illustrated by the students.

Welcome to Dodge Intermediate School!

Introduction

Welcome to Dodge! It is a fun school with many opportunities! Dodge is a very nice school (the cafeteria food is even good!) and, until the high school was built, it was the newest school in town!

We bet you have A LOT of questions about Dodge—everyone does! That's why we put this booklet together.

Our most important advice for the first day of school is to just act like yourself. There are TONS of teachers and older kids to ask where to go if you get lost.

So . . . here are our suggestions about having a good year at Dodge. Enjoy fourth grade!

The school is so big! Will I get lost?

Yes, Dodge is bigger than the other schools you went to, but you probably won't get lost because teachers take you around the school a lot. After a week, you'll know where everything is.

Dodge is pretty much a square. The library is the center. Around it are upstairs and downstairs classrooms. There are some other hallways, but your teacher will take you through them.

continued . . .

How do I make the first few days easier?

Here are ideas from Dodge students:

"I practiced the combination to my locker about five times when I first got it so now I know it so well that I can open it in about ten seconds!"

"If you need any help, ask a teacher, NOT a student (at least not the first few days."

"At first, all the stairs are a pain, but you'll get used to them."

"Just ignore kids who say you are short or whatever. They are SO annoying!"

"If you buy lunch, have your money ready as you stand in line."

How will I ever stay organized?

Keep your desk organized by putting your books on one side and your trapper on the other. Take home all the papers you don't need at school any more. Also, have a folder for each subject (like math, science, and social studies) and keep these folders in your trapper, too.

Always put your stuff back in the right spot, because once it is in the wrong spot you will never have time to put it back where it belongs.

Lastly, clean out your trapper once a month and don't clutter up your locker with all kinds of junk and papers.

What can you tell us about teachers and homework?

You're probably wondering if all the good things you heard about the teachers are true. Well, we can't say that all of the teachers are nice, because that will have to be your opinion. But what we CAN say is that every good thing we ever heard about them WAS true. It's NOT true that the teachers are mean, but it IS true that they may be a little stricter than you're used to.

Teachers don't give as much homework as people say they do. But, when you do get homework, you should finish it right after school, because then you'll have the rest of the night to yourself. We know we probably sound like your mother, but doing your homework DOES help!!

continued . . .

What other stuff should we know?

Here's what Dodge students say:

"If you want the older kids to like you, don't show off, be snotty, or try to annoy them."

"Do not write on the bathroom walls—ever! The janitor will make you wash it off!"

"You can't sit wherever you want in the cafeteria. There aren't fights during lunch, and there is a much larger selection of food than at your elementary school."

"If you have a problem with another kid, tell an adult or (if you can't leave) ignore the person. DON'T FIGHT THEM!!"

"Don't worry about the locker rooms—just like the stairs, you get used to them pretty quickly. Also, don't be scared, because the boys and the girls are kept separated."

Activity: Just Like Me

Students have a lot in common with each other, whatever the depth or range of their intellects. After all, humanity being what it is, there is more that ties us together than what separates us.

In this activity, students first get to express how much alike they really are. This is followed by a "personal inventory" that invites them to share other, more detailed aspects of their lives and personalities.

Begin the activity by having students sit in their chairs, at desks or tables, but far enough back that they can stand up readily. Tell them that you're going to read a series of statements aloud. For each statement that's true for them, they should stand up, raise their arms, and shout, "That's just like me!" You might use the statements below or create your own. Tip: Be prepared for loudness and laughter.

Stand up and shout if . . .

- Pizza is my absolute favorite food.
- Someday I'll own a fancy sports car.
- I cry as easily as I laugh.
- I dream in color.
- I want to have more than five kids when I grow up.

- I wish I could be 5 years old again.
- I want to be 21 years old right now.
- My best friend is at least two years older than I am.
- My best friend is at least two years younger than I am.
- I make up my own rules in the games I play.

Afterward, ask the students to take their seats and settle down. Then explain the next part of the activity: Each student will now write a description of himself or herself, using the letters from "Just Like [his or her name]." The letters can appear anywhere in the words. Here's an example for a student named Joe:

well-ad**J**usted

not too h**U**mble

love**S** beaches

Traveler

Laid-back

wr**I**ter

Kind

Easygoing

Jovial

kn**O**wledgeable

Effervescent

You might make this into an advanced vocabulary lesson, challenging students to find difficult synonyms for common words. (For example, "happy" for someone needing an A can become either "elated" or "ecstatic.") Finally! A use for those classroom thesauruses!

Hang these self-portrayals on a classroom wall—or in the hall—so students can see their common bonds through a unique perspective.

Activity: *Symbolic Scavenger Hunt*

We all remember scavenger hunts from summer camp, school field trips, or birthday parties. No matter what we were told to search for, all scavenger hunts had something in common: They were concrete. We worked our way down a list, looking for specific objects. There wasn't much creativity or self-expression involved.

Our "Symbolic Scavenger Hunt" is different. The object of this game is to locate items that symbolize or represent ideas, concepts, or relationships. Students are also asked to locate items that represent *themselves* as people—past, present, and future.

For example, on a recent field trip to a nature center, Jim had his seventh-grade students do the following:

Find one thing that . . .

. . . represents mathematical precision in nature

. . . represents nature's way of recycling

. . . represents what a friend is

. . . indicates positive and negative changes

. . . proves that nature has a sense of humor

. . . looks like something you might find on another planet

. . . reminds you of someone you know

. . . has been changed by human intervention

. . . is natural, but not native, to this area

. . . symbolizes the best part of being a kid

. . . you think no one else will find

. . . is used or made by an animal

. . . is living and is older than you are

. . . is living and is younger than you are

. . . has been shaped by wind

. . . has been shaped by water

. . . represents something you enjoy

. . . represents the person you are now

. . . represents the person you once were

. . . represents the person you will someday be

The students were given 40 minutes to locate as many items as possible from this list. They worked in teams of three or four. They were told to write descriptions of the items they found—and not to take anything from nature. Later, when the students returned to the classroom, they reported on their discoveries and why they thought specific ones made good symbols.

Not only did students learn something about themselves, they also became careful observers of nature, looking for personal meaning in the trees, plants, and animals they saw. A class discussion of their responses could have gone on forever, as students jumped at the chance to express who they were and what was important to them.

Activity: *Who Knew?*

If your experience is the same as ours, this activity is one your students will want to repeat. Why? First, because it's fun (and funny). Second, because it reveals something about memorable events in a person's life. Third, because it gives students a chance to stretch the truth legitimately, all in the name of self-disclosure.

Have each student write down five statements about himself or herself. The rules: Four statements must be true, and one must be a lie. Allow 10 to 15 minutes for this. Surprisingly, some students may have trouble coming up with legitimate-sounding lies.

You might start by sharing a list of your own. Here are two lists we came up with, followed by two lists submitted by sixth-grade students Melissa and Kent.

Jim's List

1. I had to take over the controls of a small plane when the pilot got sick.

2. I almost drowned when I fell off a boat into the ocean.

3. I like listening to alternative rock music.

4. I bought a sports car without knowing how to drive a stick shift.

5. I took my first trip overseas by throwing a dart at a world map and going where it landed.

Judy's List

1. I love dogs of all shapes and sizes, but I can only have a terrier or a poodle because they don't shed. (I'm allergic to animal hair.)

2. I jumped off a sailboat off the coast of Africa, without any idea how I was going to get home. I landed in Mozambique!

3. I have traveled to more than 12 countries around the world.

4. I speak several languages fluently.

5. I love cheese and have been called a cheesehead.

Melissa's List

1. I almost got lost at the Grand Canyon.

2. I hit my head on four metal bars while falling off a jungle gym.

3. I've been to Canada.

4. I have a sister named Sara who doesn't lie.

5. I know someone who guards the Dalai Lama.

Kent's List

1. I pulled the fire alarm when I thought it said "free."

2. I cried when my fish got flushed down the toilet.

3. I'm scared of my grandmother.

4. I can't bend my big toe backward.

5. I took a knife out of a drawer and stabbed the kitchen wall.

What you find out from this activity is fascinating. You learn about your students' talents, skills, and quirks; you learn about their families and social relationships; you learn about places they've lived and visited, languages they speak or understand, and dreams they aspire toward. Indeed, you learn more from their truth-telling than their lie-sharing.

In case you want to know the lies in the lists above: Jim's is #1. Judy's is #4. Melissa's is #4 (her sister lies all the time—according to Melissa, that is). And Kent's is #5 (thank goodness).

More Ways to Promote a Positive Classroom Environment

1. Grade papers with the number correct, not the number wrong.

If a student takes a 20-item quiz and gets two wrong, don't take the easy route and write "–2" on the paper. Instead, write "+18" or 18/20. A small thing, but it sends a big message: "You did a fine job, and you got a lot more right than you missed."

continued . . .

2. Once in a while, write a positive comment.

Matt (Jim's son) once received an assignment back from his eighth-grade language arts teacher. Attached to it were two self-sticking notes on which these words were written:

> *Matt—I have figured out why I enjoy reading your work so much. You give yourself permission to dream, to think wild thoughts, and to record those thoughts. Remember, Matt, continue dreaming BIG DREAMS and focus on pleasing yourself, your own creative mind. In that way, you'll never stifle yourself or become a robotic writer.—**Mrs. Setter***

This was the only extended note from Mrs. Setter that Matt received all year—and it was the only one he needed to receive, for it validated not only Matt's work, but also his sense of self.

Make yourself a promise to write each of your students at least one note this year, a note that acknowledges not only what they do but who they are. It might hang on a refrigerator for months—like Mrs. Setter's note to Matt.

3. Post your own Points of Pride.

Several teachers we know hang their high school and college diplomas in their classrooms. Others post positive notes on bulletin boards that they received in previous years from parents or students. Still more bring in trophies won in sports, T-shirts worn in 5K runs for Muscular Dystrophy, or blue ribbons won for pie-baking or flower-growing at a county fair. (One brave teacher actually posted "before" and "after" photos of a successful diet where she had lost 75 pounds.)

In each instance, these teachers are sharing pieces of themselves and their lives with students. In the process, they are also letting their students know that learning extends beyond the school years and goals continue to be attained, even in adulthood.

Invitational Education in Establishing Disciplinary Procedures

Strategy: Avoid Group Punishments

Your students are chatty in general, and your requests for quiet go unheeded—at least by some. Unable to determine exactly which children are responsible for the noise, you give one final warning: "If it's not quiet by the time I count to three, you will all lose your recess. One . . . two . . . three!"

It isn't quiet, so you smugly (or sternly) follow through with your plan: "Okay, that's it. I'll see you all at 10:15."

There, you've done it—ruined recess for everyone, yourself included. Gifted students in particular hate this form of punishment, although all students can see the inequity inherent in punishing en masse. It's easy to see why the nontalkers get upset; after all, it wasn't *their* fault. Yet even those who are "guilty as charged" realize how unfair it is to punish others who are innocent. Some may appear at your desk, repentant and pleading, asking you to lift the punishment from those who are blameless.

Avoid these situations at all costs. It's hard to argue with the logic of a student whose only guilt is by association, or whose sense of justice demands to know why "innocent until proven guilty" applies in the courthouse but not in your classroom.

Strategy: Reward Incremental Improvements

Many gifted youngsters are stingy when it comes to giving themselves credit for a job well done. If there's a flaw, they'll find it; if there's a higher grade to be gotten, they'll wish they attained it. Too few of them notice incremental improvements in performance and, therefore, downplay their efforts until perfection is reached.

Educators can help students enjoy the fruits of their labors by pointing out to them their small successes. Comments such as "Ann, your cursive handwriting is really improving; I noticed it on the poster you designed yesterday," or "Compare these two assignments, Joey. Notice how much more complete this second one is" go a long way toward sharing your satisfaction with day-to-day growth or progress.

Strategy: Catch Them Being Good

It's easy for educators to ignore or take for granted situations that neither bother us nor demand our attention. It's quite difficult, though, to tolerate a child who is misbehaving, disturbing others, or causing a general ruckus. In fact, we react strongly and swiftly to point out and curb these actions.

As R.L. Thorndike might say, "How soon they forget." Thorndike's "law of effect" (we all learned about it in Educational Psychology 101) rests on the idea that animals (people included) are likely to repeat those behaviors for which they are rewarded. Thus, if we want to see a particular behavior repeated in someone's repertoire, we reinforce it, and if we want to extinguish a particular behavior, we douse it with feigned ignorance and make believe it isn't there.

However, behaviorists usually work in labs, not schools, and it's easier to ignore rats in a cage than children in a classroom. This behavioristic theory collapses as soon as it confronts a child who perceives negative attention (such as when a teacher chastises a child's behavior) as preferable to no attention at all.

Still, the impact of emphasizing the positive to children can't be argued. Imagine the surprise of a group of first-graders who hear, "I really appreciate the way you are sharing your crayons. It makes my job more pleasant when you behave so well." "Who is this?" they'll wonder. "The teacher from planet Nice-Nice?"

Yet they'll listen and incorporate this statement into their ever-growing reserve of comments that prove their value, their ability, or their responsibility. Pick on the positive, and see how much more pleasant a place school can become.

Strategy: Avoid Fear-Based Discipline

Sometimes, it's easier to learn what to do by seeing an example of what *not* to do. In this case, a second-grade teacher—sweet, kind, and misinformed—presented us with this illustration:

Her explanation? "I went to a workshop where the speaker said that children had to know the reasons they might have lost a special privilege, like extra recess. So, every morning I give each of my students a fresh happy face and, when I catch them doing something wrong, I punch a hole in their face with my paper punch. At the end of the day, we each count how many holes we have in our faces. Anyone with more than five holes cannot go out for extra recess."

Did her plan work? Yes. Negative behaviors diminished. Did her plan respect students or encourage them to pursue new, positive behaviors? Doubtful. Her students behaved out of fear, and all you learn from fear is more ways to avoid punishment.

Strategy: Discipline in Private

Nobody's perfect. Every student will misbehave at some time. Every student—even the most able and conscientious—will need an occasional talking to. When this time comes, discipline in private. Though this is more time-consuming, it's a more personal, respectful, and meaningful way to point out the connection between the child's action and your reaction. Examples:

- *(Said in front of class):* "That's inappropriate language, Sue. Let's talk about it after class."

- *(Said in private):* "Erin, Mike told me how bad he felt when you called him 'stupid' because he's not in the top reading group. Were you trying to make him feel bad?"

- *(Said in private):* "Santo, I was going to stop my lesson when you wouldn't stop talking during math, but I'd rather talk with you privately about your behavior."

Each of these statements conveys respect to the student, and each one begs the student to forge the connection between actions and consequences. Especially effective with intelligent children (who can see the correlation between their action and your response) and students who seldom get punished (and think it's the end of the world when they do), private disciplining can help students save face in front of their classmates. It also teaches an important lesson that an off-the-cuff public reprimand ("Behave yourself, Margaret! I expect better behavior from a smart girl like you.") can never achieve.

Invitational Education Through Self-Satisfying Behaviors

When you read the following strategies, you may tell yourself, "Wait—these are about *me*, not about creating a positive classroom environment for my students." There's an old saying: "If Mama ain't happy, ain't nobody happy." The better you feel about yourself as a teacher (and a human being), the better you'll be at teaching.

Strategy: Start and Maintain a Feel-Good Folder

Even eternal optimists have their down days. Whether caused by biorhythms, bad karma, or distressing news, every teacher has occasional second thoughts about our chosen profession. *There must be easier jobs,* we think, *not to mention more lucrative.* Still, we persevere. We get through. We find that second wind. And we go on.

To make the journey more manageable, keep track of the "invitations" you have received as an educator. Gather together some of the little rewards of our profession—the happy face drawn by a first grader and given to you as a present; the former sixth grader, now in college, who wrote to you once "just to say thanks"; the note from two parents who appreciated the "shoulder to cry on" you provided when they needed it most. Place them all in a file and label it your Feel-Good Folder. Then, on days that are rougher than you would like, open the folder and re-read the messages that meant so much. You'll be surprised at how special those notes still are.

Samples from Our Feel-Good Folders

Jim:
Thank you so much for taking the time to get the names of counselors for my daughter. You always amaze me because you are such a busy person, but you always take time to go the extra mile for someone. Thank you!

Jean

Mom and Dad,
I'm in Positano, on the Amalfi Coast. I can't believe you sent me on this trip, and here I am, at a place between heaven and Earth (I don't know which is closer), thanks to you.

Love, Matt

Jim:
Please keep writing. Your articles are like "word candy" to me. I keep chewing on them for a long, long time.

Doris

continued . . .

Dear Judy:

Thank you for writing back to me. You are the only person I know who actually writes nice, decent, long letters. You spend time and make the effort. I really admire that, and you always make me feel good because you really know how to handle things. Gosh, you should be a psychiatrist!

Later . . . Thomas

Dear Judy:

This letter is years late, but I wanted to thank you for all that you have done to help me through your book. My education has greatly improved because I took your suggestions to heart. I've pulled through some tough times because of your encouragement. I've been inspired by lessons instilled from your writing . . . you have really made a difference.

Sincerely, Amie

Strategy: Leave School at School

Anyone who thinks that education is an 8 A.M. to 3 P.M. job, or an occupation chosen by those who appreciate summer too much to work, need to have their eyes opened and their mouths closed. In any human services career, teaching included, your job follows you home (where you get telephone calls from parents), to the mall (where you see your students), and on vacation ("Hey, isn't that Mrs. Jackson over there in the bikini?").

This reality isn't necessarily stressful, but if you find yourself talking about your job to people who aren't involved in education—spouses, neighbors, grandchildren— you might need to learn how to leave school at school. Because this is easier said than done, here are some tricks you can try:

- Grade papers or plan tomorrow's lessons before you leave the school building. On some days, leave school empty-handed.

- Plan an exercise routine—even 30 minutes three times a week—and stick to it. This could be as serious as racquetball or as leisurely as a walk around the neighborhood. Just do it!

- Splurge occasionally. Have a massage. It's so invigorating and therapeutic that the 50 dollars you spend ought to count as a medical tax deduction.

■ Make a "school conversation schedule." Promise yourself that you'll talk shop with colleagues or family for only 30 minutes a night. After that, all talk of school is verboten. (Even better: Attach a 25-cents penalty for every infraction of this rule. With luck and a little effort, the pot will be empty and you will be happier.)

Strategy: Avoid Comparing Yourself to Others

How frequently we downplay our efforts and accomplishments by comparing them with those of our colleagues! In our attempts to become "superteacher," we look around us and see what others have done that we have not. Even as the ink is still drying on the parent newsletter we're sending home on a monthly basis, we belittle its importance because "so-and-so down the hall thought of it first."

Educators' worst enemies are often themselves. To break this cycle of accomplishment-disappointment-accomplishment-disappointment, we need to learn a lesson we so often teach our students: Compare your efforts *today* with *your own* efforts of yesterday or last week or last year, never with the efforts of the person down the hall. Remember: You're not the teacher next door, and that's okay.

Strategy: Know That You Don't Have Total Control

This vital understanding—that you don't have control over your students' lives—is the one taught so well by Mrs. Sanders, the teacher we met at the beginning of this chapter. An excellent educator and a caring individual, she realizes the limits of her powers. She knows too well that the lives of her students are not always easy or pretty. She acknowledges that some pupils enjoy homes of privilege, while others are never free from want—physical, environmental, or emotional.

Still, she goes on . . . because she *can* help and she *does* help, every day between 8 A.M. and 3 P.M., in a place called a classroom.

So do you.

The Magic of Teaching

by Scott Stuart, fifth-grade teacher

I believe that educators are yearning to get back in touch with their "first love." I think that for people to go into teaching in the first place, they had to be called by a dream. A dream that they could make a difference. Educators need to be encouraged to capture that dream once more. Sure, there are difficulties and walls to climb, but the "raw materials"—our students—often have no awareness of the pressures with which we deal. We don't have to transfer them on! Even though we fight the politics of schools, we can still enjoy the pleasure of seeing children grow and develop. I think that is the magic of teaching.

A Final Thought

The invitations to learn that we give our students on a minute-by-minute, day-to-day basis are very efficient ways to enhance both achievement and self-esteem in the classroom. Students who feel good about themselves as human beings, not just scholars, grow to become (in the words of William James) "effective geniuses": young people in touch with both their hearts and their minds, and eventually adults as willing and able to *care* deeply as to *think* deeply.

Notes

1. William W. Purkey and John M. Novak, *Inviting School Success: A Self-Concept Approach to Teaching, Learning, and Democratic Practice,* 3rd ed. (Belmont, CA: Wadsworth, 1996).

2. Donald W. MacKinnon, *In Search of Human Effectiveness: Identifying and Developing Creativity* (Buffalo, NY: Creative Education Foundation, 1978), p. 171.

3. Alfie Kohn, *Punished by Rewards: The Trouble with Gold Stars, Incentive Plans, A's, Praise, and Other Bribes* (Boston: Houghton Mifflin Company, 1993), pp. 49–67.

4. Ibid., p. 52.

5. Ibid., p. 63.

BUG ROLL

CONGRATULATIONS, _____ !

You "**B**rought **U**p your **G**rade" in

_____

and didn't go down in any subject.

KEEP UP THE GOOD WORK!

Teacher's Signature: _____

Date: _____

Resources

Books/Periodicals

The Autonomous Learner Model: Optimizing Ability by George Betts and Jolene Kercher (Greeley, CO: ALPS Publishing, 1999). This revised edition of a classic shows teachers and gifted coordinators how to plan gifted programs for grades 6 and up that focus on the emotional as well as the cognitive abilities of students.

Barefoot Irreverence: A Guide to Critical Issues in Gifted Child Education by James R. Delisle (Waco, TX: Prufrock Press, 2002). Reviews all aspects of emotional development of gifted students, as well as other topics such as standardized testing, parenting gifted children, and continuing controversies in gifted child education.

Crossover Children: A Sourcebook for Helping Children Who Are Gifted and Learning Disabled, 2nd ed., by Marlene Birely (Reston, VA: Council for Exceptional Children, 1995). Resource material and information for helping twice-exceptional kids.

Duke Gifted Letter A publication of the Talent Identification Program at Duke University and edited by Steven I. Pfeiffer, this newsletter is published quarterly and provides timely and interesting articles and resources appropriate for both parents and educators of gifted kids. Available through Duke University Press and online at *www.dukeupress.edu.*

Emotional Intelligence by Daniel Goleman (New York: Bantam Books, 1995). A well-researched volume that looks at the link between intellectual and emotional intelligence, and examines the inner characteristics of people who excel in life.

The Gifted Kids' Survival Guide: For Ages 10 & Under, by Judy Galbraith, M.A. (Minneapolis: Free Spirit Publishing, 1999). A friendly, straightforward guide for younger gifted kids which explains what giftedness is all about, how to make the most of school, and how to socialize successfully.

The Gifted Kids' Survival Guide: A Teen Handbook by Judy Galbraith, M.A., and Jim Delisle, Ph.D. (Minneapolis: Free Spirit Publishing, 1996). A guide for older gifted kids with strategies, practical how-to's, and surprising facts (as well as essays and quotes from teens themselves) on how to survive and thrive as a gifted teen.

Handbook of Gifted Education, 3rd ed., edited by Nicholas Colangelo and Gary A. Davis (Needham Heights, MA: Allyn & Bacon, 2002). Experts in the field address a wide variety of topics, including identification, classroom practices, creativity, and counseling.

Handbook of Intelligence edited by Robert J. Sternberg (New York: Cambridge University Press, 2000). A broad review of current research into the nature of intelligence, includes discussions of emotional intelligence, measuring and testing intelligence, and information processing.

Intelligence Reframed: Multiple Intelligences for the 21st Century by Howard Gardner (New York: Basic Books, 1999). A further examination and elaboration on the theory of multiple intelligences, with its implications for education in the new century.

Multicultural Gifted Education by Donna Y. Ford and J. John Harris, III (New York: Teachers College Press, 1999). A concrete and thorough resource that bridges the fields of gifted and multicultural education. Contains case studies of multicultural gifted education, classroom methods, sample activities, and guidelines with a checklist to help evaluate current multicultural education programs.

Multiple Intelligences in the Classroom, 2nd ed., by Thomas Armstrong (Alexandria, VA: ASCD, 2000). Tools, resources, and ideas teachers can use to help students of all intelligences achieve their full potential.

Once Upon a Mind: The Stories and Scholars of Gifted Child Education by James R. Delisle (Belmont, CA: Wadsworth Publishing Company, 2000). This is a "user-friendly text" in which the history of gifted child education is told through a series of personal reflections of practitioners in the field. There is a special focus on the emotional lives of gifted children and those who have promoted this in their work.

Reaching New Horizons: Gifted and Talented Education for Culturally and Linguistically Diverse Students edited by Jamie A. Castellano and Eva Díaz (Needham Heights, MA: Allyn & Bacon, 2002). Examines how gifted children from backgrounds of bilingualism or culturally different settings can be identified, appreciated, and served in our schools.

Reversing Underachievement Among Gifted Black Students: Promising Practices and Programs by Donna Y. Ford (New York: Teachers College Press, 1996). This landmark book offers a new beginning on the often ignored subject of underachievement among black youth. The author's hope is to "desegregate" gifted education and ensure equity on behalf of black and other minority students.

Some of My Best Friends Are Books: Guiding Gifted Readers from Preschool to High School, 2nd ed., by Judy Halsted (Scottsdale, AZ: Great Potential Press 2001). Offers many good and current suggestions for children's literature appropriate for gifted kids.

Talented Children and Adults: Their Development and Education by Jane Piirto (Upper Saddle River, NJ: Prentice Hall Inc., 1999). This is a general text on giftedness, but one of the few that focuses significantly on gifted secondary students and adults. Very complete, especially for those who are looking for a more comprehensive view of the entire field of giftedness and talent development.

Teaching Gifted Kids in the Regular Classroom: Strategies and Techniques Every Teacher Can Use to Meet the Academic Needs of the Gifted and Talented by Susan Winebrenner, M.S. (Minneapolis: Free Spirit Publishing, 2001). A classic for teaching gifted kids, loaded with references and resources.

Teaching Young Gifted Children in the Regular Classroom by Joan Franklin Smutny, Sally Yahnke Walker, and Elizabeth A. Meckstroth (Minneapolis: Free Spirit Publishing, 1998). Designed to help teachers identify, nurture, and challenge the younger gifted child (ages 4–9).

Organizations

Council for Exceptional Children
1110 North Glebe Road, Suite 300
Arlington, VA 22201
1-888-232-7733
www.cec.sped.org
A complete database of research and intervention methods for children who are gifted, twice-exceptional, or have other special education needs.

Davidson Institute for Talent Development
9665 Gateway Drive, Suite B
Reno, NV 89511
(775) 852-3483
www.ditd.org
The Institute seeks out profoundly gifted young people and supports their educational and developmental needs. They host an array of resources for educators, and the PG CyberSource on their Web site is a deeply comprehensive and searchable listing of valuable information and resources for teachers *and* parents.

ERIC Clearinghouse on Disabilities and Gifted Education
1110 North Glebe Road
Arlington, VA 22201
1-800-328-0272
www.ericc.org
ERIC stands for Educational Resources Information Center and is an invaluable resource, particularly online. It gathers and disseminates professional literature, information, and resources on the education and development of individuals of all ages who have disabilities and/or who are gifted.

National Association for Gifted Children (NAGC)
1707 L Street NW, Suite 550
Washington, DC 20036
(202) 785-4268
www.nagc.org
A national advocacy organization for parents and educators that addresses the needs of gifted and talented children and youth. The Web site is a comprehensive resource and features easily accessible links to every state's gifted organization.

National Research Center on the Gifted and Talented (NRC/GT)
University of Connecticut
2131 Hillside Road, Unit 3007
Storrs, CT 06269
(860) 486-4676
www.gifted.uconn.edu/nrcgt.html
Visit the Web site for a plethora of research-based resources, links, and more.

Supporting the Emotional Needs of the Gifted (SENG)
PO Box 6550
Scottsdale, AZ 85261
(206) 498-6744
www.sengifted.org
Helps parents identify giftedness in their children, helps children understand and accept their unique talents, and provides a forum for parents and educators to communicate.

Web sites

Hoagies' Gifted Education Page
www.hoagiesgifted.org
The site contains a wide variety of resources, links, articles, and information for gifted kids, their educators, and their parents. A valuable and friendly Web site.

Haven
www.geocities.com/havensrefuge
A Web site and multilayered chat forum created by and for gifted kids. It features a variety of message boards where members discuss a range of topics from the academic to the philosophical to the social. An excellent online resource for gifted youth and teens.

Tagfam
www.tagfam.org
An online organization and community that serves the families of intellectually gifted children to ensure that their chidren's emotional, social, and physical needs as well as intellectual needs are met. The site provides resources, links, and several themed email discussion forums where members can seek emotional support and information.

Pace
www.yale.edu/pace
Run by noted intelligence researcher Robert Sternberg, PACE is the Yale Center for the Psychology of Abilities, Competencies, and Expertise.

Index

About the Authors

Jim Delisle, Ph.D., is a Professor of Education at Kent State University in Ohio, where he directs the gifted child education programs at both the undergraduate and graduate levels. He also teaches gifted students in grades 6–8 in Twinsburg, Ohio, one day each week. Jim is the author and coauthor of over 200 articles and

eleven books, including *Growing Good Kids* (with Deb Delisle), *Kidstories,* and *The Gifted Kids' Survival Guide: A Teen Handbook* (with Judy Galbraith). His work has been featured in the *New York Times, Washington Post,* and *People,* and on National Public Radio and *Oprah.*

Jim lives in Kent, Ohio, most of the year and in North Myrtle Beach, South Carolina, when school is out. Jim and his wife, Deb, enjoy cruising the Caribbean and dropping in unexpectedly on their son, Matt, who lives in Oakland, California.

Judy Galbraith, M.A., has a master's degree in guidance and counseling of the gifted. She has worked with and taught gifted children and teens, their parents, and their teachers for over 20 years. In 1983, she started Free Spirit Publishing, which specializes in SELF-HELP FOR KIDS® and SELF-HELP FOR TEENS® books and other learning materials.

Judy is the author of *The Gifted Kids' Survival Guide for Ages 10 & Under* and *You Know Your Child Is Gifted When . . . A Beginner's Guide to Life on the Bright Side.*

She is the coauthor of *The Gifted Kids' Survival Guide: A Teen Handbook* (with Jim Delisle), *What Kids Need to Succeed: Proven, Practical Ways to Raise Good Kids* (with Peter L. Benson, Ph.D., and Pamela Espeland), and *What Teens Need to Succeed: Proven, Practical Ways to Shape Your Own Future* (with Peter and Pamela).

Judy lives in Minneapolis, Minnesota, with Chloé, her comic Airedale "terror." Her hobbies include sailing, traveling, scuba diving, and tennis.

Other Great Books from Free Spirit

The Gifted Kids' Survival Guide
For Ages 10 & Under
Revised & Updated Edition
by Judy Galbraith, M.A.
First published in 1984, newly revised and updated, this book has helped countless young gifted children realize they're not alone, they're not "weird," and being smart, talented, and creative is a bonus, not a burden. Includes advice from hundreds of gifted kids. For ages 10 & under.
$9.95; 104 pp.; softcover; illus.; 6" x 9"

The Gifted Kids' Survival Guide
A Teen Handbook
Revised, Expanded, and Updated Edition
by Judy Galbraith, M.A., and Jim Delisle, Ph.D.
Vital information on giftedness, IQ, school success, college planning, stress, perfectionism, and much more. For ages 11–18.
$15.95; 304 pp.; softcover; illus.; 7¼" x 9¼"

Perfectionism
What's Bad About Being Too Good?
Revised and Updated Edition
by Miriam Adderholdt, Ph.D., and Jan Goldberg
This revised and updated edition includes new research and statistics on the causes and consequences of perfectionism, biographical sketches of famous perfectionists and risk takers, and resources for readers who want to know more. For ages 13 & up.
$12.95; 136 pp.; softcover; illus.; 6" x 9"

You're Smarter Than You Think
A Kid's Guide to Multiple Intelligences
by Thomas Armstrong, Ph.D.
In clear, simple language, this book introduces the theory, explains the eight intelligences, and describes 22 ways to develop each one. Kids will learn how they can use all eight intelligences in school, expand their multiple intelligences at home, and draw on them to plan for the future. Resources point the way to books, software, games, and organizations that can help kids develop the eight intelligences. This timely, important book is recommended for all kids, their parents, and educators. For ages 8–12.
$15.95; 192 pp.; softcover; illus.; 7" x 9"

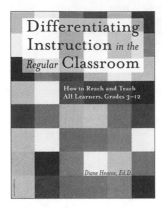

Differentiating Instruction in the Regular Classroom
How to Reach and Teach All Learners, Grades 3–12
by Diane Heacox, Ed.D.

Differentiation—one of the hottest topics in education today—means changing the pace, level, or kind of instruction in response to learners' needs, styles, and/or interests. Here's a menu of strategies and tools any teacher can use to differentiate instruction in any curriculum, even a standard or mandated curriculum. Drawing on Bloom's Taxonomy, Gardner's Multiple Intelligences, other experts in the field, and the author's own considerable experience in the classroom, this book explains how to differentiate instruction across a broad spectrum of scenarios. Recommended for all teachers committed to reaching and teaching all learners. For teachers, grades 3–12.
$29.95; 176 pp.; softcover; 8½" x 11"

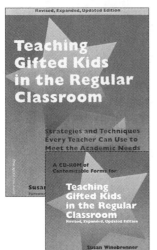

Teaching Gifted Kids in the Regular Classroom
Strategies and Techniques Every Teacher Can Use to Meet the Academic Needs of the Gifted and Talented
Revised, Expanded, and Updated Edition
by Susan Winebrenner

Teachers call it "the orange bible"—the book they count on for insight, advice, and strategies that work. The revised and updated edition of a proven best-seller (over 160,000 in print) includes a new chapter on the characteristics of gifted students and one on parenting gifted kids. Throughout, the compacting and differentiation strategies that were the core of the first edition have been greatly expanded. For teachers, all grades.
$34.95; 256 pp.; softcover; 8½" x 11"

Teaching Gifted Kids in the Regular Classroom CD-ROM
This CD-ROM includes all of the reproducible forms from the book plus many additional extensions menus in several subject areas—80 forms in all. Teachers can print them out when they need them and even customize most of the forms for their classrooms and students.
$12.95; Macintosh and PC compatible, 5" CD-ROM, 80 reproducible handout masters.

Up from Underachievement
How Teachers, Students, and Parents Can Work Together to Promote Student Success
by Diane Heacox, Ed.D.

This step-by-step program helps students of all ages, with all kinds of school problems, to break the failure chain. Students are motivated to succeed because they are part of the team. Includes reproducible handout masters. For parents and teachers of all grades.
$18.95; 144 pp.; softcover; 8½" x 11"

Challenging Projects for Creative Minds

12 Self-Directed Enrichment Projects That Develop and Showcase Student Ability
for Grades 1–5

by Phil Schlemmer, M.Ed., and Dori Schlemmer

The best way to prepare children for the future is to teach them how to learn, and that's just what these projects do. Each project sparks kids' imaginations, calls on their creativity, and challenges them to solve problems, find and use information, and think for themselves. For teachers, grades 1–5.

$29.95; 144 pp.; softcover; illus.; 8½" x 11"

Challenging Projects for Creative Minds

20 Self-Directed Enrichment Projects That Develop and Showcase Student Ability
for Grades 6 & Up

by Phil Schlemmer, M.Ed., and Dori Schlemmer

Give your students opportunities to explore beyond core curriculum by completing in-depth projects that promote lifelong learning skills. Reproducible forms help students choose and plan a project, report their progress and problems, keep a record of their work time, and evaluate the project after completion. For teachers, grades 6 & up.

$34.95; 168 pp.; softcover; illus.; 8½" x 11"

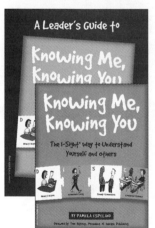

Knowing Me, Knowing You

The I-Sight® Way to Understand Yourself and Others

by Pamela Espeland

Using the DiSC® dimensions of behavior (direct and active, interested and lively, steady and cooperative, concerned and correct), teens learn how their personal styles change from one situation to the next and explore ways to use this knowledge for more effective interactions with others. For ages 12 & up.

$13.95; 128 pp.; softcover; illus.; 7" x 9"

A Leader's Guide to Knowing Me, Knowing You

by Pamela Espeland

For teachers, grades 6–12.

$21.95; 96 pp.; Otabind lay-flat binding; 8½" x 11"

To place an order or to request a free catalog of SELF–HELP FOR KIDS® and SELF–HELP FOR TEENS® materials, please write, call, email, or visit our Web site:

Free Spirit Publishing Inc.
217 Fifth Avenue North • Suite 200 • Minneapolis, MN 55401-1299
toll-free 800.735.7323 • local 612.338.2068 • fax 612.337.5050
help4kids@freespirit.com • www.freespirit.com

Visit us on the Web!
www.freespirit.com

Stop by anytime to find our Parents' Choice Approved catalog with fast, easy, secure 24-hour online ordering; "Ask Our Authors," where visitors ask questions—and authors give answers—on topics important to children, teens, parents, teachers, and others who care about kids; links to other Web sites we know and recommend; fun stuff for everyone, including quick tips and strategies from our books; and much more! Plus our site is completely searchable so you can find what you need in a hurry. Stop in and let us know what you think!

Just point and click!

new! Get the first look at our books, catch the latest news from Free Spirit, and check out our site's newest features.

contact Do you have a question for us or for one of our authors? Send us an email. Whenever possible, you'll receive a response within 48 hours.

order! Order in confidence! Our secure server uses the most sophisticated online ordering technology available. And ordering online is just one of the ways to purchase our books: You can also order by phone, fax, or regular mail. No matter which method you choose, excellent service is our ultimate goal.

1.800.735.7323 • fax 612.337.5050 • help4kids@freespirit.com